ENTERPRISING WOMEN IN TRANSITION ECONOMIES

Enterprising Women in Transition Economies

Edited by

FRIEDERIKE WELTER
University of Siegen and RWI Essen, Germany,
DAVID SMALLBONE
Kingston University, UK
NINA ISAKOVA
National Academy of Sciences of Ukraine, Ukraine

LONDON AND NEW YORK

First published 2006 by Ashgate Publishing

2 Park Square, Milton Park, Abingdon, Oxon OX14 4RN
711 Third Avenue, New York, NY 10017, USA

Routledge is an imprint of the Taylor & Francis Group, an informa business

First issued in paperback 2016

British Library Cataloguing in Publication Data
Enterprising women in transition economies
1. Businesswomen - Former Soviet republics 2. Women-owned business enterprises - Former Soviet republics
3. Entrepreneurship - Former Soviet republics
4. Businesswomen - Europe, Central 5. Women-owned business enterprises - Europe, Central 6. Entrepreneurship - Europe, Central
I. Welter, Friederike II. Smallbone, David III. Isakova, Nina B.
338'.04'082' 0947

Library of Congress Cataloging-in-Publication Data
Enterprising women in transition economies / edited by Friederike Welter, David Smallbone and Nina B. Isakova.
p. cm.
Includes index.
ISBN 0-7546-4232-1
1. Businesswomen--Former communist countries. 2. Women-owned business enterprises--Former communist countries. 3. Entrepreneurship--Former communist countries. I. Welter, Friederike. II. Smallbone, David. III. Isakova, Nina (Nina B.)

HD6072.6.F6E58 2006
338'.04082091717--dc22

2005034912

ISBN 978-0-7546-4232-9 (hbk)
ISBN 978-1-138-26664-3 (pbk)

Transfered to Digital Printing in 2010

Contents

Part 3: Women Entrepreneurship in Central Europe

Part 4: Policy Issues and Policy Perspectives

List of Figures

List of Tables

List of Contributors

Elena Aculai is a Senior Research Officer at the National Institute of Economy and Information of the Ministry of Economy of the Republic of Moldova. She is also the member of the board of directors of The International Center for Advancement of Women in Business. Dr. Aculai has been acting as a research group director at the Academy of Sciences of Moldova for many years. Her research interests include small private business development especially during the start-up period; business management, first of all business-planning and financial analysis; development of industry. Dr. Aculai has been involved in a number of international projects on small business development in the states with transitional economies in Eastern Europe and Asia.

Ruta Aidis is a Lecturer in Entrepreneurship and Governance at the School of Slavonic and East European Studies, University College London. From 1996 to 1998, she was a Fulbright fellow in Lithuania researching female entrepreneurs. In 2003, she received a PhD degree in Economics from the University of Amsterdam. Dr. Aidis is the author of several publications on small and medium-sized enterprises including: *Laws and customs: Entrepreneurship, Institutions and Gender during Economic Transition* (SSEES/UCL 2004), and articles in *Small Business Economics, Post-Communist Economies* and *Feminist Economics*. Her main research interests include entrepreneurship, migration, gender, and institutional development.

Dr. Gül Berna Özcan is Senior Lecturer in European Business and Corporate Governance at the School of Management, Royal Holloway, University of London. She holds a PhD in economic geography from the London School of Economics and is the author of several publications on small and medium-sized enterprises including *Small Firms and Local Economic Development: Entrepreneurship in Southern Europe and Turkey* (Avebury Press, 1995), 'Small business networks and local ties in Turkey', in *Entrepreneurship and Regional Development* (1995), and 'Limitations to alternative forms of capitalisation: the case of Anatolian holding companies', in *World Development* (2003). Entrepreneurship and enterprise promotion in the Kyrgyz Republic is one of her current research projects and it is funded by the Nuffield Foundation. She also holds a Leverhulme Trust Fellowship to conduct research in Uzbekistan, Kazakhstan and the Kyrgyz Republic. Her forthcoming book is *Building States and Markets; enterprise development in Central Asia* is due to be published by Palgrave/Macmillan in 2007.

Mateja Drnovšek has been a post-graduate research assistant at the University of Ljubljana since 1997, recently finishing her PhD thesis on the growth potential of young technology-based firms. Her professional interests are focused towards entrepreneurship, business environment and employment. She has participated in several projects dealing with different topics of entrepreneurship, in particular female entrepreneurship in Slovenia.

Miroslav Glas is Professor at the University of Ljubljana in Slovenia, and the Head of the Centre for Entrepreneurship Development at the Faculty of Economics. Professor Glas is an internationally recognised expert on entrepreneurship and small business development, having been working in this area of research and policy for 18 years. He has participated in a number of international collaborative research projects (PHARE, PHARE-CBC) in Slovenia and he has co-ordinated three national projects on the development of SME support services (on financial scheme for SMEs, on the 'voucher' scheme for advisory services, on the development of business support centres). He is a member of the national team for GEM study, starting from 2002.

Nina B. Isakova holds a scientific degree of Candidate of Sciences in Economics from the National Academy of Sciences Ukraine. Currently she is a senior researcher at the Center for Scientific and Technological Potential and Science History Studies at the National Academy of Sciences Ukraine. She does research on small business and entrepreneurship in transition economies, science and technology policy and innovation. Her recent research work focuses on female entrepreneurship. In addition to her academic pursuits, Nina was a co-founder of a private consulting centre in Kiev, VENTURE centre (1993-1998) and has had work experience at USAID-funded NEWBIZNET project in Kiev as Deputy Director in Small and Medium Enterprise Policy (1997-1998).

Olha Krasovka holds a scientific degree of Candidate of Sciences in Economics from the National Academy of Sciences Ukraine. She is a researcher at the Center for Scientific and Technological Potential and Science History Studies at the National Academy of Sciences Ukraine. Her recent research work focuses on innovation and venture capital, small business and female entrepreneurship in transition.

Lidia Kavunenko holds a scientific degree of Candidate of Sciences in Economics from the National Academy of Sciences Ukraine and is working as Deputy Director and a senior researcher at the Centre for Scientific and Technological Potential and Science History Studies at the National Academy of Sciences Ukraine. Among the wide range of her research interests there are women and youth entrepreneurship and education.

Alexander Lugovy was a post-graduate student during the research project on women entrepreneurs in the Ukraine, working closely with Nina Isakova. He is now working as Head of Marketing in the Ukrprombank in Kiev.

Charos Maksudova graduated from the University of Tashkent, with a master thesis on women's entrepreneurship in Uzbekistan. She is currently working for Tadbirkor Ayol, the Business Women Association in Uzbekistan, having participated in a large-scale research project on women entrepreneurs in Uzbekistan.

Damira Mirzakhalikova also graduated from the University of Tashkent, after which she worked for a USAID project. Since 1996, she is employed by Tadbirkor Ayol as a business consultant. Damira participated as junior researcher in a large-scale research project on women entrepreneurs in Uzbekistan, being responsible for leading and analyzing in-depth interviews with Uzbek women entrepreneurs.

Nelly Rodionova has a broad background in researching SMEs and competition in Moldova. She works at the National Institute of Economy and Information of the Ministry of Economy of the Republic of Moldova and participates in international research projects within Dr. Aculai's research group in Chisinau, Moldova.

Natalja Ju. Schakirova is Deputy Director for International Relationships in Tadbirkor Ayol, the Business Women Association of Uzbekistan, which was set up by women entrepreneurs in the early 1990s. She holds a scientific degree of Doctor of Philosophy of the Humboldt-University of Berlin. Dr. Schakirova's main areas of interest deal with business trainings for women start-ups, women entrepreneurs in small enterprises and re-training unemployed women in handicraft professions. She has broad international experiences in how to prepare women for entrepreneurial activities.

David Smallbone is Professor of Entrepreneurship and Small Business and Associate Director of the Small Business Research Centre (SBRC) at Kingston University. In 2004, he was awarded the degree of doctor honoris causa by the University of Lodz, Poland for his contribution to the study of entrepreneurship. David is also a Visiting Professor in Entrepreneurship at the China University of Geosciences, Wuhan. He is President of the European Council for Small Business and Entrepreneurship and a Director of the Institute of Small Business and Entrepreneurship (ISBE) in the UK. David has 20 years of experience of SME research on a variety of topics, focusing particularly on applied policy issues, on which he has published widely. David's current research interests include entrepreneurship and SME development in transition and emerging market economies; black and minority enterprise; entrepreneurship and small business development in rural areas; innovation and innovation policy relating to small firms; growth processes in small firms; and social enterprise. Professor Smallbone has acted as a policy consultant to the OECD and an expert on matters related to entrepreneurship in transition countries for UNECE and OSCE.

Natalia Vinogradova works at the National Institute of Economy and Information of the Ministry of Economy of the Republic of Moldova, participating as a junior researcher in Dr. Aculai's research group in Chisinau, Moldova. She is also a post-graduate student in the area of SMEs studies.

Friederike Welter is Professor for SMEs at the University of Siegen and on leave of absence as deputy head of the research group 'Entrepreneurship and Enterprise Development' in the Rhine-Westfalia Institute for Economic Research (RWI). She also is affiliated as visiting professor in business administration/entrepreneurship at the Jönköping International Business School, Sweden, and she holds the TeliaSonera Professorship for Entrepreneurship at the Stockholm School of Economics in Riga, Latvia. She is President Elect of the European Council of Small Business and Entrepreneurship. For more than 10 years, Friederike has been involved in research projects both on behalf of German ministries and international organizations. In addition, she works as a consultant for various governments. Her main research interests, on which she has published widely, are entrepreneurial behaviour, (female) entrepreneurship and support policies in mature markets and the emerging market economies in post Soviet countries. Published and forthcoming related books include an edited book on *Trust and Entrepreneurship: A West-East Perspective* (Elgar, 2005) and a monograph jointly authored with Professor Smallbone on *Entrepreneurship and Small Business Development in Central and Eastern Europe and Former Soviet Countries* (Routledge, 2006).

Part 1
Women's Entrepreneurship in a Transition Context: Key Issues

Chapter 1

Introduction

Friederike Welter, David Smallbone and Nina B. Isakova

Aims and Rationale for the Book

This book examines female entrepreneurship in countries that are at different stages of transformation from centrally planned into market economies. Interest in female entrepreneurs has increased during recent years throughout the world. Women in business are a growing force in the economy, and in transition environments, their contribution extends from the economic sphere to include the wider process of social transformation. The wide political, economic and social reforms in former socialist countries deprived many women of the paid jobs and social security provided by government, thereby forcing them to find alternative ways of generating income. In this context, starting a business was one of the options facing entrepreneurial women, shaped by a combination of push and pull factors.

There is an increasing awareness among policy makers and scholars that female entrepreneurship in transition countries can no longer be ignored. Although the topic has not been completely neglected by researchers, the present book presents recent research findings on women doing business in different transition environments. The volume includes examples from countries that are different in historical background, the pace of market reforms and cultural distinctiveness. The book contains research performed in more progressive countries, in terms of market reforms, (Slovenia and Lithuania); less fortunate states (Ukraine and Moldova); two Central Asian countries; and the specific case of East Germany.

This book is distinguished from existing books on gender issues in transition economies (e.g., Ashwin, 2000; Buckley, 1997; Lazreg, 2000) and on small business development in transition in one important respect. Although focused on distinctive issues, all of the country chapters are empirically grounded using original material. In the case of Ukraine, Uzbekistan and Moldova, this involves previously unpublished survey results and case study evidence drawn from a research project on female entrepreneurship (supported by INTAS, project number 00-0843). The major objectives of this project were to investigate this phenomenon in three different countries in an attempt to assess its contribution to economic and social development. A wider international perspective was attained by the editors by adding research findings on enterprising women in East Germany (compared to

West Germany), Kyrgyzstan, Lithuania and Slovenia, which provide rich evidence and data for further conceptualisation and policy implications.

All chapters combine research into the nature and extent of female entrepreneurship in transition economies, with a discussion of the specific role of these women in the process of social and economic transformation. Female entrepreneurship is defined as economic activity of women small business (firm) owners, including sole proprietors. Female entrepreneurs are women sole proprietors; small (micro) business owners; or co-owners of businesses with male partners. By focusing on the nature and extent of female entrepreneurship in relation to the role of women in society, the different chapters provide new insights into the involvement of women entrepreneurs in transition, as well as barriers and enabling factors and strategies used to solve problems. The evidence presented in this book thus contributes to a deeper understanding of the current and potential contribution of women to economic and social development in these countries. Furthermore, this allows for comparisons and conclusions with respect to female entrepreneurship in countries with differing political and economic environments and with a distinctive cultural and historical background. Key themes discussed in the book include:

- Conceptualisations of female entrepreneurship under transition conditions, taking into account the socialist legacy; as well as the routes that women take into business; and the development potential of the enterprises they set up. It is argued that an institutional approach is helpful in interpreting women's entrepreneurship and private enterprise development under transition conditions (Welter et al., 2003).
- An overview of the transition context in the different countries concerned, with special attention paid to the institutional; social and political settings for women entrepreneurs.
- A discussion of the varying nature and extent of women's entrepreneurship in the countries concerned that reflect differences in the pace of market reform and wider transformation processes, as well as specific Soviet legacies and differing cultural values.
- The role of policy in influencing the extent of women's entrepreneurship that has occurred so far, together with the specific forms of women's entrepreneurship that have evolved. The role of institutional development is emphasized, within the context of a broadly based view of what constitutes public policy (Smallbone and Welter, 2001b). Following an analysis of what has been achieved so far, the book identifies the policy priorities for fostering women's entrepreneurship, appropriate to the different national contexts in the countries concerned.

The Transition Context

Processes of Market Reform and Stages of Transition

Although sharing many common processes, a combination of different starting points; differences in the nature and pace of market reforms (such as with respect to privatization); and in the wider process of social and economic change during the transformation period, has resulted in considerable differences in transition environments in practice. This affects both the nature and the extent of women's entrepreneurship, reflected in the number of women-owned businesses, and the nature of the contribution of women entrepreneurs to the transformation process. Moreover, when researching female entrepreneurs in formerly centrally planned economies it is important to recognise the differing cultural background between, and even within, countries as well as varying historical paths and differences in the current role of women in society. Female entrepreneurship in transition countries such as Ukraine and Moldova differs from that in Central Asian countries, because here traditional cultural values survived throughout the Soviet period, gaining in importance during the transition period. As chapters 6 and 7 demonstrate, in policy terms, female entrepreneurship in EU candidate countries can contribute to both the competitiveness and social inclusion agendas; although it can be argued that the role of women in informal markets in Lithuania is particularly distinctive in the latter respect. Germany serves as an example where within one country we can observe regional differences in women's entrepreneurship, which partly results from path-dependent developments over the past 40 years.

In this context, there is a need to review market reforms in different countries, taking into account the different stages of market development to be observed in transition economies and the relation between the development of women's entrepreneurship and the overall transformation process. The nature and extent of the contribution of women entrepreneurs to economic development is very much related to the external conditions in which they are operating, including the extent of market reforms, such as the privatization of former state-owned firms; establishing a legal frame; creating the overall institutional conditions; and the policy stance adopted by government. A comparison between Central European and former Soviet countries reveals a considerable difference in this extent.

Although Curran (2000) has criticised the use of 'transition indicator models' to assess progress towards introducing a market economy in transition countries, the approach enables us to summarise a number of aspects of market reform that have potential implications for the nature and pace of development of women's entrepreneurship. For example, the privatization of former state-owned assets is one of the processes contributing to the development of a private sector, either directly through the transfer of all, or part, of former state-owned companies into private ownership and/or indirectly through the use of the premises or equipment of former state-owned enterprises by new private firms.

In this context, indicators of the European Bank of Reconstruction and Development (EBRD) show wide variation between countries on various dimensions. In terms of small-scale privatization, for example, it varies from Croatia, the Czech Republic, Hungary, the three Baltic States, Poland, the Slovak Republic and Slovenia at one extreme (high) to Belarus and Turkmenistan at the other (low). In terms of price liberalisation, the spectrum varies from Hungary, Poland, Slovenia, Romania and Moldova at one extreme (high) to Belarus, Turkmenistan and Uzbekistan at the other (low). However, any transition model based solely on economic and political reforms neglects the wider social, historical and cultural context of these countries which in turn influences their transition path. Transition has been described as an 'open-ended search for an adequate systemic setting' (Dembinski and Unterlerchner, 1993, p. 153) and cannot be explained by economic and political reforms alone. In this regard, other researchers have sought to explain a quicker or slower pace of transformation through the differential influence of 'communist legacies' on different transition paths (Panther, 1998; Raiser, 1997, 1999; Smallbone and Welter, 2001b). Thus, in situations where market reforms have been slow or only partially installed, the institutional context becomes a critical factor for entrepreneurship, since government still has to create the framework conditions for private sector development to become embedded and sustained. In this respect, we differentiate between transition countries with a slow reform progress and those transition countries, where reforms progressed quicker, mainly the new member states of the European Union and upcoming candidate countries, taking into account that differences in the extent of market reforms, combined with other economic, social and historical differences limit the scope for generalisation across the variety of countries that comprise Central and Eastern Europe and the former Soviet Union.

Entrepreneurship in the Transformation Process

In considering (women's) entrepreneurship in a transition context, it may be helpful to briefly clarify some definitional issues such as what is meant by entrepreneurship. Broadly defined, entrepreneurship includes all business owners and self employed people, involved in some form of wealth generating activity, although narrower definitions that emphasize innovation and value added are useful in helping to identify the nature and extent of the contribution of entrepreneurship to economic and social change.

Entrepreneurship is a multidimensional concept, which can be analysed at different levels. Firstly, entrepreneurship is concerned with individuals in terms of their roles, traits and actions, integral to which are their learning abilities and behaviours (Pedler et al., 1998). The second dimension is at the firm level and the third at the aggregate level of industries, regions and nations. A consideration of the role and characteristics of entrepreneurship in a transition context involves linking the individual level to the aggregate level, as the context for entrepreneurship is a distinctive one, with a much stronger influence on the nature and extent of entrepreneurship compared to mature market economies.

Alongside the liberalisation of prices and the creation of market institutions, the transformation of centrally planned into market economies involves the development of a privately owned business sector, through a combination of the privatization of former state-owned companies and the creation of completely new enterprises. In principle, entrepreneurship (particularly in the form of the creation of new ventures) can contribute to the process of transforming former socialist countries into democratic, market based systems in a variety of ways. The potential role of entrepreneurs includes generating employment; using privatised property for production; contributing to the development of a diversified economic structure; contributing to the innovative capability of the economy; and contributing to economic development through the generation of foreign sales and/or import substitution. In addition to these essentially economic roles, entrepreneurship can also contribute to the emergence and development of a middle class that is fundamental to the wider process of transformation to a market based democracy.

However, achieving this potential contribution has presented many challenges in a context where, in most socialist countries, private business ownership was previously considered illegal; the resources for establishing and developing businesses extremely limited and the external environment contains many institutional deficiencies, compared with most mature market economies. Not surprisingly, some 15 years after the start of the reform process, there is considerable variation between countries in the extent to which a facilitating environment for the development of entrepreneurship has been created. As a result, it is inappropriate to refer to transition countries as if they are an undifferentiated, homogeneous group, any more than so-called market economies may be considered as a uniform group. Instead, it may be appropriate to think in terms of a continuum from central planned economies at the one extreme to liberal market economies at the other, with individual countries situated at different points along it. In the context of former socialist economies, positioning along this continuum is heavily influenced by the extent of the commitment of government to market reforms. This commitment is demonstrated through their actions with respect to progress with privatization; the extent to which there is price liberalisation; and the role of government with respect to the creation and effective operation of market institutions as well as their attitude towards entrepreneurship.

One issue that arises in countries that until the early 1990s were operating under a centrally planned system, concerns the potential of entrepreneurial activities during the socialist period to 'breed capitalism' (Kornai, 1992). Although in Central and Eastern European countries private entrepreneurship lost its major role with the introduction of a centrally planned economic system, different forms of private entrepreneurship co-existed beside state ownership and entrepreneurship within state enterprises during the socialist period (Welter, 1996; Smallbone and Welter, 2001a). In this regard, we can distinguish between the formal and the grey economy (consisting of the second and the illegal economy), where 'boundaries' frequently changed following political trends of liberalising and restricting private ownership and entrepreneurship.

In addition, Rehn and Taalas (2004) have emphasized how entrepreneurship flourished during the Soviet period in the daily lives of individuals, as they struggled to cope with the material shortages that were a common occurrence in the Soviet system. In pointing out the importance of interpreting entrepreneurship in its specific social context, Rehn and Taalas raise definitional issues concerning the nature of entrepreneurship, which they interpret as a 'search for opportunities and beneficial outcomes in economic interactions' (p. 246) which, through necessity, made most citizens of the USSR entrepreneurs.

All this contributes to a different background of (women) entrepreneurs in transition conditions, which interacts with characteristics of the institutional environment to influence the specific patterns of their entrepreneurial behaviour. For example, in early stage transition countries, where progress with market reforms has been slow or stalled, we can frequently observe a persistent type of behaviour that may be characterised as 'muddling through' and 'rule avoiding', but which nevertheless represents a learned response to a particular set of external environmental conditions (Welter, 2003, 2005; Welter and Smallbone, 2003). Examples include economic activity that is at least partly in the shadow economy, tax evasion, and a heavy reliance on personal network contacts in daily business life.

Women's Role in Economy and Society

In this context, gender could represent an additional dimension, in that the evolving institutional framework might affect women's formal integration into the emerging market economy due to redefined and changed gender roles, which restricts their access to external resources and organizations which are needed in order to realize a venture.

In post Soviet countries women entrepreneurs often lack the established networks their male colleagues brought with them from Soviet times (Welter et al., 2003). Men held most leading positions in politics and in state enterprises, which resulted in women being omitted from the Soviet nomenclatura, 'parallel circuits' in state firms and other high level networks, which have previously been suggested to be important influences on the development of entrepreneurship during the transition period (Smallbone and Welter, 2001a). As a result, at the beginning of the transition process, women had fewer opportunities both to enter entrepreneurship through privatising large state firms or through setting up small spin-off firms from larger state enterprises, as well as using 'old' contacts for their business. Only where they could transfer their management position from Soviet time into ownership, were women successful in entering entrepreneurship through the small-scale privatization of shops, restaurants, pharmacies.

On the other hand, networking contacts, especially where they involve strong ties, might be more important for women entrepreneurs in post Soviet societies than men in order to overcome traditional role patterns. Business is considered a predominantly 'male territory', requiring so-called 'male' qualities, such as strength and assertiveness. This is not surprising in Central Asian countries, for example, where traditional values with an emphasis on family relations played an important role both throughout the Soviet period and when transition started. However, there is a similar trend in the European post Soviet countries, such as the Ukraine or Moldova, reflected in 'widely held public assumptions that business is a masculine occupation' (Zhurzhenko, 1999, p. 246). 'Male guardianship' (Akiner, 1997, p. 287) gains momentum, which is a trend with enormous potential consequences for female entrepreneurship and for the role that social capital will have to play. For example, research on young entrepreneurs in transition economies revealed that female entrepreneurs in NIS countries were more likely to pursue a business with their husband/friend or father as partners or guardians, whilst in Central European countries it was apparently easier for women to act as entrepreneurs on their own (Roberts and Tholen, 1999).

Previous research on female entrepreneurs in transition countries has concentrated on the characteristics of women entrepreneurs, but most of these studies neglect both the heterogeneity of female entrepreneurship and the influence of the role attributed to women in society on the nature and extent of their involvement in entrepreneurship. Society as it manifests itself in cultural norms, traditions and religion might result in presuppositions concerning the roles ascribed to men and women (Chell and Baines, 1998). This in turn could influence the routes for women into entrepreneurship as well as the extent of female entrepreneurship, the form their entrepreneurial activities take and also their success. Therefore, when researching female entrepreneurs in transition economies it is important to recognise the differing cultural background between, and even within, countries as well as varying historical paths and the current role of women in society. Regional differences could aggravate constraints on female entrepreneurship not only where the business environment and the access to external resources and support are concerned, but also with respect to the role of women when traditional clan and patriarchal family structures restrict female roles.

Structure of the Book

This book incorporates an introductory chapter, seven country-specific chapters, each focused on a particular topic, and a concluding chapter ending up with policy recommendations. Each of the country-based chapters includes firstly, an overview of the development of entrepreneurship (small firms) so far, and the policy context; secondly, an evaluation of the role of women within society under previous regime; and thirdly, an in-depth discussion of a selected theme. The thematic sections of the chapters are based on unique empirical data drawn from research projects in which the different authors have been involved either alone, or as part of a research team.

In *Chapter 2*, contributed by Nina Isakova, Olha Krasovska, Lidia Kavunenko and Alexander Lugovy, the focus is a central theme in gender studies on entrepreneurship, i.e., gender differences (similarities) identified in the Ukraine. Female entrepreneurship is a new area of research in the Ukraine. Descriptive studies of small business and entrepreneurship performed in the country, did not aim to compare female and male entrepreneurs in order to identify differences in their personal characteristics, business goals and performance, barriers to business start-up and development; and perceptions of business environment. This chapter is an attempt to fill the gap by describing research results of a study, which concentrated on female entrepreneurship in a transition environment, whilst also including a male control group. The authors of this chapter are looking for answers to the following questions: are female entrepreneurs the same or different from their male counterparts in terms of personal characteristics and characteristics of their businesses; are there any gender differences in business start-up, motivations and business development; is there any impact of gender on finance related issues; are female and male networks similar; are women more or less successful with regard to business performance? The Ukrainian authors examine the data and evidence on male female differences in small business in one of the 'slower pace' transition countries.

In *Chapter 3* the authors, Friederike Welter, David Smallbone, Damira Mirzakhalikova, Natalja Schakirova and Charos Maksudova, consider the influence of inherited cultural tradition on modern state-of-the-art of female entrepreneurship in Uzbekistan. The chapter describes the nature and extent of female entrepreneurship in one of the former Soviet Asian republics, depicting ways women cope with barriers created to doing business by Muslim tradition and Soviet inheritance. Traditional values and norms have an important impact, as do religion, although in this case the influence is a more subtle one. In this context, the chapter studies the nature of women's entrepreneurship in Uzbekistan, where transition towards a market-based economy has been slow and where society shifts between traditions and modernity. Female entrepreneurship could play an important role in modernising Uzbek society and changing public attitudes towards women, which in turn will enable the government to make better use of the economic potential of female entrepreneurs.

Chapter 4 is discussing another important theme in the field of small business research in transition: are there any (female) entrepreneurs in new market economies or just business owners (proprietors)? The authors from Moldova, Elena Aculai, Nelly Rodionova and Natalja Vinogradova, provide a classification of female business owners based on a number of indicators characteristic of entrepreneurial people: namely, business aptitude, motives for starting a business, business performance, entrepreneurial behaviour and objectives. Innovative behaviour, defined as a type of dynamic behaviour, which has a strong effect on business, orientated to a long-term business development, is argued to be the most important indicator for defining entrepreneurs and proprietors. Drawing on a combination of survey data and case studies, a classification is introduced, together with a discussion of its contribution and limitations.

Chapter 5, written by Gül Berna Özcan, is based on 35 in-depth interviews with female entrepreneurs and numerous observations in various bazaars across Kyrgyzstan. De-industrialisation, poverty and disorientation have forced women to seek new ways of surviving, supporting their families and preserving their dignity.

This chapter analyses how women entrepreneurs shape their lives in these bazaars, to what extent their enterprise is generating income and job opportunities for their families and others, and how they cope with the risks and uncertainty of their business environment. The Kyrgyz findings show rapid growth in the number of both female and male entrepreneurs in bazaars, which increasingly evolve into entrepreneurial hubs with newly emerging business/entrepreneurial networks, providing the externalities of a capitalist market economy. The author argues that while academic and policy studies on Eastern Europe have been rapidly increasing, there is very little empirically informed research on Central Asian development in general and Kyrgyzstan in particular. At the same time multi-ethnic Kyrgyzstan is striving to develop its own form of nation state, beyond the old Russian domination and ethnic and tribal rivalries.

Female traders in informal markets in Lithuania are the focus of *Chapter 6*, contributed by Ruta Aidis. One of the main aims of this chapter is to provide a further understanding and insight into this category of female SMEs. The other aim of this chapter is to provide an introduction to the situation for women, in general, in Lithuania, which is one of the EU's new member states, as well as specific information on SME owners. Traders at open air markets are especially interesting from a gender point of view because in many cases, women make up the majority of traders. For many women trading is still an activity of the last resort to earn income, for others open air markets could be a starting point to expand their activities, in the long run leading to viable businesses. Drawing on a study of traders at one of the largest open air markets in Lithuania, the author sets out to explore these questions.

Chapter 7, which has been written by Mateja Drnovšek and Miroslav Glas, recognizes the gap in female entrepreneurship studies in Slovenia and draws from projection theory. The following questions are addressed: what is the contribution of women-managed businesses to gross output and employment growth in Slovenia; what are the overall characteristics of companies managed by women entrepreneurs in Slovenia compared to their male counterparts; what kind of strategies and related business challenges do Slovenian women entrepreneurs undertake; what are the gender-specific characteristics of managing a growing business? The authors used qualitative and quantitative research methods combined with several statistical sources. First, the present state of the development of female entrepreneurship in Slovenia is assessed through a univariate analysis of an economy-wide database of incorporated and sole-proprietor companies. Second, in order to gain an insight into the business and strategic characteristics of women-managed companies a questionnaire-based survey on a sample of the 500 fastest-growing companies in Slovenia in 2003 was analysed. The authors offer implications to different groups of readers, including academic researchers, policy-makers, entrepreneurs, managers and business students. For local academic researchers this study makes important theoretical and empirical contributions to the changing role of women in Slovenian society. In relation to policy-makers, this study brings useful insights on how to design policy measures to foster dynamic entrepreneurship and entrepreneurs.

Chapter 8, contributed by Friederike Welter, discusses differences and similarities of female entrepreneurship in West and East Germany, highlighting the peculiarities of the development of this important sector in the specific conditions of a post-socialist country. Because of the massive transfer of capital, know-how and institutions one would expect little differences between West and East German entrepreneurs. On the other hand, East German female entrepreneurship might also show some distinctive characteristics because of the rapid transformation process, which was accompanied by a massive loss of employment and a renaissance of conservative values. This question so far has not been explored systematically. Overall, this chapter draws attention to the institutional embeddedness of women's entrepreneurship, which is influenced by the regulatory frame, societal values and norms of behaviour, thus allowing an exploration and partial explanation of differences observed between women's enterprises, their routes into entrepreneurship and motivations, all of which are influenced by institutional legacies.

The final *Chapter 9* presents conclusions with respect to the current state of women's entrepreneurship in different transition economies and former planned economies; the role of women entrepreneurs in relation to the wider social, economic and institutional change; and finally, policy priorities for fostering women's entrepreneurship in countries at different stages of market reform and an outlook comparing women's entrepreneurship in transition economies and more developed countries.

References

Akiner, S. (1997), 'Between tradition and modernity: the dilemma facing contemporary Central Asian women', in M. Buckley (ed), *Post-Soviet women: from the Baltic to Central Asia*, Cambridge University Press, Cambridge, pp. 261-304.

Berger, B. (1991), Introduction. In B. Berger (ed), The Culture of Entrepreneurship, ICS Press, California, pp. 1-12.

Chell, E. and Baines, S. (1998), 'Does gender affect business performance?', *Entrepreneurship and Regional Development*, vol. 10, no. 2, pp. 117-135.

Curran, J. (2000), 'Small and Medium Enterprise Development: Borrowing from Elsewhere? A Research and Development Agenda – a comment on Allan Gibb's Paper', *Journal of Small Business and Enterprise Development*, vol. 7, no. 3, pp. 212-219.

Dembinski, P.H. and Unterlerchner, H.C. (1993), 'Barriers to Entry for Private Enterprises: The Muddling through of State Enterprises', *Revue européenne des sciences sociales*, vol. 31, no. 96, pp. 151-166.

Kornai, J. (1992), 'The Affinity between Ownership and Co-ordination Mechanisms: The Common Experience of Reform in Socialist Countries', in K.Z. Poznanski (ed), *Constructing capitalism: the re-emergence of civil society and liberal economy in the post-communist world,* Westview, Boulder, Colorado, pp. 97-116.

Panther, S. (1998), 'Historisches Erbe und Transformation: "Lateinische" Gewinner - "Orthodoxe" Verlierer?', in G. Wegner and J. Wieland (eds), *Formelle und informelle*

Institutionen: Genese, Interaktion und Wandel, Metropolis Verlag, Marburg, pp. 211-251.

Pedler, M., Burgoyne, J. and Boydell, T. (1998), *The Learning Company: A Strategy for Sustainable Development*, McGraw Hill.

Raiser, M. (1997), *Informal Institutions, Social Capital and Economic Transition: Reflections on a Neglected Dimension*, Working Paper 25, EBRD, London.

Raiser, M. (1999), *Trust in Transition*, Working Paper 39, EBRD, London.

Rehn, A. and Taalas, S. (2004), ''Znakomstva I Svyazi' (Acquaintances and connections) – Blat, the Soviet Union and mundane entrepreneurship', *Entrepreneurship and Regional Development*, vol. 6, pp. 235-250.

Roberts, K. and Tholen, J. (1999), 'Junge Unternehmer in den neuen Marktgesellschaften Mittel- und Osteuropas', in D. Bögenhold (ed), *Unternehmensgründungen und Dezentralität – Eine Renaissance der beruflichen Selbständigkeit?* Westdeutscher Verlag, Opladen, pp. 257-278.

Smallbone, D. and Welter, F. (2001a), 'The distinctiveness of entrepreneurship in transition economies', *Small Business Economics*, vol. 16, pp. 249-262.

Smallbone, D. and Welter, F. (2001b), 'The Role of Government in SME Development in Transition Countries', *International Small Business Journal*, vol. 19, no. 4, pp. 63-77.

Welter, F. (1996), 'Unternehmer in Osteuropa', *Berliner Debatte INITIAL*, no. 3, pp. 100-107.

Welter, F. (2003), *Strategien, KMU und Umfeld*, Schriftenreihe des RWI, 69, Duncker and Humblot, Berlin.

Welter, F. (2005), 'Entrepreneurial Behavior in Differing Environments', in D.B. Audretsch, H. Grimm and C.W. Wessner (eds), *Local Heroes in the Global Village*, International Studies in Entrepreneurship, Springer, New York, pp. 93-112.

Welter, F. and Smallbone, D. (2003), 'Entrepreneurship and Enterprise Strategies in Transition Economies: An Institutional Perspective', in D. Kirby and A. Watson (eds), *Small Firms and Economic Development in Developed and Transition Economies: A Reader*, Ashgate, Aldershot, pp. 95-114.

Welter, F., Smallbone, D., E. Aculai, E., Isakova, N. and Schakirova, N. (2003), 'Female entrepreneurship in post Soviet countries', in J. Butler (ed), *New perspectives on Women Entrepreneurs*, Information Age Publisher, Greenwich, pp. 243-270.

Zhurzhenko, T. (1999), 'Gender and identity formation in post-Socialist Ukraine: The case of women in the shuttle business', in R. Bridgman, S. Cole and H. Howard-Bobiwash (eds), *Feminist Fields: Ethnographic Insights*, Broadview Press, Ontario, pp. 243-263.

Part 2
Women's Entrepreneurship in Former Soviet Republics

Chapter 2

Entrepreneurship in the Ukraine: A Male Female Comparison

Nina B. Isakova, Olha Krasovska, Lidia Kavunenko and Alexander Lugovy

Introduction

In the Ukraine, women-owned businesses constitute a significant part of small business sector. In spite of the growing role of women's participation in business, little is known about female entrepreneurs. The novelty of the phenomenon of female entrepreneurship in transition economies is the reason why it did not receive much attention of SME researchers. The more so, descriptive studies performed in the country did not aim to compare female and male entrepreneurs to identify differences in their personal characteristics, business goals and performance, barriers to business start-up and development, perceptions of business environment. This chapter is an attempt to fill the gap by describing research results of a study,[1] which concentrated on female entrepreneurship in a transition environment. The following issues, popular in the literature on female entrepreneurship, will be discussed:

- Are female entrepreneurs the same or different from their male counterparts in terms of personal characteristics and characteristics of their businesses?
- Are there any gender differences in business start-up, motivations and business development?
- Is there any impact of gender on finance related issues?
- Are female and male networks similar?
- Are women more or less successful with regard to business performance?

The main objective of this chapter is to examine the evidence on male female difference in small business in one of the 'slower pace' transition countries. This discussion is preceded by a general description of small and medium-sized enterprise (SME) development and policies, and the role which Ukrainian women were playing in the pre-reform period.

Entrepreneurship and SME Development in the Ukraine

Since 1991 the Ukraine, like other Soviet successor states, had to undergo a complex three-fold transition – to independent sovereignty, democracy and a market economy. Like all former communist countries, the Ukraine faced the task of building a new economic system based on free market and private sector development despite the absence of an adequate legal framework, hyperinflation, production crisis and lack of business tradition and skills.

Bottom-up entrepreneurial initiative of people, who were confronted with the necessity to survive in the years of economic crisis and high level of unemployment, and top-down actions of the government, consisting in the introduction of new legislation to allow and promote private entrepreneurship development, have resulted in creation of a new sector in the economy – the small business sector. At present, in the Ukraine the development of entrepreneurship and SME sector is considered to be one of the most significant factor in macro economic stabilization, solving the unemployment problem and fostering innovation.

The development of the small business sector has undergone and is still experiencing a number of political and economic difficulties caused by the overall social and economic crisis in the country and the transition from the centrally planned to a market economy. Two primary ways to create private enterprises were used, namely, the registration of new businesses and the privatization of former state companies. In the first case, scarce personal savings and a lack of start capital had urged entrepreneurs to look for and select activities with low capital requirements and low barriers of entry, which, as a rule, were to be found in retail and intermediary activities. The pace of development was much slower for manufacturing or technology-based companies. With regard to privatization of state-owned companies the main problem was restructuring and changing the management styles to keep the profiles of operations and retaining the markets. Between 1992 and 1998 the number of privatized small enterprises totalled 46,355 entities, of which 82 per cent had been privatized in 1995-1998. Among these 'small privatization' objects the majority were retail trade and service firms. The financial crisis in Russia in 1998 had a major impact on the process of private entrepreneurship development in the Ukraine. As of now, the capacity of private entrepreneurship is still underused in solving the problems of unemployment, and in increasing state and local budget revenues, the supply of goods, the income level of population, as well as solving social problems.

It is difficult in the Ukraine to obtain reliable data on the number of small enterprises. Researchers on entrepreneurship and small business development are using three main sources of information: official statistics gathered by the Statistics Committee of the Ukraine, sociological surveys performed by projects with foreign/international funding and anecdotal evidence. Official statistics do not reflect the real situation because of a considerable number of shadow businesses and/or shadow operations. Even registered and operating enterprises conceal turnover from state authorities: half of the respondents in a survey in 1999 admitted the shadow operations at their enterprises amounting to between 20 and 50 per cent (Yacoub and Senchuk, 2000). However, the high level of unofficial (shadow) business is argued by Kaufmann (1994, p. 66) to demonstrate the entrepreneurship, creativity and ability to adapt and survive of Ukraine's citizens. Despite the mentioned drawbacks of official statistics it does help to see the general tendencies and dynamics of small business development. As data in Table 2.1 demonstrate, the rate of small business development had been slowing down since the late 1990s.

Table 2.1 Main indicators of small enterprise development in the Ukraine during the 1990s

Indicators	1991	1998	2000	2002
number of small enterprises (SE)	47,084	173,404	217,930	253,791
in % to previous year	-	127.3	110.6	108.6
SE per 10,000 inhabitants	9	35	44	53
average annual SE employment, in 1,000 persons	1192.4	1559.9	1709.8	1918.5
in % to previous year	-	111.8	101.9	106.1
average employment per SE	25	9	8	8
% of SE employment in total employment	4.9	9.0	10.8	13.2

Source: Osaulenko (2003, p. 338).

In 2002 the number of small enterprises equalled 253,791 which is five times higher compared to 1991, while the growth of small business employment was only 2.7 times, reflecting a decrease in the average number of employees per business (25 in 1991 and 8 employees in 2002). In 2002 the share of small enterprises employment was 13.2 per cent of the total employment.

The year 2000 was the first year of Gross Domestic Product (GDP) growth since independence, which was reflected in enterprise performance over the year: a larger proportion of Ukrainian firms were profitable in 2000 than in 1999 and there has been almost universal growth in value added activities. According to a survey of Ukrainian enterprises, smaller firms were more dynamic, and more of them were profitable than larger firms; further, start-up firms generally performed much better than either state-owned or privatized firms (Yacoub, Senchuk and Tkachenko, 2001).

With regard to the main types of activities small enterprises concentrate in wholesale and retail trade, industrial production, realtors' operations and construction (Table 2.2).

Table 2.2 Sectoral structure of small business sector (in per cent)

Basic type of economic activity	1998	2000	2002
Wholesale & retail trade	51.9	46.4	40.0
Industrial production	15.0	15.8	16.0
Realtors operations	9.9	12.1	15.6
Construction	8.6	8.4	8.6
Agribusiness, hunting, forestry	2.0	3.6	4.6
Transport, communications	3.1	3.9	4.5
Collective, public & personal services	3.7	3.4	3.8
Hotels & restaurants	3.4	3.5	3.4
Healthcare	0.9	0.9	1.1
Education	0.7	0.8	0.8
Other	0.8	1.2	1.4
Total number of SE	173,404	217,930	253,791

Source: Authors' calculations based on Osaulenko (2003, p. 339).

Official statistical data suggest that the number of small companies in trade is decreasing, while other sectors demonstrate a slight increase, in particular transport and communications sector and agribusiness. When summing up all types of service activities (realtors, transport and communication, collective, public and personal services, hotels and restaurants, healthcare and education), the share of service businesses amounts to 29.2 per cent in 2002.

Noticeable regional variations in small business development are one of the characteristic features of the Ukraine. Indeed, since the beginning of economic reforms great regional variations in small business development have been reported in the country, which can be attributed to the regional economic situation, available regional resources, economic activity of population, and the attitude of local authorities to business development (Klochko and Isakova, 1996). Using the number of operating small enterprises per 10,000 inhabitants as an indicator for regional comparison, there are roughly three main groups of regions: Kiev city (151 small enterprises – SE – per 10,000 inhabitants), several regions, which demonstrate better or approximately the same results as the Ukrainian average (61 to 51 SE per 10,000 inhabitants) and those regions, which are less developed in terms of small business (48 to 32 SE per 10,000 inhabitants). Regions with big industrial cities, a developed infrastructure, state industrial plants (the assets of which were successfully 'used' in new private companies started by top managers), bigger local markets, high qualification manpower and innovation potential typically report more progress in small business development. Some regions provide a better economic environment for new enterprises to start, survive and grow compared to less fortunate areas, and in such regions the input of small business into regional economic development is higher.

Although there are no official statistical data available on female enterprises, surveys of entrepreneurs and anecdotal information testify that women tend to do business in retail trade, catering, services of all kinds, which is supported by data of a baseline survey conducted in 1999 (Kiev International Institute of Sociology, 2000). According to this survey 98 per cent of all women-owned business are small and employ fewer than 50 employees. 69.6 per cent of women-businesses are in wholesale or retail trade. Different types of services make up 23.2 per cent of female enterprises, while manufacturing (and mining) and construction are less popular amounting to just 3 per cent of female enterprises.

The Policy Environment for (Female) Entrepreneurship

The Ukrainian case serves a good example of how business can develop 'from the creativity, drive and commitment of individuals rather than as a result of government actions'. (Smallbone and Welter, 2001, p. 259) What is the policy environment for small (female) enterprises development in the country?

A retrospective analysis of the Ukrainian government actions (policy) to support private entrepreneurship suggests that the first steps with regard to promoting private entrepreneurial initiative were related to the formation of a legal framework for entrepreneurship. The main action taken by the state was the adoption of the Law on Entrepreneurship (February 1991) to allow legal private entrepreneurial activities. The legal framework for private enterprise activities established, no other components of a state policy to support private entrepreneurship were in place, such as macroeconomic stability, national currency, taxation to allow business growth, favourable social environment, positive attitude at the level of regional and local authorities, a business support infrastructure or any other direct support measures. It took years for some of the components of an adequate business environment to be developed. Thus, during the first years of SME development in the Ukraine the majority of private entrepreneurs perceived the overall business environment as unfavourable (Klochko and Isakova, 1996). It used to be a common saying among entrepreneurs addressing authorities: 'There is no need to help us; please, don't interfere'. Private entrepreneurship was developing despite any government policies and unfavourable economic conditions. By the mid-1990s government started to recognise the significant role private entrepreneurs may play in regeneration of economy and country's welfare. That was not a sudden insight: international economic advisers working in the Ukraine were persistent advocates of supporting and developing a viable SME.[3]

Ukrainian officials at all levels of responsibility have been widely utilising this notion to demonstrate their commitment to economic reforms and their progressive views. In late 1996, the government announced a major tax reform package intended to reduce the tax burden and improve tax collection. The proposals included reductions in payroll tax and in personal income tax rates, higher allowances for depreciation as well as reductions in the contributions to various funds including the Employment Fund. The government intended to offset part of the revenue loss by a reduction in tax exemptions and by introduction of a property tax.

In 1997, the State Committee for Issues of Entrepreneurship was established to elaborate and implement policies, which would eliminate barriers in registration and licensing of entrepreneurial activities, significantly simplify reporting procedures, diminish the tax burden and the number of inspections by local authorities. These tasks were to be fulfilled through drafting new legislation acts and launching a vast deregulation programme in the framework of the President's of Ukraine administrative reform. Further restructuring of the Committee (now the State Committee of Ukraine in the Issues of Regulatory Policies and Entrepreneurship) took place during 2000 with the objective to strengthen its deregulation function and regional outreach.

The President of the Ukraine's Executive Order 'On Introduction of a single state regulatory policy in the area of entrepreneurship', the Laws of the Ukraine 'On State Support of Small Enterprises' and 'On the National Small Business Support Programme' are appraised highly by government officials and are considered important documents for the further development of private business sector. The Law of the Ukraine 'On the National Small Business Support Programme' determines the main objectives of the Programme as follows:

- improvement of the normative and legal base in the sphere of entrepreneurial activities;
- formation of a single state regulatory policy in the sphere of entrepreneurship;
- improvement of financial, credit and investment support of small enterprise;
- promotion of creation of infrastructure for small enterprise development; and
- implementation of regional policies to promote small enterprise development.

The expected results, as written down in the document, are described rather fuzzy: acceleration of small enterprise development, utilisation of its hidden capabilities, making small enterprise an effective instrument to solve economic and social problems, promotion of structural change of the economy, sustainable tendency in increase of number of small enterprises, reduction of shadow turnover in small business, increase in input of small business to the economy of the Ukraine and strengthening the economic base of regions, a positive impact on solving unemployment problems, saturation of national market with goods and services. The Programme foresees annual elaboration of concrete measures to implement its tasks, and the Cabinet of Ministers is responsible for these measures to be implemented by local authorities. However, interviews with entrepreneurs and survey data suggest that the Programme and implementation measures have little effect on SME development in the regions.

Entrepreneurs as a rule do not know about the existence of this Programme, or they do not benefit from these measures, which is proven by our survey results and case study interviews. Similar to ten years ago, Ukrainian entrepreneurs rely on their own capabilities or the support from friends and families (Smallbone et al., 1999).

Female entrepreneurs experience the same difficulties in dealing with government at the local level. In our study, female respondents did not perceive they have been discriminated in any way, but considering the scale and sector of businesswomen activities (micro enterprises mostly in services and trade) one might argue that the insufficient attention to the needs of micro and small businesses is significantly limiting the growth of small business sector on the account of new women-owned businesses.

The Role of Ukrainian Women in Society during the Past Decades

The role of women in society during the Soviet period was to a great extent determined by the gender policies of the communist party, which aimed at increasing the total labour force by means of attracting as many women as possible to work. Before the Soviet era marriage and family responsibilities were perceived as the main social goals of a Ukrainian woman and women were mostly deprived of any political and economic independence in society. This traditional patriarchal gender order was changed with the establishment of a state based on communist ideology. The first years of the new state were characterized by an active transformation of the basic social institutes, which resulted in providing political and civil equal rights to women, including the spheres of education, occupational choices and freedom of travel.

However, this boom in gender equality was limited both geographically to large industrial cities and socially to working class and professionals ('intelligentsia'). An important social event with a long-lasting effect on the status of women was the 'illiteracy liquidation', which covered women as well as men. This campaign, unprecedented in scale, had allowed women to become a noticeable part of the workforce and enlarged the place of women in labour market. For example, in the early 1920s 12 million people were illiterate in the Ukraine, including 8 million women. The efforts of a network of special schools for grown-ups and the All-Ukrainian society 'Down with illiteracy' headed by V.O. Meschaninova had resulted in an increase in literate women from 37.2 per cent in 1921 to 57.5 per cent by 1929 (Stefanenko, 1999).

According to Soviet ideology, women were supposed to have equal rights to men and to be actively participating in the 'construction' of communism in the country. This policy was consistently pursued for almost two decades, made even more important by the significant decrease in the male population, following the First World War, the revolution and the civil war (Barsukova, 2001). Starting from the 1930s a shift towards 'double burden' responsibilities of women had taken place, as the state had placed on women the responsibility for performing simultaneously the roles of a successful worker and a successful mother. At the same time men were looked upon as agents of political, economic and social changes and progress. In the families the patriarchal order prevailed with women in charge of family budgets, household activities, raising children and serving the husband. The Second World War and the post-war period had only aggravated the double burden: women had to work harder in order to replace men who were serving in the army and lost in the war. According to statistics, the share of women among workers and office employees in the Ukrainian SSR in 1943-1945 was much higher and amounted to 74 per cent (Stefanenko, 1999a, p. 153).

In the following years the state also aspired to involve women as much as possible into the national economy, which by the end of 1980s has resulted in female employment being equal to that of male employment (Table 2.3).

Table 2.3 Share of women in the number of employed in Soviet Republics (in per cent)

Soviet republic	1940	1960	1970	1980
USSR	39	47	51	51
Russian SFSR	41	50	53	52
Ukrainian SSR	37	45	50	52
Moldavian SSR	35	43	51	51
Uzbek SSR	31	39	41	43

Source: Sivko (1983, p. 70).

Educated women in the Soviet Ukraine were employed in a variety of sectors, which is illustrated in Table 2.4, demonstrating employment preferences of women. Jobs in such sectors as education, healthcare, industrial production (mainly, light industry and food processing) and science were selected by women with university education or maybe left for them by men because of lower salaries. Women with a secondary vocational education preferred industrial production, healthcare and trade. 1980 showed an increase in the share of women (both university and secondary vocational education) in construction – a traditionally male-dominated sector.

More recently, in the 1970s and 1980s the extensive development of economy determined the social status of the Ukrainian women: 90 per cent were working and the percentage of employed women was rising (Stefanenko, 1999a). The majority of women had to work because it was impossible to keep the family having just one (husband) breadwinner, which was another reason contributing to a high level of female participation in the labour market. However, a higher level of education did not influence the status of working women: men were occupying leading positions in politics, economy and society, while women were perceived as 'second class' employees. The average income of female employees was, as a rule, lower than that of male employees; women were the last to be hired and the first to be fired. The priority placed by the Soviet state on developing heavy industries resulted in a situation where few resources were delivered to the light industry and other sectors with a high share of female employment. This in turn resulted in inferior working conditions and lower wages. Even in industries with a high percentage of female employment, such as light industry, food industry, teaching, medicine, men would execute the supervision and decision-making. Bohachevska-Homyak (1995) argues that the number of Ukrainian women who had well-paid job in production, government or party was very small compared to their total employment in these sectors. She calls the tendency to keep salaries and wages (and hence the prestige) lower in sectors with a high concentration of women employment the 'feminisation of certain professions' (Bohachevska-Homyak, 1995, p. 363), which is a well-known phenomenon in Western economies.

Table 2.4 Share of women specialists with university and secondary vocational education by sector in the Ukraine (in per cent)

Sectors	As of 16 November 1970 University education	As of 16 November 1970 Secondary vocational education	As of 14 November 1980 University education	As of 14 November 1980 Secondary vocational education
Industrial production	13.2	20.5	18.2	24.5
Agriculture	2.6	6.2	3.1	7.1
Transport	1.1	2.2	1.5	2.7
Communication	0.2	1.0	0.4	1.2
Construction	2.2	3.2	7.5	5.4
Trade, catering, supply	3.2	11.2	4.8	14.7
Communal and services to population	0.3	0.9	0.8	1.7
Healthcare, physical culture and social welfare	11.9	26.7	9.4	20.4
Education	44.5	14.3	34.4	9.5
Culture	1.5	2.6	2.0	2.8
Science	8.3	2.6	9.9	2.8
Credit and insurance	0.5	1.5	0.7	1.8
Government bodies and cooperative management	5.7	4.9	6.5	4.5
Total	100	100	100	100

Source: Sivko (1983, p. 23).

According to Pavlychko (1997), nowadays women in public service constitute the majority (in some ministries women dominate, for example they account for 67.2 per cent in the Ministry of Economy and up to 95 per cent in the Ministry of Social Welfare), but only between three and four per cent occupy top positions. Considering the low labour turnover in public services, we may argue that the situation is similar to that to be observed in the last years before the reforms. Notwithstanding the high representation of women in ministries and other government structures, these females were (and are) not advocates of gender equality and did not 'change the nature of authority and its ideology in the interest of women' (Pavlychko, 1997, p. 224).

During Soviet times, Ukrainian women never played a significant role in politics. In accordance with party recommendations there was a special quota for women representation in the Verhovna Rada (as well as female membership in the party, female participation in the party congresses), which increased up to 36 per cent by 1980. However, this made no difference under the highly centralized power of the Communist party and direct 'instructions' from Moscow on the laws to be adopted and decisions to be made. Women had no impact on social and economic development. In our view, women were neither among the 'nomenclatura' (well connected party members and other elite positions), nor were they perceived as potential politicians by society. This is reflected in the low share of women in the Verhovna Rada after perestroika, when no quota for women was foreseen in free elections (Table 2.5).

Table 2.5 Women in the Verhovna Rada of the Ukraine (in per cent)

Verhovna Rada convocations	Per cent of women
1st convocation (1938-1947)	24.8
4th convocation (1955-1959)	34.5
7th convocation (1967-1971)	34.1
10th convocation (1980-1985)	36.0
12th convocation (1990- 1994)	3.0
13th convocation (1994-1998)	5.7
14th convocation (1998-2002)	8.1

Source: Kalacheva (1999, p. 63).

Any discussion of the role of women in society should not be missing such an important role as social reproduction. Women remained responsible for their families and children upbringing despite the necessity to work full-time. The participation of a vast majority of the female population in the labour market has led to a change in reproduction behaviour. According to Zhurzhenko (2001), the cities experienced a shift from large families to families with four and less children. In describing the evolution of government measures to support maternity and childhood, she concludes that the Soviet model of social reproduction was a 'mobilising model', which implied, on the one hand, the maximum use of women as labour resource and, on the other hand, the use of their biological reproduction function to increase labour resources (Zhurzhenko, 2001, p. 87).

Until 1985, when the 'perestroika' started and the first shy feminist activities commenced, the socialist gender order remained in place. However, feminism and feminist ideas have not found a wide dissemination in the Ukraine. The majority of the Ukrainian population feel sceptical towards the need to change the existing gender order. Men in politics and authorities do not take gender studies and feminist organizations seriously, even if they never would admit this in public. What is more, women themselves are not in favour of feminism movement either. Although the majority would admit that their life is hard and tedious, they would not blame the existing order of things. Rather a woman would blame herself for not being able to marry more successfully and/or make a better professional carrier.

Women in the Ukraine are not (and never were) a homogeneous group and there is no a single women's identity (Pavlychko, 1997). At the same time, there are features, which are typical for all Ukrainian women such as a high level of involvement in social production and on average a high level of education. In our view, these factors had allowed for the emergence of female entrepreneurship, even if in many cases it was necessity-driven.

Are Women and Men Entrepreneurs in the Ukraine Different or Similar?

Female entrepreneurship and gender differences in small business development continue to be at the forefront of research in many countries. Studies focus on identifying female entrepreneurs' characteristics and gender differences in such areas as characteristics of businesses and entrepreneurs, motivation, education and previous experiences, psychological characteristics, financing, barriers to development and growth, and networking (Scott, 1986; Cromie, 1987; Aldrich, 1989; Brush, 1992; Fay and Williams, 1993; Catley and Hamilton, 1998; Isakova, 2001).

Brush (1992), in having reviewed 57 papers on women business owners, concludes that women entrepreneurs are similar to men in some aspects, such as basic demographic factors, business characteristics and problems, but are different in work experience, education, skills, business goals and performance. Based on a literature review of some 400 academic articles on women entrepreneurs Carter et al. (2001) have revealed that literature on the topic is developing in the direction to investigate more specifically gender differences in business management, finance, business networks and performance; these authors conclude that cumulative knowledge and explanatory theories are still lacking. Research results which are presented in this chapter aim to add to the bulk of knowledge on differences and similarities of female and male entrepreneurs, focusing on a transition country. The data which are obtained from a survey of 297 female and 81 male small business owners in four regions of the Ukraine, and case study interviews are used to examine whether there are any gender differences with regard to:

- characteristics of entrepreneurs and their motivations;
- start-up patterns, resources and constraints;
- management of small firms;
- issues of financing;
- business networks; and
- business performance and growth.

The findings will be compared with previous research to see if gender variations in selected areas in the transition conditions are similar to those identified in Western countries. Discussion will focus on the topics identified by Carter and her co-authors (2001) as those dominating in academic literature concerned with female entrepreneurship.

Characteristics and Motivations of Entrepreneurs

Female entrepreneurs are a heterogeneous group with variations in their backgrounds, motivations and goals. Still certain common characteristics can be traced, which was done by Baygan (2000) on the base of data of several surveys conducted in the 1990s in different countries. This author comes to the conclusion that 'on average female entrepreneurs are in the age group of 35-44, married and have children; have less formal or business related education. In industrialized countries women entrepreneurs have relatively higher educational levels but still often lack prior entrepreneurial or management experience' (Baygan, 2000, p. 19). Broad descriptions of personal characteristics of female entrepreneurs, including demographic features, education, previous work and business experience find more similarities than differences with male counterparts (Carter et al., 2001).

In the Ukraine, female entrepreneurs are typically in the age groups of 40-49 or 30-39, married and have children. The majority are highly educated and competent people with university degrees and work experience (mostly in non-production sphere of economics) but they often lack formal business training and business experience. The latter is explained by the fact that private business sector had only started to develop since the political and economic reforms in the late 1980s. A typical male entrepreneur has much in common with the female counterpart: no differences were observed in terms of education, business training or prior business experience but male entrepreneurs were on average slightly older (40-49 age group is the most representative), there were more married men and men tended to have previous work experience in production sphere.[2]

Women start a business for the following three main reasons: they are looking for job satisfaction, independence and achievement; and men come into business for the same reasons (Carter et al., 2001). Such reasons for start-up as 'independence', 'controlling time', 'flexibility for personal and family life' and 'freedom to adapt one's own approach to work' were found to be the same for women and men by Shane et al. (1991).

However, there are studies to suggest that there exists a difference in motives of men and women, or emphasis they attach to motives (Catley and Hamilton, 1998). According to other sources (Baygan, 2000), women come into business to generate extra income for household, or to be independent and creative. Although the 'push group', which includes women who are forced into business, is comparatively larger, the 'pull group' of those who are looking for independence and self-realization in business, is argued to be growing (Baygan, 2000).

The wish to be independent (to work independently) was the most frequent motive for the Ukrainian women to start business, which does not necessarily mean that women come to business to be financially independent from their husbands or family. Disappointment with the government that was unable to provide decent jobs during the years of political and economic reforms urged women to take their destiny in their own hands. In this respect women do not differ from men, who also indicated this motive most frequently.

Starting business as an alternative to unemployment was the second priority in motivation of women, but not for men. Male entrepreneurs more often than women came into business because they had resources (finance, skills, social capital) available. Although such push factor for starting business as generation of 'income to live or survive' was important for female entrepreneurs, the share of those women who indicated that they started business just because they wanted 'to have own business' was very close in number.

For example, a female entrepreneur owning a clothing factory and a shop in Kharkiv, always wished to have her own business. This 25-year-old married woman had set her mind on starting her own business after graduating from a university with the diploma in accounting and audit. She did not want to work as a hired employee. Her education, a bit of working experience and money received from selling an inherited apartment of her grandmother served a base to create this company, with 8 employees, bought-out premises, and profit, which exceeded expenditures. She was competent in economics, accounting and business planning. She knew her business plan would be correct and feasible. She was dreaming about a clothing factory as a child, when she wanted to be a clothing designer. She did not become a designer but owns a business in this sphere. When she met a middle-aged female friend who spent all her life making clothing, this helped a lot in making the dreams of the respondent come true.

In the Ukraine, not unlike in other transition economies women tend to do business in selected sectors, which supports the suggestion by Bruno (1997), that 'women who succeed in becoming entrepreneurs are usually limited to specific sectors, such as services or the production of cultural/educational activities or textile and fashion businesses where interference of organized crime and perceived risks are lower' (Bruno, 1997, p. 57). This corresponds to the data of a survey of female entrepreneurs in Russia in 1997, which depicts a distinct sectoral preference of women owning businesses: According to Basurkova (1999), they are most active in retail trade, catering, science, culture, and healthcare.

The Ukrainian women surveyed in this study owned small companies operating in services, trade, small-scale manufacturing and agriculture. The agricultural businesses were engaged in growing vegetables and poultry in the backyards of own homes at the outskirts of the cities. Manufacturing firms were producing food products (oils, diary, bread, cakes), textiles and textile articles, including wearing apparels; knitted wear. There were companies engaged in production of wood articles and carpentry. Some firms indicated production of books or periodicals or printing materials as the first type of activities. Plastic products, flat glass, ceramic articles, metal structures, imitation jewellery, optical instruments, electricity apparatus are also among the products of the surveyed manufacturing firms. Trade firms were spread along wholesale and retail trade activities in specialized stores, in non-specialized stores and in the market places. They were engaged in selling food products and a wide range of consumer goods. Repair services, photo shops, hairdressing, catering, canteens, real estate, renting premises, travel agency, education, medical care, legal, audit, recruitment, software, business consulting were among the services provided by the female firms.

The sectors preferred by women are not exclusively female; as our results demonstrate, men business owners are to be found in all types of activities described above.

Business aptitude is an important personal characteristic to influence success in starting and running a company. According to self-evaluation of respondents, Ukrainian women are less oriented to risk taking, planning and problem solving in comparison with men (Table 2.6).

Table 2.6 Perceptions of entrepreneurs of their business aptitude*

Features	Female	Male
Risk orientation	3.54	4.14
Planning orientation	3.91	4.36
Preference to determine one's own professional future	4.64	4.65
Achievement motivation	4.08	4.47
Problem solving orientation	3.78	4.38

*Mean on a five-point Likert scale.

Source: Own survey 2002.

Start-up: Patterns, Resources and Constraints

The topic of start-up patterns, resources and constraints is related to analysis of characteristics and motivations of female entrepreneurs and most researchers agree that start-up is more difficult for women (Carter et al., 2001). The heterogeneity of female entrepreneurs is reflected in business start-up patterns in the Ukraine: a small group of entrepreneurial entrepreneurs came into business to respond to market opportunities as soon as private entrepreneurship was legalized in the country. The so-called small privatization in the Ukraine had significantly added to the number of female small business owners. Managers of former state-owned small shops, restaurants, hairdressing shops did not choose to be business owners, but few of them left their enterprises after privatization. Professionals constitute another large category among Ukrainian female entrepreneurs, which includes women (teachers, lawyers, auditors, medical doctors, translators, nurses) who come to business with the 'capital' of their knowledge, skills and desire to work independently.

Forced female entrepreneurs were the most numerous categories in the first years of reforms. These women had to come into business to earn a living for themselves and their families. As a rule, they used to start up with working in the shadow in retail activities or services. They would register officially with some capital accumulated and a market niche occupied. There are variations observed in the business development of forced entrepreneurs. Some of them are marginal entrepreneurs looking for opportunities to find a well-paid job and to stop business activities. Others are comparatively successful and satisfied with their present situation.

There are also examples when forced female entrepreneurs 'move' into the category of conventional entrepreneurs looking for business development and growth. A former librarian in Kharkiv had to leave her job because she received no salary. She first worked in her brother's business (retail trade of milk and diary products) and later became the owner. At the time of the interview in 2002 her business was profitable and provided jobs for four employees. The knowledge and business experience acquired in this line were pushing her towards manufacturing and she was planning to start a diary products processing business. She became more independent and was happy to be an entrepreneur. Another example of forced entrepreneurship is a female respondent in Chernivtsy who was in retail trade selling clothing imported from Poland. She had no people working for her and her business was at the verge of failure because of the new rules of visiting Poland. She was not satisfied with the situation. Making money for her family was her only motive at the beginning and at the time of the interview. She admitted she would be glad to leave this business and have a job of a hired employee if she would be paid a good salary.

Start-up patterns of male owners of companies employing less than 50 people are similar to those of women.

The Ukrainian results justify that the external business environment is producing major constraints both for female and male small entrepreneurs; nevertheless certain gender variations can be distinguished. The gender comparison of start-up barriers in the Ukraine allow concluding that women are more preoccupied with lack of finance and regulations and laws, while men have more problems with skilled employees (Table 2.7).

Both women and men feel that lack of premises and high taxes impede business development at the initial stage and there is no gender difference in evaluation of these two start-up constraints. Although the majority of female and male entrepreneurs were able to cope with these constraints, we may argue that external barriers significantly hamper the development and growth of businesses regardless of gender. Women were able to overcome start-up constraints to a considerable extent in 33.3 per cent, while men succeeded to do so in 46.3 per cent.

Table 2.7 Top five constraints at start-up (in per cent)*

Constraints	Female	Male
Lack of capital, finance	51.2	37.0
Lack of premises	47.5	49.4
Lack of skilled employees	29.8	43.2
Taxes	31.5	35.8
Regulation & law	31.2	21.0
Number of respondents	295	81

*Multiple responses, percentages based on number of respondents. Respondents could give up to three answers.

Source: Own survey 2002.

The Management of Women-owned Firms

The research area of management of women-owned firms encompasses a wide range of issues, including employment relations, management processes, the style of managing and leadership, the effect of gender on the experience of self-employment and business performance, operational problems and strategies used to overcome them, and connections between women, entrepreneurship and family (Carter, 2000; Carter et al., 2001).

Ukrainian female entrepreneurs are similar to their male counterparts in strategies to solve business problems, and this is justified by the priorities in improvement of business performance (Table 2.8). Similar to men female entrepreneurs take efforts to improve product/service quality, to increase advertising and promotional activity, to modernize technologies and equipment. At the same time, more women than men are concerned with upgrading their management skills. This is the only gender difference identified with regard to performance improvement measures.

Thus, women at large do not differ from men in what they do to increase performance, but are they similar to men in how they do it? Both female and male entrepreneurs did apply for external support in terms of advice, consultation or information, but they had different preferences in the types of sources. Women were more inclined to use assistance from local officials, while men preferred more to consult fellow entrepreneurs. This may be an indication of a still lower level of integration of female companies into the business community. On the other hand, women may be inclined to use more formal methods in solving business problems.

Table 2.8 Priorities of entrepreneurs for improving business performance (in per cent)[a]

Measures	Female	Male
To improve product/service quality	69.8	71.4
To increase advertising and promotional activity	48.0	51.9
Technological modernization	33.8	36.4
To reduce non-wage/salary costs	28.8	32.5
To upgrade management skills	25.3	15.6
To improve the quality of supplies	25.3	20.8
To improve channels of distribution	13.5	14.3
To modernise/extend buildings	16.0	19.5
Number of respondents[b]	281 (95%)	77 (95%)

a Multiple responses based on number of respondents. Respondents could give up to three answers.

b Number of respondents seeking to improve performance, in brackets: per cent of total number.

Source: Own survey 2002.

The last two arguments apply to gender differences in product/services promotion methods used by the Ukrainian entrepreneurs. Female business owners prefer to promote their products/services to the market by advertising in mass media and dissemination of brochures and flyers, while male business owners are using more recommendations from customers and suppliers, own sales representatives and agents. The gender difference in promotion methods may be part of the reasons why female businesses with an increase in home region sales are far less numerous than male (46.6 per cent female, 82.2 per cent male).

Are women more successful or less successful than men with respect to certain aspects of running a business? The answers to this question, addressed to both female and male respondents, revealed gender differences in assessment of women's management skills. Indeed, almost half of the interviewed women considered that gender did not matter in business management, the percentage of male of the same view was lower (44.4 to 22.2 per cent for different aspects of management). On the other hand more men felt that women were less successful in running a business (72.8 to 43.2 per cent for different aspects). In particular men would rate lower the abilities of women in production management, in exporting, innovation, networking, market development and growth of sales. To a certain extent, these evaluations of male entrepreneurs are supported by our performance data for female businesses.

Financing and Related Issues

Sources of finance are a popular area in research to look for gender differences. Verheul and Thurik (2001) identify direct and indirect effects on start-up capital. Having analysed 2,000 cases of Dutch starting entrepreneurs (500 female) these authors conclude that both equity and bank loans in women-owned companies do not differ from male-owned businesses, although, women do have a smaller amount of start-up capital. Limited access to capital and other resources is often cited as a typically female problem. One of several international studies gives an idea on the sources of finance women entrepreneurs are using in different countries. According to the results of a project carried out by the National Foundation of Women Business Owners, which was focused on growth of female entrepreneurship, very frequently own savings are the sources of finance. Own savings were cited as the source of finance by 65 per cent of respondents in Canada, 48 per cent in Mexico, 39 per cent in Ireland, 28 per cent in Brazil and 26 per cent of respondents in Argentina (NFWBO, 1999). Results of a study in Finland have demonstrated gender differences with regard to applying for a bank loan (Hokkanen et al., 1998).

Table 2.9 Start-up capital sources

	Female			**Male**		
Sources of start-up capital	**Mean (median)[a]**	**N[b]**	**%[c]**	**Mean (median)[a]**	**N[b]**	**%[c]**
Own savings	73.25 (100)	217	73	73.95 (90)	76	94
Family	43.79 (40)	99	33	23.83 (20)	30	37
Friends	46.25 (40)	76	25	17.38 (20)	21	26
Customer	58.72 (50)	39	13	46.00 (35)	10	12
Supplier	30.00 (20)	12	4	0.00 (0)	-	-
Bank	44.07 (40)	27	9	53.00 (50)	10	12
State programmes, donors	61.94 (50)	18	6	48.33 (45)	6	7

a Mean and median based on respondents that reported use of a particular source of finance.
b N: number of respondents who reported the use of a particular source of finance.
c In per cent of total number of respondents.

Source: Own survey 2002.

In the Ukraine, small business owners use own savings most frequently as start-up capital, but the share of women who had money to start their businesses was smaller in comparison with men (Table 2.9). Women may have less personal savings because of on average lower salaries paid before they come into business or maybe they know better the needs of their households, feel a higher responsibility and do not wish to risk the scarce, as a rule, resources.

Although both sexes applied to their families and friends for finance, women were relying more on these two sources. The same holds for using financial means provided by customers. With regard to bank loans, there is almost no gender difference – only a small minority is using this source of funding; still the share of bank loans in start-up capital is at average 10 per cent higher in male businesses.

Ukrainian female entrepreneurs are not as active as male entrepreneurs in investing in their business. For example, 41 per cent of female businesses operating for more than 12 months by the time of the interview have indicated they had investments, while the share of male businesses amounted to 66 per cent. The same differences are also observed with regard to using own savings for investment, i.e. women are less inclined to invest their own money into business development (Table 2.10). Approximately the same is the structure of external sources used for investment by women and men; still sometimes women choose to use such options as customer, bank, family, and friends, the percentage of these particular sources are higher than in male cases. This data may indicate that a typical female investment sources' structure may be less diversified than a male one.

Table 2.10 Investment capital sources in 2001-2002 (in per cent)

	Female			Male		
Sources of investment capital	**Mean (median)[a]**	**N[b]**	**%[c]**	**Mean (median)[a]**	**N[b]**	**%[c]**
Own savings	85.99 (100)	76	28	87.93 (100)	46	57
Customer	80.47 (100)	32	12	65.00 (65)	12	15
Family	46.79 (27)	14	5	21.67 (20)	3	4
Friends	24.09 (20)	11	4	13.33 (10)	3	4
Supplier	25.00 (20)	4	1	50.00 (50)	2	2
Bank	53.33 (45)	12	4	26.67 (20)	3	4
State programme, donors	62.00 (50)	5	2	45.00 (45)	2	2

a Mean and median based on respondents that reported use of a particular source of finance.
b N: number of respondents that reported the use of a particular source of finance.
c In per cent of respondents working for 12 months and more.

Source: Own survey 2002.

An interesting and important question is why the practice to apply for a bank loan is not so popular with small business owners in the Ukraine. Although only a minority of entrepreneurs of both sexes were using bank loans for starting their businesses and even less for investments, almost one third of female entrepreneurs and male entrepreneurs did approach the banks since the start-up of their businesses. Our results support the view of Coleman (1998), who argues, that it is not gender of business owner which is a hindrance in relations with banks, but characteristics of a typical female company, and primarily, size, age and sector. In this respect, a comparison of the Ukrainian female and male businesses, which were the same in their characteristics, demonstrates that women are similar to men in applying for bank loans and reaching success. Almost one third of female respondents (29.7 per cent) have reported they had applied for a bank loan since the start-up and 65.9 per cent of these applications were successful. In the male control group 24.7 per cent of respondents had applied for a bank loan and 60 per cent of the applications were successful. The main differences between sexes with respects to the reasons why entrepreneurs are not seeking a bank loan are as follows: women had less confidence in success and did not wish to take a risk. However, women and men evaluated reasons such as 'unfavourable conditions', 'lack of security', 'did not need a bank loan' in the same way.

The female dislike for taking risks on their business is very well illustrated by an owner of a construction company from Sumy, who started her business with the money paid by the first customer. At the beginning deficiency of working capital was the greatest problem in business, but she never took any external financial assistance. She understood that not to use external finance is a wrong approach, as 'the civilized world is working using other people's money', still she could not force herself to get a loan. Not to make debts was her habit since Soviet times, and she could not sleep when she had debts. In future she is planning to have her own production of construction materials, as she is not happy with the quality of construction materials (metal and wooden) available in the market. Would she overcome her aversion against debts (i.e. take a bank loan), her business would receive the impulse needed for growth.

Gender and Business Networks

According to Carter et al. (2001) gender and business networks is an under-researched area; still gender differences were revealed in the process of networking and contents of social networks. Gender composition of business networks may have an influence on business development. Our results have demonstrated that although Ukrainian female entrepreneurs have more female business links in their networks in comparison with their male counterparts, still almost half of customers, business partners, business consultants and other business links are male (Table 2.11). Suppliers are more frequently male than female. On the other hand, male entrepreneurs do have women among their business links.

Judging by the female case study interviews gender had no influence on the choice of business partners; entrepreneurs were choosing business partners by their professionalism and competence. There were cases, when women were mostly dealing with other women, but only because the sector was "female" and there were no fellow businessmen in this business. When female entrepreneurs had male business partners, they felt neither discomfort, nor discrimination. Similar to women male entrepreneurs felt that gender of business contacts was not so significant as personality and skills.

Table 2.11 Per cent of women in business links of entrepreneurs

Types of business links	Female	Male
Suppliers	38.4 (30)*	23.6 (20)
Customers	51.3 (50)	40.0 (50)
Business partners	47.9 (50)	31.5 (30)
Other business links	46.2 (50)	30.0 (20)
Business consultants	62.7 (60)	36.1 (30)

*Men and women business links make up 100% in each type of business link. Mean values are given, and the median in brackets.

Source: Own survey 2002.

Table 2.12 Types of external cooperation links (in per cent)

Types of external links	Female	Male
Same sector private enterprises	37.6	50.0
Adjacent fields private enterprises	21.8	27.8
Individuals	11.3	11.1
Private enterprises in general	9.8	2.8
State enterprises	6.0	-
Number of respondents[a]	133 (45%[b])	36 (44%[b])

a Number of respondents, who had external links.
b In brackets: per cent of total number.

Source: Own survey 2002.

Previous research on small business suggests that because of their limited internal resources companies of this size should learn to use external resources and assistance (Smallbone et al., 1999). Limited resources of small firms make it expedient for them to cooperate with other firms and entrepreneurs, thus placing networking as one of the success factors in survival and growth of companies, which also may conceal some gender differences. Almost half of female entrepreneurs cooperate with other businesses in ways other than selling to them or buying products/services. No gender difference in percentage of 'cooperators' was revealed (Table 2.12). Although the preferences in external links are very much the same (both female and male entrepreneurs choose to cooperate primarily with entrepreneurs from the same sector or from adjacent fields private enterprises), female entrepreneurs mentioned private enterprises in general more often than men; besides women cooperated with state enterprises, the type not chosen by men at all.

Ukrainian female and male entrepreneurs differ in their motives for cooperation with external links. Female entrepreneurs set and maintain external cooperation primarily aiming at 'exchange of information', 'exchange of experience and ideas' and 'advice and consultancy' more often than men. Male entrepreneurs are looking for 'higher profits', 'joint production and servicing' and 'share of physical infrastructure'. Comparison of this data with the performance indicators of female and male businesses described below leads to an argument that motives selected by men in networking prove to be more productive.

Case studies provide evidence that when women are using external business links not only for exchange of information or experience, this cooperation is very efficient. A female manufacturer of knitted wear in Kiev has a practice to share client with similar businesses when she has big orders of corporate clients. She highly evaluates such cooperation, which is profitable for her business and helps her to keep the clients. She also is using external links with other entrepreneurs for exchange of information. Another female entrepreneur from Kiev, who grows flowers, imports flowers from Poland and has two stalls in the market place to sell them, is using cooperation in the form of advice of other entrepreneurs in legal issues and reporting; but also she has an agreement with two business partners, according to which the three of them hire a bus together for business trips to Poland. This helps her to spend more time on growing flowers and develop business.

In general, both women and men tend to perceive the cooperation with external links to be of high value for success of their business; 85 per cent of female and 81 per cent of male respondents selected this assessment.

Performance and Growth

Studies on the influence of gender on business performance and growth conclude that women-owned businesses perform less well, and this may be caused by under-resourcing at start-up (Carter et al., 2001). Some authors argue that women perform less well because financial gain is not so important a start-up goal as, for instance, independence or flexibility to meet family and work commitments (Brush, 1992, Rosa et al., 1996). Is there any gender difference with respect to business performance and growth of the Ukrainian small businesses? Income and expenditures comparison was one of the indicators to evaluate business performance used in the study.

Business performance among other factors is influenced by the objectives set by entrepreneurs. Both female and male respondents have selected growth more frequently than other objectives, but the share of male growth-oriented entrepreneurs was higher (Table 2.13). On the other hand, female entrepreneurs were less ambitious; one third of them were aiming at a more modest objective of survival, which can be treated as an indirect indication of a lower performance of female entrepreneurs. The share of female respondents who aimed at providing a living for their families was also larger than in the male control group. In relation to the objectives specified entrepreneurs were asked to assess the performance of the business in 2001-2002 by selecting one of three suggested answers: unsatisfactory, satisfactory and successful performance. Judging by the assessments of respondents, male entrepreneurs were more successful in achieving their objectives. Female entrepreneurs tend to evaluate their performance with regard to achieving objectives as 'satisfactory' in 77.5 per cent (compared to 50 per cent of the male entrepreneurs). Men more often assessed their performance as 'successful' (43.8 per cent men and 15.3 per cent women).

Table 2.13 Objectives for the past 12 months, 2001-2002 (in per cent)

Objective	Female	Male
To grow	46.9	67.5
To survive	32.4	15.0
To prepare for selling	0.4	0
To provide a living for family	12.4	5.0
To improve personal/family income	4.7	10.0
Other objectives	3.3	2.5
No of enterprises*	274	80

*refers to enterprises operating 12 months and more.

Source: Own survey 2002.

There was almost no gender variations revealed with respect to the type of growth chosen by entrepreneurs: majority of both female and male entrepreneurs mentioned the growth of profits and growth of sales turnover. Less significance was attached to the growth of fixed assets and growth of employment, which may be related to limited financial resources in the first case and reluctance to increase obligatory payments in the second case.

Table 2.14 Income in the last 12 months, 2001-2002 (in per cent)

Indicator	Female	Male
Income does not cover expenditures	12.4	1.3
Income covers expenditures	59.9	36.3
Income exceeds expenditures	27.7	62.5
Number of respondents*	274	80

*Businesses operating 12 months and more.

Source: Own survey 2002.

The comparison of income and expenditures indicates a similar tendency: women are performing less than men. The income covered the expenditures for the majority of female respondents and exceeded expenditures in approximately one third. Still, businesses owned by men demonstrated better results: there were more companies with income exceeding expenditures and only one firm where income did not cover expenditures (Table 2.14).

Gender differences in business performance, growth orientation and success in goals achievement of the Ukrainian entrepreneurs can be related to a higher percentage of male respondents who indicated that availability of resources was their motive to start business, while we can observe a small number of female entrepreneurs who were motivated by a wish to have own business. A lower performance level of women-owned businesses partly also results from their lower investment level and a lower level of use of own savings when starting. This is aggravated by the scarcity of external funding opportunities, females' risk adversity demonstrated by their self-evaluations of business aptitude and the reasons female entrepreneurs stated for not applying for a bank loan.

Conclusions

The findings of the research study presented in the chapter were supposed to explore the question whether women and men entrepreneurs in the Ukraine are different or similar. Not surprising, the key conclusion arising from our empirical data is that women and men entrepreneurs in the Ukraine are similar in some respects and different in others. More specifically, the similarities of entrepreneurs encompass the following:

- Female and male entrepreneurs in the Ukraine are similar in their personal characteristics, such as age, education, previous work experience, business experience and management training. Most women and men were highly educated, but they had little knowledge of business management when starting their business and no formal business training.
- Women and men start businesses for largely the same reasons, with the wish to be independent or to work independently being the most frequently mentioned motive.
- Women and men start businesses using mainly own savings. Only a small minority are applying for banks loans for start-up or investment.
- The share of entrepreneurs who had applied for external funding since start-up and success rates, were almost the same in female and male enterprises.
- Entrepreneurs regardless of sex have to start and run their businesses in mostly unfavourable external environment, which is testified by the major constraints when starting and at present. Both female and male entrepreneurs cited lack of finance (related to a lack of external financing), high taxes, regulations and laws as the most pressing barriers for starting and developing a business.
- In order to compensate for scarce internal resources, both women and men are cooperating with other entrepreneurs and they apply for external assistance.

Differences by sex can be found in business performance, financing, motives for cooperation with other businesses and business aptitude or management abilities evaluations:

- In comparison with men, female entrepreneurs have fewer resources to start businesses and they are investing less. According to their self-evaluation, Ukrainian women are less oriented to risk taking, planning and problem solving. On the other hand, male entrepreneurs demonstrate better results in business goals achievement, business performance and growth, and they are more growth oriented.
- With regard to the relations between business management and gender, female entrepreneurs considered gender as having a neutral effect, while men would rate lower women's abilities in production management, exporting, innovation, networking, market development and sales growth.
- Gender differences also can be observed with regard to motives for cooperation. Motives of female entrepreneurs mainly include 'exchange of information', 'exchange of experience and ideas' and 'advice and consultancy'. The preferences of male entrepreneurs are 'higher profits', 'joint production and servicing' and 'sharing physical infrastructure'.

In the context of the results obtained for the Ukraine, it is advisable to improve information on female entrepreneurs by gathering statistics with a gender component (OECD, 2000) and encouraging further research in the area. Moreover, improvement of legislation, tax and regulation policies in the country would remove the most distressing obstacles in starting and developing small companies, including women-owned firms. In addition, it is advisable to develop further a system of micro financing institutions in order to foster female entrepreneurs in number and to improve the quality of female businesses.

Notes

1 'Female entrepreneurship in transition economies: the example of Ukraine, Moldova and Uzbekistan', funded under the INTAS programme (contract no. 00-0843).

2 TACIS programmes of the European Union, German Government Programmes, World Bank, and the U.S. Agency for International Development were and are the most active Western donors in technical assistance and advice.

3 Gender comparison is made for the category of owners of small businesses employing less than 50 employees and operating in manufacturing, construction, services and trade. Conclusions may not be true for gender comparison of larger businesses' owners.

References

Aldrich, H. (1989), 'Networking among women entrepreneurs', in O. Hagan, C. Rivchun and D. Sexton (eds), *Women owned businesses*, Praeger, New York, pp. 103-132.

Barsukova, S. (1999), 'Female entrepreneurship: specifics and perspectives', *Sotsiologicheskie issledovaniya*, vol. 9, pp. 75-84 (in Russian).

Barsukova, S. (2001), 'Success models of women of Soviet and post-soviet periods: ideological myths creation', *Sotsiologicheskie issledovaniya*, no. 2, pp. 75-82 (in Russian).

Baygan, G. (2000), *Improving knowledge about women's entrepreneurship*, paper presented at the OECD Second Conference on Women Entrepreneurs in SMEs: Realising the Benefits of Globalisation and the Knowledge-Based Economy, 29-30 November, http://www.oecd.org/dsti/sti/industry/indcomp.

Bohachevska-Homyak, M. (1995), *White on white: women in social life of Ukraine, 1884-1939*, Lybid, Kiev (in Ukrainian).

Bruno, M. (1997), 'Women and the culture of entrepreneurship', in M. Buckley (ed), *Post-Soviet women: from Baltic to Central Asia*, Cambridge University Press, Cambridge, pp. 56-74.

Brush, C. (1992), 'Research on women business owners: past trends, a new perspective and future directions', *Entrepreneurship: Theory & Practice*, vol. 16, pp. 5-26.

Carter, S. (2000), 'Gender and enterprise', in S. Carter and D. Jones-Evans (eds), *Enterprise and small business: principles, practice and policy*, FT Prentice Hall, London, pp. 166-181.

Carter S., Anderson, S. and Shaw, E. (2001), *Women's business ownership: a review of the academic, popular and Internet literature*, Report to the Small Business Service, University of Strathclyde, Glasgow.

Catley, S. and Hamilton, R.T. (1998), 'Small business development and gender of owner', *Journal of Management Development*, vol. 17, pp. 75-82.

Coleman, S. (1998), 'Access to Capital: A Comparison of Men and Women-Owned Small Businesses', *Frontiers of Entrepreneurship Research*, www.babson.edu/entrep/fer.

Cromie, S. (1987), 'Similarities and differences between women and men who chose business proprietorship', *International Small Business Journal*, vol. 5, pp. 43-60.

Fay, M. and Williams, L. (1993), 'Gender bias and the availability of business loans', *Journal of Business Venturing*, vol. 8, pp. 363-376.

Hokkanen, P., Lumme, A. and Autio, E. (1998), 'Gender-Based Non-Differences in Bank Shopping and Credit Terms', *Frontiers of Entrepreneurship Research*, www.babson.edu/entrep/fer.

Isakova, N. (2001), 'Gender similarities and differences in performance and evaluations of the Ukrainian entrepreneurs', *Sociology: Theory, Practice, Marketing*, vol. 2, pp. 144-153 (in Ukrainian and Russian).

Kalacheva, I. (1999), *Women and men in Ukraine: Statistics collection*, State Statistics Committee of Ukraine, Kiev.

Kaufmann, D. (1994), 'Diminishing returns to administrative controls and the emergence of the unofficial economy: a framework of analysis and applications to Ukraine', *Economic Policy*, no. 19, Supplement, pp. 52-69.

Kiev International Institute of Sociology (2000), *Women and Entrepreneurship*, USAID Newbiznet project, Kiev.

Klochko, Y. and Isakova, N. (1996), 'Small Business Sector in Ukrainian Transition Economy: achievements to date', *Entrepreneurship & Regional Development*, vol. 8, pp. 127-140.

National Foundation for Women Business Owners (NFWBO) (1999), *Report*, Center for Women's Business Research, www.nfwbo.org.

OECD (2000), *OECD Second Conference on Women Entrepreneurs in SMEs: Realising the Benefits of Globalisation and the Knowledge-Based Economy*, Conference Recommendations. 29-30 November, http://www.oecd.org/dsti/sti/industry/indcomp.

Osaulenko, O. (2003), *Statistic yearbook of the Ukraine for 2002*, State Statistics Committee of Ukraine, Kiev.

Pavlychko, S. (1997), 'Progress on hold: the conservative faces of women in Ukraine', in M. Buckley (ed), *Post-Soviet women: from Baltic to Central Asia*, Cambridge: Cambridge University Press, pp. 219-234.

Rosa, P., Carter, S. and Hamilton, D. (1996), 'Gender as a determinant of small business performance: Insights from a British study', *Small Business Economics*, vol. 8, pp. 463-478.

Schwartz, E.B. (1976), 'Entrepreneurship: a new female frontier', *Journal of Contemporary Business*, Winter, pp. 47-76.

Scott, C.E. (1986), 'Why more women are becoming entrepreneurs', *Journal of Small Business Management*, vol. 4, pp. 37-44.

Shabbir, A. (1995), 'How gender affects business start-up – evidence from Pakistan', *Small Enterprise Development*, vol. 6, pp. 35-42.

Shane, S., Kolvereid, L. and Westhead, P. (1991), 'An exploratory examination of the reasons leading to new firm formation across country and gender', *Journal of Business Venturing*, vol. 6, pp. 431-446.

Sivko, B. (1983), *Women of the Ukrainian SSR*, Central Statistics Department of the Ukrainian SSR, Kiev.

Smallbone, D. and Welter, F. (2001), 'The Distinctiveness of entrepreneurship in transition economies', *Small Business Economics*, vol. 16, pp. 249-262.

Smallbone, D., Welter, F., Klochko, Y., Isakova, N., Aculai, E. and Slonimski, A. (1999), *Identifying support needs of small enterprises in Ukraine, Moldova and Belarus to develop an agenda for policy at national and regional levels*, Final report on TACIS ACE project (Contract no: T95-4139R), CEEDR, London.

Stefanenko, L. (1999), 'Womanhood of Ukraine in the pre-war period', in L.O. Smolar (ed), *Women studies in Ukraine: woman in history and today*, Yastroprint, Odessa, pp. 131-153 (in Ukrainian).

Stefanenko, L. (1999a), 'Status of women in the post-war period', in L.O. Smolar (ed), *Women studies in Ukraine: woman in history and today*, Yastroprint, Odessa, pp. 153-163 (in Ukrainian).

Verheul, I. and Thurik, R. (2001), 'Start-up capital: Does gender matter?', *Small Business Economics*, vol. 16, pp. 329-345.

Yacoub, M. and Senchuk, B. (2000), *The state of small business in Ukraine: an IFC report on the results of survey of enterprises in Ukraine*, non-published report, IFC, Kiev.

Yacoub, M., Senchuk, B. and Tkachenko, T. (2001), *Enterprises of Ukraine in 2000: an IFC report on the results of survey of enterprises in Ukraine*, non-published report, IFC, Kiev.

Zhurzhenko, T. (2001), *Social reproduction and gender policy in Ukraine*, Folio publishers, Kharkov (in Russian).

Chapter 3

Women Entrepreneurs between Tradition and Modernity – The Case of Uzbekistan

Friederike Welter, David Smallbone, Damira Mirzakhalikova, Natalja Ju. Schakirova and Charos Maksudova

Introduction

The process of transformation towards market economies deprived a majority of women in the former Soviet states of their paid jobs, as well as most of the social security provided under socialism. On the other hand, the needs of women to earn additional income have grown during the transition period. Here, female entrepreneurship is important not only to alleviate growing unemployment, but also to take advantage of the potential contribution of women entrepreneurs to economic and social transformation. An important research question for female entrepreneurship in transition countries concerns the extent to which any distinctive characteristics of women-owned businesses that are observed, may be attributable to gender-related factors, such as the position of women in the economy and society, or instead to the overall business environment.

In this context, this chapter researches the nature of women's entrepreneurship in Uzbekistan, where transition towards a market-based economy has been slow and where society shifts between traditions and modernity, in an attempt to make a contribution to our understanding of women's entrepreneurship under 'early stage' transition conditions. After examining the overall development of SMEs and the policy environment, the chapter analyses the role of Uzbek women in Soviet times and during transition. Survey and case study data from our joint research project[1] is used to analyse the behaviour of women entrepreneurs in relation to their stated aims for starting and running their businesses, and seeking particularly (through the case studies) to identify any change in their motives and business behaviour over time. Empirical data also is employed to explore the effect of the environment on women's entrepreneurship, asking whether the specific Uzbek conditions restrict women entrepreneurs and under which conditions they might assist women business owners. The chapter concludes with a short summary and outlook.

Development of Small and Medium-Sized Enterprises during the 1990s

The development of small and medium-sized enterprises (SMEs) in Uzbekistan can be divided into three stages (Kurmanbaeva et al., 2000). During the *first stage* (1991-95) Uzbekistan observed a dramatic increase in SMEs, which were mainly created as individual or family enterprises, limited-liability companies or cooperative entities. The number of SMEs in Uzbekistan increased over 4.5 times during this period, and the number of their employees almost doubled. All this was mainly due to the programme of smallscale privatization, the transformation of illegal and semi-legal entities of the Soviet period into legal ones, combined with the liberal economic environment, which existed prior to 1994, when small enterprises were not controlled by the government, in practice.

During the *second stage* of reform (1996–1999) the development of SMEs in the republic slowed down. Increasing competition, tighter import controls from 1996 onwards and more privileges for larger firms either crowded out some SMEs, or made their operations less profitable. Thus, between 1996 and 1998, the number of employees in SMEs decreased, to reach 54 per cent of the 1995 level by 1998. Moreover, a considerable number of those new companies registered in the second half of the 1990s never actually started business operations, because they were only registered for tax purposes. The 14th session of Olii Majlis [parliament] in 1999, marked the start to *the third stage* of SME development, as it explicitly established conditions for development of small and medium business (Schakirova et al., 2002). However, by the end of 1999, the number of SMEs continued to decrease, and a considerable number of registered small and medium business entities stayed idle. As a result, the government had to introduce a package of legal and institutional measures to address these problems, which included resolutions to improve the legal framework for small business operations, as well as creating incentives for its development, and to ensure its sustainability. The Law 'On Guaranteed Freedoms of Business Activities' (passed in May 2000) played an important role in this process and this package of measures have already yielded some results.

As a result of the positive development of SMEs, they contribute to the supply of domestically produced goods and services to the domestic consumer market, including products as household goods, furniture, textile and ready-made garments, construction materials, and foodstuffs.

By the end of 2000, the number of functioning SMEs had increased by 1.1 times, compared with the start of the year, reaching 165.5 thousand by 2001, or 5.6 functioning SMEs per 1,000 people (in 2000). In addition, some progress has also been made with respect to the sectoral structure of SMEs, since manufacturing, construction, and services have developed faster than retail and trading activities. As Table 3.1 shows, SMEs have been making an increasing contribution to GNP since the year 2000 to reach 35.5 per cent in 2003. At the same time, as in other transition economies, this contribution varies between regions, reflecting differences in the pace of restructuring and in the overall level of economic development. The highest proportional contribution is in Dzizak, Samarkand and Syr-Darya and the lowest in Navoi and Kashkadarya (Table 3.1).

Table 3.1 Contribution of SMEs to gross national product, 2001-2003 (in per cent)

	2000	2001*	2002	2003
Republic of Uzbekistan	31.0	24.4	34.6	35.5
Regions:				
Andizhan	32.9	24.1	36.6	39.4
Bukhara	33.0	24.1	35.0	39.8
Dzizak	37.1	27.4	52.3	56.9
Kashkadarya	25.8	19.1	33.7	34.9
Navoi	21.5	14.5	22.3	22.1
Namangan	33.4	22.8	40.0	44.4
Samarkand	44.3	29.8	47.9	48.9
Surkhandarya	39.1	29.8	44.5	44.5
Syr-Darya	38.9	29.3	46.8	47.8
Tashkent	34.0	24.6	36.0	38.2
Ferghana	32.0	23.8	39.6	42.1
Khorezm	34.2	25.7	40.4	40.5
Tashkent city	41.5	45.1	45.2	46.6

*In 2001, the data did not take into account farms.

Source: Own calculations based on official statistical data from 'Social and Economic Position of Uzbekistan'.

Interestingly, the role of women in business ownership shows even more regional variations, at least, based on official data (Table 3.2). In Uzbekistan as a whole, less than one in 10 registered businesses are owned by women, and in some regions, such as Namangan and Khoresm this is less than one per cent. However, in the city of Tashkent and in Bukhara and Ferghana regions, around one in five registered businesses are owned by women, suggesting significant differences in the social context for women in various parts of the country.

Table 3.2 Statistical data on women managers in SMEs in Uzbekistan, 2003

Territory	Registered businesses	Of them controlled by women	In per cent
Republic Karakalpakstan	12,279	1,608	13.1
Andizhan	23,573	719	3.1
Bukhara	19,972	4,004	20.0
Dzizak	17,701	241	1.4
Kashkadarya	18,499	1,545	8.4
Navoi	9,373	1,093	11.7
Namangan	11,903	752	6.3
Surhandarya	11,785	72	0.6
Syr-Darya	11,460	669	5.8
Samarkand	26,795	298	1.1
Tashkent	17,758	1,791	10.1
Ferghana	19,656	3,848	19.6
Khoresm	16,326	135	0.8
City of Tashkent	20,355	4,747	23.3
Total republic	237,435	21,522	9.1

Source: Own calculation by Business Women Association, based on registry data from the Chamber of Commerce.

Policies for SME and Entrepreneurship Development

Numerous *laws and regulations* for private entrepreneurship exist in Uzbekistan, although there have been some recent attempts to limit the intrusion of state officials into business activities. For example, since 2001, all private firms have been issued with record books to record checks by official bodies of private firms, which are now limited to 1-2 times a year. For additional checks, the controlling bodies must produce special permissions. This measure has significantly reduced the number of unscheduled check-ups by different controlling bodies, as well as the possibility for their misuse. At the same time, in 2002 the government introduced new import and currency regulations in order to assist domestic production, which severely affected shuttle traders with neighbouring Central Asian republics (most of them women), micro enterprises as well as those domestic SMEs depending on imported goods. So, whilst some government policies may have helped the development of the small business sector since 2001, other policies have had counteracting tendencies.

As in other transition economies, laws adopted in the Republic are typically changed frequently, often involving the issuance of contradictory regulatory acts and by-laws, which is a major constraint on the development of entrepreneurship. This hampers the development of entrepreneurship.

Uzbekistan appears to have an elaborate business support infrastructure, most of which has been donor-initiated. Over the years of reform in Uzbekistan, institutional and legal conditions as well as *institutional structures* were established to support the development of SMEs. Among these are the Chamber of Commodity Producers and Entrepreneurs; the Business Fund; 'Madad' insurance company; a network of consulting, engineering and leasing companies; and business incubators. The Chamber was established to ensure the design of an integrated market infrastructure, to support small and medium business, as well as individual entrepreneurship; to expedite the formation of proprietors, and to protect their rights and interests. It aims to assist and support private businesses of all sizes. The Business Fund of the Republic of Uzbekistan was established by Presidential Decree to finance investment projects through extending credits to small businesses, and to provide technical assistance such as consulting and information services.

The infrastructure supporting small and medium business also includes a network of insurance agencies, such as 'Madad', 'Uzbekinvest', 'UzinvestAIG', and 'Uzagrosugurta,' established by government resolutions. The purpose of these insurance agencies is to secure credits, protect against business risks, insure borrower's liability for non-repayment of credits and provide insurance protection for foreign investments to develop private and small business. The insurance agencies also offer credit guarantees for SMEs.

In addition, Uzbekistan has a large number of *non-governmental and not-for-profit organizations* (NGOs). According to official data from the Ministry of Justice, 2,310 organizations were officially registered in the Republic as of May 1, 2000. However, estimates by the Institute of Macroeconomics and Social Research of Uzbekistan find twice as many such organizations. NGOs act both as employers and as service providers. Each active organization has its target group, focusing its efforts on solving the problems and issues facing its target group.

One such example is the Business Women Association of Uzbekistan (Tadbirkor Ayol), which participated in the particular research project the chapter is drawing on in terms of empirical data. The Association was the first NGO focusing on creating a conducive environment for women in the transition process. During its life span over more than ten years, the Association has managed to rally over 4,000 businesswomen throughout the country. With the help of various programmes and projects, around 1,200 women have been trained in 12 handicraft professions, more than 200 have received business education, 300 have been trained in venture creation, and another 1,000 in marketing and management. In addition, 130 young women from rural areas have received basic computer training, and over 30 persons have been trained in export management.

'Olima', the Association of Women Scientists, also offers training, such as 'Fundraising', 'Women and Business', and 'Women's Self-concept', in which women are trained how to present themselves in the labour market and sell their knowledge and experience. 120 women attended a training programme on

'Adaptation to a Market Economy', which was held in Great Britain. The trainees of these seminars have begun to participate more actively in the economic reforms of the state, as well as in the organization of scientific and production associations and creating new jobs.

In 1999, the NGO Centre 'Nash Dom' [Our Home] was established to assist in improving economic and social protection for mothers and children. The organization conducts free training and seminars to develop the professional skills of socially vulnerable women. Training courses such as 'Legal Foundation of Business' and 'How to Start Your Business', are offered on a regular basis. Lawyers, business consultants, and specialists in microlending are regularly available for free advice. In Tashkent and Tashkent province, more than 200 women from socially vulnerable segments of the population have participated in seminars and trainings conducted by 'Nash Dom'.

Whilst the economic reality requires their increased entrepreneurial engagement, the specific cultural traditions in Uzbekistan re-enforce the traditional role of women in society. However, since 1995 the state has adopted a number of protectionist measures regarding women[2] to strengthen and raise their rights and rendering support to women's movement. Active government measures, which are aimed at supporting the development of SMEs in the country, assisted women in setting up small businesses, although the recent shift towards an import-substitution policy tends to drive small (female) traders and female entrepreneurs relying on imported raw materials out of business.

The Role of Uzbek Women in Soviet Times and Today

The Soviet Gender Legacy

Fajth (2000, p. 90) describes many achievements of the Soviet period as superficial and the underlying process as authoritarian rather than rights-based. Despite an ideological commitment to promoting emancipation through the participation of women in the labour market (Kerblay, 1977); women still faced conflicting roles in economy and society. Although the Soviet state sought to redefine the role of women in society, in order to utilise their economic potential, the preferred Soviet role model was still the worker-mother whose duties were to work, produce children and run the household. The state assisted them in meeting their competing role demands by providing the legal and institutional framework that included benefits for working mothers, job protection and childcare systems (Ashwin, 2000). Even though the Soviet state partly socialised the male role to provide for the family, traditional gender relations persisted (Kiblitskaya, 2000a). As in other Soviet republics, the boom in policies and practices with respect to equal rights for men and women was limited geographically to large industrial cities and socially to working class and professionals.

Nevertheless, an important social development, with a long-lasting effect on the status of women, especially in the Central Asian republics, was the policy of 'illiteracy liquidation', which covered women as well as men. This campaign allowed women to become a notable part of the workforce, enlarging their place in the labour market. The situation of women improved during this period, compared with pre-Soviet times, when Uzbek women had to live according to the rules of 'shariah', which prohibited Muslim women from working outside their house. On the whole, the difference in the position of Uzbek women in the early and late Soviet periods is huge. Each family can narrate examples, which illustrate the changes in women's position. For example, among women of the first Soviet decade, few worked outside of their house and only a few gained access to modern education, including higher education. Whereas in the beginning of the 1990s nearly half of all Uzbek women worked, 49 per cent of high school graduates were girls and the share of women in higher administrative and management positions amounted to 17.5 per cent (Tokhtahodjaeva, 2000).

Although such indicators in Uzbekistan were below the average for the USSR, even today they remain much higher than in other Muslim countries, with a comparable level of income. Nevertheless, despite these positive indicators of the social status of Uzbek women during the Soviet period, the situation varied for women from different social segments, and from both urban and rural areas. The essentially top-down emancipation process failed to involve women from all layers of society, as it failed to overcome cultural traditions. This particularly affected young women and girls whose rights were limited to a considerable extent by the family context (Tokhtakhodjaeva, 2001). In Uzbekistan, girls were still expected to obey to the eldest person in the family and/or their husband, and these values were particularly pronounced in the countryside.

As a result, the Soviet state placed a dual responsibility on women for performing the roles of successful worker and successful mother (Aivazova, 1998), whilst men were looked upon as agents of political, economic and social changes and progress. In Uzbekistan, this was re-enforced by dominant traditional values. For example, in families, the patriarchal order prevailed with women being in charge of family budgets, household activities, bringing up children and serving their husbands. As a result, alongside the dominant official system of education, an alternative system of education for women existed, and within families they were educated according to the traditional way of life (UNDP, 1999).

Gender role stereotypes continued to define the household as a female sphere and work as essentially a male sphere of activity (Turetskaya, 2001). This led Bruno (1997) to refer to distinctive styles of female entrepreneurship in post Soviet countries, because of the effect of women's experiences during the Soviet period in organizing their household consumption. These experiences allowed women during the transition period to manage shortages through a complicated system of bartering goods and favours and cultivating informal knowledge and information networks.

Although theoretically based on concepts of equality, in practice, the Soviet system discriminated against women, who experienced a glass ceiling in politics and economy. Despite its commitment to working women, the state tacitly acknowledged and supported the male dominance in the public sphere (Ashwin, 2000). Men held most leading positions in politics and in state enterprises, which resulted in women being omitted from the Soviet nomenclatura, 'parallel circuits' in state firms and other high level networks, which have previously been suggested to be important influences on the development of entrepreneurship during the transition period (Smallbone and Welter, 2001b). As a result, at the beginning of the transition process, women consequently had fewer opportunities to enter entrepreneurship through privatizing large state firms or through setting up small spin-offs firms from larger state enterprises.

The Transition Context: a 'Renaissance of Patriarchy'

During the transition period, the *economic and social roles* of women underwent an enormous *change*, leading to conflicts between family needs, women's responsibilities and their individual wishes. With respect to women's roles the Soviet state left a 'paradoxical legacy, with 'strong and independent women who nevertheless ended up doing all the housework' (Ashwin, 2000, p. 18). Whilst the Soviet working-mother contract is responsible for the ongoing interest of women in work, the responsibilities of motherhood became redefined. Following the destruction of the state social welfare and childcare system, post Soviet governments transferred motherhood and family responsibilities back into the private sphere, which post Soviet societies such as Uzbekistan, where patriarchal values had survived anyway, were quick to accept.

Even though modern societies theoretically offer a broad range of gender role models, post Soviet societies tend to emphasize a housewife identity for women (Zhurzhenko, 2001). This *predominance of traditional gender roles* goes hand in hand with a '*renaissance of patriarchy*' (Zhurzhenko, 1999, p. 246). This is not surprising in the Uzbek context because in Central Asia generally, cultural values emphasizing family relations survived throughout the Soviet period, gaining momentum since transition started (Tabyshalieva, 2000), re-enforced by religious norms. At the beginning of 1990s, Uzbek society tended to reject all that belonged to the Soviet period; and women's position was the first to be criticized. Suddenly, the society built on religious norms appeared an attractive alternative for the majority of the population. Many writers and even politicians began to advocate full restoration of traditionalism and Islamic values. Utopian ideas (i.e. that if all start living like our ancestors, justice will be restored) were put into minds with the reference to the authority of Islam freed from the pressure. The battle to return woman to her initial focus on the family, and restricting her world to the care for children and husband was the first step on the way to the restoration of religious norms. In the early 1990s, endless articles in both official and opposition publications portrayed women as men's shadow, obedient to his will, satisfied with what she has and serving her family (Tokhtakhojaeva, 2000).

Until today, traditional cultural values and norms continue to influence a positive attitude of the majority of people towards a submissive behaviour of women. Men have not been freed from the feeling of absolute superiority over women, with the intra-family roles largely being determined by tradition; this requires a family to be headed by a man, where the younger members give deference to the elders, and the wife to the husband. Being greatly burdened with housework in all social, age and educational groups, women's public activity is lower than that of men. Boys must never undertake 'female' work even if they wish to help with the housework. Moreover, the dominant public opinion is that any physical work classified as 'female' is shameful for a man to undertake, as it disgraces him in the eyes of the public. As this opinion is rooted in the minds of boys, they are guided by it in their future lives.

Since childhood, a future woman is taught how to undertake household tasks for her future husband. A commonly recognized 'good' daughter-in-law gets up at 6 o'clock in the morning, cleans the house, makes breakfast, then wakes up the rest of the family. When the family sits for meals, she must pour tea, check that anything needed at the table is in place and quickly bring what is missing. Such a traditional upbringing for women emphasizes paying particular attention to absolute resignation to the will of the parents and, after marriage, to the will of the husband. Husbands are the traditional breadwinners, while women care for family and house. If the wife knows some craft, she may earn money from this, but her earnings will not influence her status in the family. Moreover, earnings are usually given to the mother-in-law, who will hand part of it back to the woman. Divorces and other forms of protest caused by the husband's violence or the mother-in-law's pressure are subject to public condemnation. Therefore, under the influence of their own parents, women have to resign themselves to the existing order (Tokhtakhojaeva, 2001, p. 262).

Thus, the contemporary revival of patriarchal and religious values gave Uzbek women the choice of staying at home, provided that their men were willing and able to fulfil the 'breadwinner' role (Kiblitskaya, 2000b). However, widespread and rising female unemployment, combined with growing labour market discrimination also forced more and more women into business ownership, in order to be able to support their families. Although many Uzbek women require support from their spouses if they want to go into business, they also value the independence that any paid work gives them, as it helps to strengthen women's economic status.

Women's Entrepreneurship in a Traditional Environment

The Role for Women Entrepreneurs in Uzbekistan

During the 1990s, the share of economically active women decreased slightly, amounting to 44 per cent in the year 2000 compared with 56 per cent for men. At the beginning of the 1990s, 47 per cent of all women were economically active, with 18 per cent working in administration and management. Official data shows a considerably larger share of unemployed women (62 per cent) than men (38 per cent). A survey conducted by the State Department of Statistics indicates a high motivation to work on behalf of women, the majority of whom prefer either part-time employment or flexible hours (UNDP, 1999). This goes hand in hand with the decreasing number of pre-school, state institutions during the transition period. Moreover, the rising unemployment rate helps to push women into low-paid and low-valued economic activities. Women losing their jobs are generally disinclined to register as unemployed, but instead shift to (partly) informal economic activities, although this is only partly reflected in empirical data (Welter et al., 2003).

Whilst female entrepreneurs contribute to the process of transition at both the microeconomic and macroeconomic levels, their function as social role models is particularly important in a society, where cultural norms and values strongly influence the nature of female entrepreneurship. Business is still perceived as a predominantly 'male territory', requiring so-called 'male' qualities, such as strength and assertiveness. An additional factor is that in Uzbekistan, transition has been associated with the 'Uzbekisation' of society, involving the revival of patriarchal values and Islamic norms, described previously. In rural areas particularly, traditional values did not change much during the Soviet period, but after the start of transition, they have gained importance across all layers of society; and in both core and periphery regions alike. Akiner (1997, p. 287) describes this as re-establishing the 'concept of male guardianship' in public and private life, which is a trend with enormous potential consequences for female entrepreneurship.

Traditional Uzbek society has always attributed high importance to family and marriage, which typically involves female subordination. Sociological surveys have shown that this subordination serves as a major obstacle to women taking independent decisions on issues related to their own destinies. A woman does not decide herself when and whom to marry, what profession to choose, how many children to have, and what career to build (Tokhtakodjaeva, 2001). In this context, the revival of Islamic values restricts the activities of women, especially in those Uzbek regions such as the Ferghana Valley, where men enforce Islamic values on women, despite the fact that the current government is determined to control any political Islamic movement (Tazmini, 2001). Current research on the image of women in the mass media demonstrates that both radio and television portray Uzbek girls as timid and modest, having excellent housewife qualities, and answering to their parents, especially their fathers (Tokhtakhodjaeva, undated).

The collapse of the social and health systems of Uzbekistan, following the transition towards establishing a market-based economy added to the societal pressure on women to stay at home, in order to care for elderly or sick family members and children. Women also disappeared from public life. For example, the share of female politicians decreased from 35 per cent at the beginning of the transformation process to a mere 6 per cent in 1994 (Tokhtakhodjaeva, 1998).

In addition, specific territorial community structures, which nowadays operate in self-governed neighbourhood communities, are acknowledged by the Uzbek state, playing an important role in supervising women's public and private behaviour. So-called Mahallas[3] play a great role in the life of Uzbek people (Geiss, 2001). Having transformed and adjusted to current social and economic conditions in urban and rural areas, the Mahalla remains a structure regulating the public and even private life of its citizens, with breaches being censured publicly. Even today, Mahalla authorities control youth, the upbringing of youth and channels of information, as well as whether girls and women adhere to prevailing norms. This appears to operate particularly well in rural areas, where traditional norms are strong (Tokhtakhojaeva, 2001, p. 261). Thus, *regional variations,* in terms of cultural traditions, add another dimension to the possible distinctiveness of female entrepreneurship in Uzbekistan, especially considering that 70 per cent of the population live in rural areas, which are characterised by strong clan and patriarchal family structures, thereby dictating a distinctive role for women and limiting their entrepreneurial opportunities (Chakimowa, 1999). This often results in women taking up activities that are suitable for being home-based, enabling them to be combined with household responsibilities. At the same time, such activities often generate low incomes, with low growth opportunities.

While the economic reality requires their increased entrepreneurial engagement, the specific cultural traditions in Uzbekistan re-enforce the traditional role of women in society, restricting the nature and extent of women's entrepreneurship. However, since 1995 the state has adopted a number of protectionist measures regarding women, in an attempt to strengthen and increase their rights, rendering support to the women's movement. Active government measures, which are aimed at supporting the development of SMEs in the country, have assisted women in setting up small businesses, although the recent shift towards an import-substitution policy referred to earlier, has tended to drive many small (female) traders and female entrepreneurs relying on imported raw materials out of business.

In addition, the ongoing redistribution of state ownership has concentrated the overwhelming majority of income-generating resources in the hands of men, whilst the privatization process hardly benefited women at all. This was because women typically did not possess sufficient resources to allow them to become owners of large or even medium sized property. In addition, the reforms of agricultural enterprises and their privatization also took place without women's participation. As a consequence, very few women could participate in privatization and create their own firms or farms. Despite all efforts and the fact that decrees of the Constitution of the Republic of Uzbekistan concerning equal rights for women and men, progress has been slow, thereby restricting the nature and extent of female entrepreneurship.

Forms and Characteristics of Women's Entrepreneurship in Uzbekistan

Women entrepreneurs largely operate in narrow segments of the market in Uzbekistan, mainly occupying economic niches that are related to 'traditionally female' types of activity, such as trade, catering, healthcare and consumer services, or traditional handicrafts. Women are also represented in the manufacturing sector, although in this case their role is typically restricted to internal management issues. Where they own and manage manufacturing companies, this typically includes small food processing firms and similar activities. Female managers in large companies and women running small enterprises in intermediary, medical, advertising services or trade constitute only a small part of women in business in Uzbekistan. The majority of Uzbek female entrepreneurs across all age groups works as shuttle traders and street vendors, including a considerable share of women with higher education, former scientists and government employees in education or healthcare, many of whom took up business because salaries in government institutions were either low or not paid on time (Maksudova, 2000). Rural women mainly earn additional income by either selling surplus from their land, or by turning to traditional and home-based economic activities, such as silk embroidery and carpet weaving. Incomes received from these activities play an increasingly important role in family budgets in Uzbekistan.

Empirical data from our research project on women's entrepreneurship in Uzbekistan show the age of women-entrepreneurs to vary, although mainly in the range 30 to 59 years old, but with some variation between survey regions. Younger women under 20 years of age enter entrepreneurship, mainly in Tashkent, the capital of Uzbekistan, and in the Namangan region, one of the more traditional ones. This apparently was both facilitated and made necessary by the high density of population, the lack of jobs, and the need to earn the means to secure minimum family income.

Entering Entrepreneurship

Given the revival of traditional and Islamic values and attitudes, entrepreneurship could be one way for women to gain more independence. This is apparent when looking at the main motives for starting a business, by women compared with men. When asked about the main reasons for business start-up, responses indicated that women first of all strive for independence when setting up their business, followed by 'push' motives such as unemployment, whilst income reasons appeared to play a less important role (Table 3.3).

Men, by contrast, were significantly more likely to report being motivated by a desire to own and run a business e and to have taken advantage of the availability of suitable resources, which were typically less readily available to women because of their more restricted participation in the process of privatization. Women were also less likely to report they had started a business in response to specific market opportunities than men.

The survey also revealed considerable regional differences with regard to what may be interpreted as push motives for business start-up. Outside the capital city, more women mentioned entering entrepreneurship for unemployment reasons. This can be partly explained by the high proportion of women in the labour force of these regions. It is also natural, since in the rural areas the number of jobs has declined drastically, and some of the women there simply do not have any jobs.

Table 3.3 Motives for entering entrepreneurship by gender*

Motives	Female	Male	Total
to provide income to live/survive	22.5	25.0	23.1
to increase income	30.0	43.3	33.1
as an alternative to unemployment	18.0	5.0	15.0
to be independent	42.0	20.0	36.9
self fulfilment	18.0	31.7	21.2
desire to have own business	16.5	51.7	24.6
to respond to market opportunities	7.5	15.0	9.2
discontentment with previous employment	1.0	8.3	2.7
had resources available (e.g., finance, equipment, skills, contacts)	20.5	40.0	25.0
succession in a family business	2.5	8.3	3.8
social objectives	18.5	11.7	16.9
Total	200	60	260

*Respondents were invited to give three main reasons.

Source: Own survey in 2002.

Taking into account that we asked entrepreneurs for their motivations retrospectively, which is not ideal, combined with the fact that classifying motives for start-up into a crude push-pull dichotomy may be criticized as being overly deterministic (Amit and Muller, 1996), nevertheless the data do not lead to the conclusion that women's entrepreneurship in Uzbekistan is solely necessity-driven. Instead, it shows that women have a variety of motives to start a business, where both push and pull factors appear to overlap, supporting the view that these categories are not mutually exclusive. Despite the unfavourable circumstances of their lives, in many cases, Uzbek women have responded positively to engage in a new and unknown activity as entrepreneurship.

A similar finding is apparent with respect to respondents' answers to a question concerning their current business aims. Rather than showing female entrepreneurship to be mainly necessity driven, the data indicate evolving motivations (Table 3.4). Although income goals play a more important role for women compared to men, a large share of both groups is, nevertheless, growth-oriented.

Table 3.4 Most important business aim by gender (in per cent)

Business Aims	Female	Male
Growth	70.0	76.7
Survival	7.0	11.7
Providing living for family	11.5	8.3
Increasing personal/household/family income	10.0	3.3
Other aims	1.5	0
Total	200	60

Source: Own survey in 2002.

Detailed analysis of case study evidence demonstrates that women entrepreneurs are neither exclusively driven by a desire for independence or the need to earn income because of unemployment. Instead, the case study evidence suggests more complex relationships exist between 'pushed' entrepreneurship and entrepreneurs responding to potential market niches. In practice, some women entrepreneurs 'switch' between categories, as they develop their businesses, which demonstrates changing aspirations as they gain in confidence, as well as learning capacity, in some cases.

A good example is a female-owned enterprise in Tashkent, which started trading in 1994, dealing with the wholesale of imported pharmacy goods, but with smaller sidelines in selling perfumes, cosmetics and jewellery. The woman owner described herself initially as being very reluctant to act as entrepreneur, although the business has now evolved to become a fulltime activity, both for the woman entrepreneur and her husband, who had previously worked in the Ministry of Internal Affairs. Initially, the husband had encouraged his wife to act as director of the company, because his position as a government official precluded him from owning a business himself. However, since starting the business, her interest, enthusiasm and confidence in running the business had grown considerably, which indicates the pitfalls of over-emphasizing the use of static typologies of entrepreneurial motivation.

Although women entrepreneurs might be primarily survival-oriented either at business start, or subsequently, their personal ambitions could still be driven by opportunity-based elements of entrepreneurship. For example, this applies to an entrepreneur who started her metal and wood production business in order to contribute to the family income. When interviewed, the entrepreneur emphasized entrepreneurship as a possibility not only to earn money, but also to realise her own ambitions. Provided with a similar choice currently, she stated that she would still go into entrepreneurship.

By contrast, another case study demonstrates the opposite tendency. In 1995, the mother of this woman entrepreneur initiated the privatization of a hotel, which was previously her working place. Although the woman we interviewed took over as Director in 2001, referring to plans to restructure her hotel according to international standards, she also revealed conflicts between her own ambitions and interests and the dominant social background. Raised in a family, which values Central Asian traditions, she remained responsible for all household chores as well as raising her children. Being an entrepreneur helped her to acquire professional skills, enabling her to communicate with people, relying on her own capabilities and improving her societal standing. On the other hand, she stated that she would be interested in taking up a job with 'stable and decent earnings', although she claimed that her parents would not allow her to leave the hotel, which now is a family business.

In general, women entrepreneurs were able to point to ways in which running a business had been both a learning experience and a source of high personal satisfaction, without neglecting the negative aspects of entrepreneurship, such as having less time for family and friends, or health-related problems associated with working too much. Personal satisfaction was typically reported to be related to issues such as being able to realise 'childhood dreams' or finding a market niche; being in control and the leader; being independent from husband and family; as well as satisfying customer needs. All this contributes to a multifaceted picture of women's entrepreneurship in the specific social context of Uzbekistan, and to the learning experiences connected to this.

Combining Business and Family Life: A Problem for Uzbek Women Entrepreneurs?

Given the traditional attitude of Uzbek society towards women, one would expect their double workload to possibly restrict enterprise development. Survey data from our study confirms the more common involvement of women entrepreneurs in household duties, compared with their male counterparts. It also shows that women typically feel unable to complain about the unfairness of this dual workload. For example, the survey data shows that only 9 per cent of women are not involved in household duties, compared to 16 per cent of the men (Table 3.5). Moreover, most women entrepreneurs do not complain about any unfair distribution. This does not imply that the workload is fair; it just reflects the attitude of women entrepreneurs who are used to dealing with this problem. Our conclusion is that whilst it is difficult to view the household and family context in Uzbekistan as an enabling environment for entrepreneurship, the commitment of Uzbek women entrepreneurs to do something for themselves, combined with a willingness to work hard, was often associated with support from spouses and partners, as well as wider social capital.

Table 3.5 Distribution of household duties by gender (in per cent)

Household Duties	Female	Male	Total
you are not involved in household duties	9.2	16.4	10.8
you feel it is fair	62.2	63.6	62.5
you feel you could contribute more	17.3	9.1	15.5
you feel your partner/family could contribute more	11.2	10.9	11.2
Total number	200	60	260

Source: Own survey in 2002.

With regard to family and spouses, most women claimed a supportive attitude both of their families and spouses. Since women's entrepreneurship is becoming one of the primary sources of family income, the majority of spouses and other family members not only support women businesses, but also render some form of material and non-material assistance. The help provided to women is especially tangible in the rural areas, where whole families work together. In order of priority, survey data suggest that families mainly contribute through their labour input; giving emotional support; advice and capital; whilst, for men the priority order was emotional support, labour and advice). The main priority is family work, followed by capital. Spouses mainly contribute work, capital and advice. Disapproval, where it occurs, appears to be more common with respect to certain business activities, such as trade, and in the case of micro enterprises.

Developing the Business: Does being a Woman help?

Our empirical evidence shows gender to have a mainly neutral influence, from the standpoint of business development. When asked if their gender was an advantage with respect to certain aspects of business development, differences were reported across problem fields. For example, one third of surveyed women considered their gender to contribute positively to human resource management, pointing to it helping them to establish a motivating atmosphere they also perceiving themselves to be better at solving conflicts and handling employees' diversity. On the other hand, women entrepreneurs also noted certain negative aspects in this respect, such as being too soft with their employees.

When asked, whether they attributed any business problems to their gender, most women entrepreneurs denied this. At the same time, one quarter considered their gender had contributed to making their life more difficult when they started their business; third suggesting it contributed to the current problems faced. Perhaps their answers reflect the growing experience of women in dealing with all kinds of business problems, again pointing to the learning experience involved with continuous entrepreneurship for some women.

Survey respondents were also asked if they considered their gender had assisted them in dealing with the business environment. In dealing with banks, a large share of Uzbek women (43 per cent) suggested that their gender helped in this context. They also reported that their gender had assisted them in dealing with customers, authorities and other entrepreneurs, which can be illustrated with evidence drawn from case studies. Asked whether she thought that authorities, banks and similar organizations treat female and male business in the same way, one entrepreneur stressed that gender had actually helped her, especially at the start, when she had less business experience. Interestingly, however, her husband claimed that gender does not matter. She thought it easier for her, as a woman, to communicate with agencies and banks, since men are more friendly and polite with her. She gave the example of the first visit from the regional tax agency in 1995. The female inspector visiting her found a small mistake in her declaration and asked for a $2,000 penalty (which, in the eyes of the entrepreneur, was hugely exaggerated, given the amount of the unpaid tax, thereby including an element of bribe). The entrepreneur went to the office of the agency herself and asked for another tax inspector, without telling them about the demand made. When they asked her for reasons, she told them 'I am a weak woman, just starting a business, I need your help.' Now she has very good contacts with the regional tax agency, where she is well known.

A significant minority of women considered gender to be an obstacle to increasing sales, to some extent. This is illustrated by case study evidence, which shows that gender could play role in dealing with certain types of customer. For example, based on her own experience, one woman entrepreneur suggested that women are not trusted or taken seriously by male buyers/clients, especially from state companies. She quoted the example of a business deal with the army who asked for man to deal with, rather than her.

Another issue concerns whether or not women are more or less successful than their male counterparts. This question was asked to both women and men with regard to various business spheres such as finance, sales growth, business information, market development, exporting, innovation, networking, production and personnel management. Their answers show differing perceptions of women and men, in this regard. Significantly more men than women stated a negative effect of gender on the success of women-owned businesses across all spheres. This applied particularly to production, exporting and innovation. Women mainly perceived a neutral effect, but they also considered themselves to be more successful especially in fields, such as finance and, surprisingly perhaps, innovation also (42 per cent).

More detailed case evidence shows contradictory results in this regard. For example, one woman stated that today 'it is easier for a woman to be engaged in business, and she more frequently manages to be successful. Today women have become stronger. When potential entrepreneurs consult other entrepreneurs with questions related to venture creation, men only see problems, while women are more enterprising.' At the same time, another woman complained that business is more difficult for a woman, as she has to prove herself over and over again, she is not allowed to make faults.

Environment and Women's Entrepreneurship

Overall, our case study evidence draws attention to the important influence of the environment in Uzbekistan in shaping the nature of women's entrepreneurship. This refers to economic and sectoral conditions, as well as cultural influences in a broad sense. Case evidence also demonstrates the influence of particular regional conditions, as several of those women entrepreneurs who were interviewed in Namangan, appeared more ready to give up their business activities, provided they would find a job elsewhere, compared to those in Tashkent and those in the more successful ventures with growth-potential in their own region. This draws attention to the recursive links between the national/regional (economic) environments, as well as to the role of the level of personal satisfaction with regards to entrepreneurial activity. In these cases, women might not have started out of pure necessity, but staying in entrepreneurship is clearly linked to economic needs.

This can be illustrated with reference to a woman, who started a service company in the Namangan region in 2002, based on her previous working experiences and a desire to set up her own business. However, regardless of the benefits she associated with being an entrepreneur, such as gaining more independence within her family,[4] or gaining entrepreneurial knowledge and skills, this woman would readily give up her business, provided she could find a job with stable earnings.

In addition, several cases illustrate the effects of changes in the economic conditions, which can trigger a shift from initially opportunity-based entrepreneurship to more survival-oriented entrepreneurship in later years of business development. An increase in competition over the years, combined with decreasing purchase power of customers and changing laws, can lead some women entrepreneurs to take on additional activities, such as (shuttle) trading, or an extension of their production into low-cost food processing, such as dried fruits, facilitated by the fact, that most households own small plots of land. This diversification often results in a broad and unrelated portfolio of business activities, thus chiefly expressing the short-term behavioural response to overcoming pressing financial and environmental constraints (Welter and Smallbone, 2003). Such behaviour is stimulated by an attempt to secure incomes and to survive. One such example is an entrepreneur who privatised a state optics company in the Namangan region, because she perceived a niche market opportunity. Whilst a wholesale and retail trading business in medicines initially provided her with capital to privatise her previous place of work, the severe import regulations posed unsolvable problems for her, in relation to both optics and medicines. Currently she sells products from her own farm, and is considering diversifying into buying her own livestock.

Case study evidence also reveals how particular cultural influences on women's entrepreneurship in the Uzbek context fosters low-threshold and low-income business activities, with low potential for business growth. For example, another woman entrepreneur featured as a case study, reported being unable to access specialised training, because of the traditional attitude of the woman's father towards girls' education. She felt this left her with no choice but to take up a traditional business activity, namely gold embroidery and sewing, after her father's death, because this was one of the few vocational training opportunities available to her. The main motive to go into business was income-related, as the father was the sole breadwinner in the family. Similar to her own experience, two of her three sisters had set up home-based traditional business activities in carpet weaving and cookery; with all three of them involved in tutoring unemployed girls in these activities. The business had been set up in Chartak (Namangan region) in 1999, but suspended in June 2001, which the respondent explained in terms of the low purchasing power of customers and the amount of competition. The latter is not surprising, given both the low entry costs and the traditional background of this particular line of business, which is one of the few activities left for girls and women in traditional-oriented households in Uzbekistan.

Conclusions

In a situation where the overall level of entrepreneurship is at a very low level, the engagement of women in entrepreneurial activity is making an important contribution to the overall level of entrepreneurial activity in the economy. Although under-represented in the business owning population, the contribution of women to the emerging service sector is an important one in a post Soviet context. It can also be argued that the accumulated capital, knowledge and experience of women entrepreneurs are adding to what is a scarce human capital base of resources relevant to private sector development, in a country such as Uzbekistan. Moreover, although Uzbek women look for emotional, practical and financial support from their spouses, they also value the independence that any paid work gives them. Despite the fact that this type of activity is typically restricted to low-value and low-growth activities (at least from a macroeconomic point of view), this helps to strengthen women's economic status, especially where they operate in 'female market niches' (Zhurzhenko, 2001, p. 44).

With regard to women's entrepreneurship in Uzbekistan, traditional values and norms have an important impact, as does religion, although in this case the influence is a more subtle one. Most post Soviet societies have experienced a return of religious influences to some extent, in the form of either the Orthodox Church or Islam. A revival of religious values might be expected to impose strict rules on women, which could result in conflicting economic and societal roles, when women are (implicitly) forced to adhere to these regulations. This appears to be problematic for female entrepreneurship, especially in Central Asian regions, where

Islamic ideas have gained political ground during the transition years. In this situation, it has allowed Uzbek fundamentalists, for example, to extend the religious order of Islam to women's rights, affecting their personal attire and their public appearance (Ilkhamov, 2001). This partly built on the legacy from the pre-Soviet period, where the social status of a Muslim woman and her mode of life was shaped by the sexual segregation that is prescribed by the shariah. Although Muslim women could earn income through home crafts, mastership and literacy teaching, this was required to be home-based and only males could work outside home (Tokhtakhodjaeva, 2000).

All this contributes to the prevailing forms of female entrepreneurship in Uzbekistan, a large part of which involves home-based or marginal subsistence activities, in an attempt on the part of women entrepreneurs to combine family and income generation. Small-scale privatization was one way into entrepreneurship for women, as many small shops, hair dressing shops, restaurants and pharmacies had female managers in Soviet times. Women also opened small businesses in consumer- and business-oriented services; in other words, in sectors, which were underdeveloped during the Soviet period. In addition, women also constitute a significant part of the 'shuttle' trading sector importing and selling consumer goods missing in the domestic market. Thus, transition has contributed to the emergence of female entrepreneurs, despite the contradictory attitudes of post Soviet Uzbek society towards working women.

At the same time, empirical evidence suggests that generational change is associated with a challenge to the existing social order, including gender roles. Case study evidence suggests that a 'necessity push' into enterprise activity does not preclude (women) business owners acquiring those attributes associated with more opportunity driven entrepreneurship over time, such as the identification of new market opportunities, innovation and creativity and the ability to adapt to rapidly changing external conditions. As a consequence, one must be cautious about over-generalising the characteristics and behaviour patterns of female entrepreneurs in post Soviet economies. In this context, female entrepreneurship could play an important role in modernizing Uzbek society and changing public attitudes towards women, which in turn will enable governments to make better use of the economic potential of female entrepreneurs.

Notes

1 'Female entrepreneurship in transition economies: the example of Ukraine, Moldova and Uzbekistan', funded under the INTAS programme (contract no.,00-0843).

2 Decree by the President of the RU of 1995 'On Measures for Raising the Role of Women in the State and Public Development in the Republic of Uzbekistan'.

3 The Mahalla, a territorial community of neighbours, has a thousand-year history in Central Asia. The Mahalla is a structural unit of the population habitats in Uzbekistan. At present its functions of the basis of self-governance of the citizens have been legitimized by the state. The Mahalla 1) unites citizens with the purpose to address

social and economic issues in its territory, as well as to arrange cultural and mass events, assist the state authorities and management with law enforcement; 2) assists the citizens with the realization of their rights to participate in the management of community and state matters; 3) promotes international accord as many settlements are characterized of polytechnics composition of population. The Mahalla has its own property, finances, and budget, creates small enterprises, cooperatives, regular and traditional craft workshops, and takes banking credits for such purposes. One of the most authoritative functions of Mahalla is the allocation of land for possession, utilization, and lease to enterprises, establishments and citizens.

4 Although she is married and has a young son, she lives with her parents, as the husband works in Moscow.

References

Aivazova S. (1998), *Russian Women in Labyrinth of Equality of Rights*, Moscow (in Russian).

Akiner, S. (1997), 'Between tradition and modernity: the dilemma facing contemporary Central Asian women', in M. Buckley (ed), *Post-Soviet women: from the Baltic to Central Asia*, Cambridge University Press, Cambridge, pp. 261-304.

Amit, R. and Muller, E. (1996), '"Push-" und "Pull"-Unternehmertum', *Internationales Gewerbearchiv*, vol. 44, pp. 90-103.

Ashwin, S. (2000), 'Introduction: Gender, state and society in Soviet and post-Soviet Russia', in S. Ashwin (ed), *Gender, state and society in Soviet and post-Soviet Russia*, Routledge, London, pp. 1-29.

Bruno, M. (1997), 'Women and the culture of entrepreneurship', in M. Buckley (ed), *Post-Soviet women: from the Baltic to Central Asia*, Cambridge University Press, Cambridge, pp. 56–74.

Chakimowa, M. (1999), 'Wo stehen die usbekischen Frauen heute?', *Wostok-Spezial*, pp. 60-63.

Fajth, G. (2000), 'Women in transition: Themes of the UNICEF MONEE project', in M. Lazreg (ed), *Making the Transition work for Women in Europe and Central Asia*, World Bank Discussion Paper No. 411, World Bank, Washington D.C., pp. 89–101.

Geiss, P.G. (2001), 'Mahallah and kinship relations. A study on residential communal commitment structures in Central Asia of the 19th century', *Central Asian Survey*, vol. 20, no. 1, pp. 97-106.

Ilkhamov, A. (2001), 'Impoverishment of the masses in the transition period: signs of an emerging 'new poor' identity in Uzbekistan', *Central Asian Survey*, vol. 20, pp. 33-54.

Kerblay, B. (1977), *La Société Soviétique Contemporaine*, Armand Colin, Paris.

Kiblitskaya, M. (2000a), 'Russia's female breadwinners: The changing subjective experience', in S. Ashwin (ed), *Gender, state and society in Soviet and post-Soviet Russia*, Routledge, London, pp. 55-70.

Kiblitskaya, M. (2000b), ''Once we were kings'. Male experiences of loss of status in post-communist Russia', in S. Ashwin (ed), *Gender, State and Society in Soviet and Post-Soviet Russia*, Routledge, London, pp. 90-104.

Kurmanbaeva, F., Pugach, I. and Abdullaev, R. (2000), ' Small and average business in Uzbekistan: modern condition, problems, prospects', *The Economic Review*, vol. 3, no. 13, pp. 4-22.

Maksudova, Ch.M. (2000), *Marketing Research of Women's Role in Small Business*, Master's thesis, Tashkent State Economic University, Tashkent.

Schakirova, N., Mirzakhalilova, D. and Mirzaeva, M. (2002), 'Women's Entrepreneurship in the Republic of Uzbekistan', in F. Welter and D. Smallbone (eds), *Female Entrepreneurship in the Ukraine, Moldova and Uzbekistan: A Review*, RWI, Essen, pp. 41-71.

Smallbone, D. and Welter, F. (2001), 'The distinctiveness of entrepreneurship in transition economies', *Small Business Economics*, vol. 16, pp. 249-262.

Tabyshalieva, A. (2000), 'Revival of traditions in post-Soviet Central Asia', in M. Lazreg (ed), *Making the Transition work for Women in Europe and Central Asia*, World Bank Discussion Paper No. 411, World Bank, Washington D.C., pp. 51-57.

Tazmini, G. (2001), The Islamic revival in central Asia: A potent force or a misconception?', *Central Asian Survey*, vol. 20, pp. 63-83.

Tokhtakhodjaeva, M. (undated), *Traditional Stereotypes and Women's Problems over the Period of Transition* (Survey of Media in Uzbekistan), http/www.undp.uz/GID/eng/UZBEKISTAN/GENERAL/RESEARCH/uzngo_res.html.

Tokhtakhodjaeva, M. (2001), *Tired with the Past*, Tashkent.

Tokhtakhodjaeva, M. (2000), *Between Communist Slogans and Islamic Laws*, Tashkent.

Tokhtatkhodjaeva, M. (1998), *Gender Issues in Uzbekistan*, first draft, committed by UNFPA, Tashkent, http://www.undp.uz/GID/eng/UZBEKISTAN/GENERAL/RESEARCH/gender_wrc.html.

Turetskaya, G.V. (2001), 'Business activity of women and family', *Sotsiologicheskie issledovania,* no. 2, pp. 67-73 (in Russian).

UNDP (1999), *Report on the Status of Women in Uzbekistan*, UNDP, Tashkent.

Welter, F. and Smallbone, D. (2003), 'Entrepreneurship and Enterprise Strategies in Transition Economies: An Institutional Perspective', in D. Kirby and A. Watson (eds), *Small Firms and Economic Development in Developed and Transition Economies: A Reader*, Ashgate, Aldershot, pp. 95-114.

Welter, F., Smallbone, D., Aculai, E., N. Isakova, N. and Schakirova, N. (2003), 'Female Entrepreneurship in Post Soviet Countries', in J. Butler (ed), *New Perspectives on Women Entrepreneurs*, Information Age, Greenwich, pp. 243-270.

Zhurzhenko, T. (1999), 'Gender and identity formation in post-Socialist Ukraine: The case of women in the shuttle business', in R. Bridgman, S. Cole and H. Howard-Bobiwash (eds), *Feminist Fields: Ethnographic Insights*, Broadview Press, Ontario, pp. 243-263.

Zhurzhenko, T. (2001), 'Free market ideology and new women's identities in post-socialist Ukraine', *The European Journal of Women's Studies*, vol. 8, pp. 29-49.

Chapter 4

Women Business Owners in Moldova: Proprietors or Entrepreneurs?

Elena Aculai, Nelly Rodionova and Natalia Vinogradova

Introduction

The deep economic crisis of the 1990s in Moldova was accompanied by the bankruptcy of many large-scale state-owned enterprises. As a result, tens of thousand of citizens became unemployed in a short period of time. Operating a small-scale private business became one of a few methods of earning a living at that time, and this still holds true today. One implication of the existence of such strong 'push' factors into business ownership is the extent to which such people possess the characteristics and skills necessary to run a business. This is of particular importance with respect to women entrepreneurs, because of the circumstances in which many women enter business ownership.

In this context, the chapter concentrates on discussing female entrepreneurs in Moldova, firstly, because they form a significant part of Moldovan entrepreneurs contributing to economic development; and secondly, because there is a lack of empirical data and material on female entrepreneurship in Moldova. More specifically, the chapter analyses different characteristics of Moldovan female business owners, classifying them into entrepreneurs and so-called proprietors. The classification is based on several indicators said to represent entrepreneurship: entrepreneurial aptitudes, motives for starting a business, business performance, entrepreneurial behaviour and objectives. Innovative behaviour, defined as a type of dynamic behaviour, which has an active influence on every sphere of an enterprise was chosen to be the most important indicator for our classification. This indicator is of particular significance under conditions of frequent and unpredictable changes in the environment, which is typical of transition countries. Drawing on survey and case material from an international research project, we introduce an empirically-based classification and discuss its contribution and limitations.[1] It is suggested that classifying business owners on the basis of the extent to which they have the skills necessary to run a business is of potential significance for policy, because of differences in the nature of their support needs.

The chapter first sets out to discuss the development of female business ownership against the background of the overall development of private entrepreneurship and the existing political environment in Moldova. The role of women in Moldovan society during the last decades of the 20th century is briefly described, because of the need to place the involvement of women in business in the wider context of women's role in society. This is followed by a discussion of our classification of female entrepreneurs, with the last part summarising the main conclusions and possible implications for policy.

Entrepreneurship and SME Development in Moldova

In Moldova, as in other republics of the former USSR, private entrepreneurship development started during the late 1980s, gaining momentum during the 1990s. This was despite the fact that the crisis in Moldova was longer and more profound than in other transitional countries, leaving Moldova as one of the poorest countries in Europe today. During initial stages of reform, managers and workers' bodies already had obtained some independence in managing enterprises, as they had been able to lease state property and try out different models of self-supporting within state-owned enterprises. Subsequently, initial non-state enterprises appeared in the form of co-operatives. In 1991, 3,500 co-operatives existed, which were involved in construction, consumer services and the production of consumer goods (Cara and Patraşcu, 2001). After the Law on Entrepreneurship and Enterprises was adopted in 1992, many co-operatives were transformed into individual enterprises, limited liability companies, joint-stock companies, and other private forms. Furthermore, an increasing number of new ventures, mainly very small ones, were set up, particularly in low entry threshold activities. Thus, on the one hand, the state was an enabling force by approving legislation allowing for private entrepreneurship, but on the other hand, the level of unemployment rose quickly, depriving many people of their livelihood. For these reasons, people in Moldova were both pulled and pushed into entrepreneurship.

Number of Economic Units and SME Development

The number of enterprises registered in the Republic of Moldova was continually growing during the period of transition, although at varying rates. Between 1992 and 1995, the annual growth rate was as high as 150 to 200 per cent, reflecting the process of opportunity exploitation by citizens of the country, but also the overall slump in living standards which forced some citizens into starting their own businesses. Only recently did the rate of growth fell to between 4 and 5 per cent annually (DSS, 2003c). Nevertheless, the total number of enterprises is still growing, despite the fact that between 150,000 and 200,000 firms are wound up officially every year, amounting to about 30 per cent of the number of newly created enterprises (DSS, 2004). In 2003, 116,700 enterprises were registered in

Moldova, the absolute majority of which belongs to the small business sector. In 2002, small enterprises accounted for 89.7 per cent of all economic units, employed 25.4 per cent of all employees and produced 22.7 per cent of total net sales.

The overall growth in the number of small enterprises reflects a positive attitude towards private entrepreneurship within Moldova, which is supported by case study evidence drawn from a recent project on women entrepreneurs (Welter et al., 2003a, 2003b). For instance, an entrepreneur who owns a micro enterprise with three employees in retail trade, stated that 'society's attitude towards female entrepreneurs is very benevolent' and improving since she started her business. However, entrepreneurs often add that the benevolent attitude of society in this regard, is due to the hard work of business owners and their employees: 'It is possible that if private enterprises were larger, people's attitude towards them would be different as the poor do not like the rich' (Welter et al., 2003b). In addition, the small business sector is a potential source for a middle class, which is required to attain stability in society and to successfully realize social and economic programmes of the Moldovan government for the near future.

Nowadays, private firms make up the overwhelming majority of enterprises registered in the Republic (93.4 per cent) (DSS, 2003c), while state-owned and state-shared enterprises account for only 4.3 per cent, with a steadily declining share. This results from a combination of the establishment of 'de novo' enterprises, on the one hand, and the ongoing privatization of former state-owned enterprises, on the other. There also is a slowly growing share of enterprises with foreign participation: 2.4 per cent in 2003 compared with 2.1 per cent in 2001. However, foreign investors have been reluctant to invest in Moldova because of the economic and political instability in the country. This contributes to a lack of new, modern technologies, new management techniques and ways to new markets, which contributes to the slowly growing competitiveness of national enterprises. Interestingly, the share of enterprises with foreign participation is relatively high among small firms (5.8 per cent). Foreign and joint small enterprises are characterized by relatively high sales turnover: with the average sum of net sales per employee being 1.5-2.0 times the average of all small firms. However, due to their low number they do not contribute much to the country's development.

Private firms contribute 57.0 per cent of GDP and create 71.0 per cent of all working places. At the same time, state-owned enterprises account for 24.0 per cent of GDP and 22.7 per cent of employment. The discrepancy between the private enterprises' share and their contribution to GDP and employment is explained by the fact that many small, newly established private enterprises have low potential for development. There are many obstacles for their development, e.g. lack of skills and experiences in running a business, limited access to financial resources and an unfavourable business environment. Moreover, some petty entrepreneurs are not interested in business growth, especially where incomes exceed the material needs of the families. On the other hand, the public sector's potential is much higher. Some public enterprises still retain technological equipment, personnel and markets. In addition, a number of them are of strategic interest for the regional state development, thus obtaining support from government and local authorities.

Sectoral Distribution

The most widely spread type of activity among Moldovan enterprises is trade, representing 53.5 per cent of all registered economic units. The share of industrial enterprises represented 12.0 per cent in 2003, agriculture 6.6 per cent and transport enterprises 5.2 per cent. This sectoral distribution also applies to small enterprises, where most small firms are set up in trade and services which are characterized by a rapid turnover of assets and higher profitability. In particular, almost half of small enterprises are engaged in activities, such as trade, repair of motor vehicles, household commodities and articles of personal consumption. In spite of the small size of trade enterprises they are characterized by the highest labour productivity per worker (Table 4.1), which is 73.9 per cent higher than the average sum of net sales per worker in small firms.

Table 4.1 Main indicators of small business activities, by types of economic activities (1st January 2003)

	Share of enterprises, in %	Number of employees per enterprise	Net sales per employee, in % to average in republic
Total	100.0	5.9	100.0
of which:			
Agriculture, hunting and forestry	4.4	11.7	29.7
Industry	12.7	7.9	83.4
Construction	5.7	8.7	78.5
Wholesale and retail trade; repair of motor vehicles, motorcycles, household commodities and articles of personal consumption	46.9	4.4	173.9
Transport, storage facilities and communications	6.4	6.2	96.8

Source: Adapted from DSS (2003c).

Despite the predominance of trade enterprises, their share decreased in recent years, while the shares of industry and transport have increased slightly. This probably indicates the beginning economic stabilization and the beginning of

Moldova's emergence from the deep crisis of the early 1990s, which also is reflected in the growth of GDP from 1999 onwards.

Performance Indicators

According to official statistics, more than 60 per cent of enterprises in Moldova either incur losses, or only breakeven. For example, only 37.2 per cent of registered enterprises were profitable at the end of 2002. The number of enterprises which incurred losses exceeded the number of profitable ones in all sectors and types of activity, with the exception of the construction sector. Table 4.2 illustrates that for small businesses their efficiency indices are lower compared to large and medium-sized firms. For example, the net sales volume per worker of small enterprise is 13.2 thousand lei lower compared to large firms.

Table 4.2 Selected indices of enterprise activities, 2002

	small enterprises	large and middle enterprises
Share of enterprises, in %	89.7	10.3
Average share of employees, in %	25.4	74.6
Net sales, in %	22.7	77.3
Net sales per employee, thousand lei	83.1	96.3
Share of profitable enterprises, in %	83.4	16.6
Share of enterprises with losses, in %	91.6	8.4
Profit (loss) per employee, thousand lei	-1.86	0.99

Source: Adapted from DSS (2003a).

However, official data do not take into account the high share of 'shadow' activities in Moldova. The Department of Statistics estimates that 13.9 per cent of all employees are engaged in the 'shadow' economy, who are either not included in the list of employees, or their real wage is higher than the nominal one indicated in the firm's documents, with the purpose of tax evasion. Moreover, the highest share of 'shadow' employees is to be found in private enterprises (Table 4.3). Moldovan entrepreneurs are of opinion that if taxes on profit and employees amounted to no more than 25 per cent, wages would be moved out from 'the shadow', although such a taxation level may be unrealistic at the present stage of development of Moldovan economy (Kovalenko, 2004). On the whole, in 2001 the share of the 'shadow' activity of registered enterprises was estimated to amount to 6.6 per cent of GDP (DSS, 2003b).

Table 4.3 Employment in the 'shadow' economy by forms of ownership (second quarter of 2003)

Forms of ownership	Employment in the 'shadow' economy Number of employees	in % of index for Moldova
Total on republic	197,006	13.9
of which by forms of ownership:		
Public	888	0.3
Private	192,712	18.8
Other forms of ownership	3,407	5.2

Source: Adapted from DSS (2003d).

Our own survey of owners and managers of small enterprises demonstrates that the majority of entrepreneurs (64.0 per cent of respondents) considered legislation (first of all its instability) and the tax system (high tax rates, fines, customs fees) to be the main reasons for working in the 'shadow economy'. Many entrepreneurs who would like to work legally cannot do this, because their business partners work in the 'shadow', which results in illegal cash payments without proper documentation. Moreover, nearly six per cent of the respondents in our survey considered the inadequate activity of authorities (bureaucracy, bribery, corruption) and difficulties connected to registration, licensing and accounting as driving entrepreneurs to hide a part of their activity (Welter et al., 2003a). Thus, the small business sector in Moldova is still in its formation stage. In this context, government policies might assist in developing a vibrant small business sector.

The Policy Environment for (Women) Entrepreneurship

The policy environment for women's entrepreneurship in Moldova is essentially the same as that for men. The legal foundation for private business development was laid by the Constitution of the Republic of Moldova and the 'Law on Property' at the beginning of 1990s. The 'Law on Entrepreneurship and Enterprises' determined the general conditions for private and public enterprises, their activities, legal forms and size, while the 'Law on Support and Protection of Small Business' regulates micro and small enterprises' activity. Although the government regularly analyses the situation in the private business sector, updating the system of state regulation periodically, specific measures are typically just administrative decisions, which have little influence on the real sector of the economy.

Under the law, the only state structure aiming at offering financial support for small business units is the Fund for Entrepreneurship Support and Small Business Development, which has failed to perform its main role, due to financial constraints and a lack of qualified personnel. The government has tried to radically reorganize the Fund, but without success. The main factors impeding the effectiveness of the Fund include: its unclear legal status; its subordination to the state, preventing it from attracting finance from private and foreign sources. Only in the second half of 2004, which was almost 10 years after its inception, did the Fund receive 750,000 lei ($ 62,500) from the state budget. Recently, the Fund announced a competition for investment projects, in which one of the Moldovan banks will offer credits and the Fund will act as a guarantor on credits to SMEs.

One of the methods of state regulation of small business is through the adoption and execution of governmental and local programmes of small business support, which currently comprises the State Programme for Small Business Support 2002 – 2005. The main goal proclaimed by the Programme is to create stable and favourable conditions for the development of small and micro enterprises. Measures stipulated in the Programme, include legislative and normative acts, financial support for small business and building a business support infrastructure. However, once again the Programme lacks concrete measures for enterprise development. Government has also made some attempt to reduce bureaucracy. Recently, the registration procedure has been changed and simplified and a 'one-stop' mechanism has been introduced, although this has not made much difference in practice, as entrepreneurs still have to pay visits to a number of governmental establishments, and a large number of activities have to be licensed, which is a time-consuming and costly procedure.

None of the government bodies of Moldova is responsible for the elaboration, execution and co-ordination of a coherent state policy for small enterprise development. The Department of Small Business within the Ministry of Economy is the only body which partially tackles the above mentioned problems, but its status is low, and it has few labour resources. For a long time, government officials have discussed the idea of a special SME agency, which would be responsible for implementing state policies, developing links with regions, collaborating with entrepreneurs and coordinating financial support for small business. Hitherto, any discussion of entrepreneurship development and regulation is carried out mainly on the national level. Local authorities do not attach importance to this issue, considering that entrepreneurs do not need special conditions for their development. As a result, the majority of small business enterprises are found in the capital, where the infrastructure is better developed and the total demand is greater.

With regard to women, central and local government are not specifically concerned with support for female entrepreneurship, with one exception. The State Programme of Small Business Support for the years 2002 to 2005 refers to 'the expansion of possibilities of training and consulting of small enterprises' managers; their adapting to needs of state, youth, women, unemployed' (enclosure, section

4.1.2). However, as in the case of most other instruments, this one is vaguely formulated, which renders both implementation and evaluation difficult.

The business support infrastructure in Moldova consists of different components. There are private providers, which gained importance during the late 1990s, offering a wide range of services such as consultancy, business training, and information. These firms/individuals are mainly oriented towards small clients. Government representatives and clerks from local administrations also act as individual business advisors, both officially and unofficially assisting entrepreneurs (in the latter case often asking for money or gifts). The programmes and projects of Western donors have played an important role since the mid-1990s; some offering a wide range of services, while others specialize. As their services cost more than those supplied by local organizations, they are often oriented towards larger enterprises. Thirdly, there are some business associations and non-governmental organizations (NGO), which have appeared during the last three to four years. These were often set up in order to obtain donor grants, which limits their operations. In general, these NGOs specialize on certain services, although some of them are trying to lobby for their members' interests also.

There is no explicit gender orientation in the measures of these business support agencies, although women tend to prevail among the clients of women associations, which appeared in the Republic during the second half of the 1990s. Today, there are more than ten associations of female entrepreneurs in Moldova; all of them are recently created and most are but feebly developed. Currently, there are attempts to consolidate them, in order to strengthen their lobbying voice for women entrepreneurs. One way of lobbying for small business development is through business associations and networks, which can help to develop a dialogue between government and small firms. However, this form of self-support is not well developed in Moldova, mainly because small business owners have been slow to recognise the potential benefits of having a collective voice.

The Role of Women in Society

Despite a major change in the role of women in the economy in terms of employment and an increasing level of education, a traditional attitude towards women in Moldovan society still prevails. This can be illustrated with reference to a case study of a female entrepreneur, conducted by the authors, who stated that she was too shy and lacking in self-confidence when she started her business, which she considered a great obstacle. She pointed out that she had been brought up in a way which cultivated shyness and a lack of self-confidence, as those features were considered attributes of an ideal woman. In the following sections, we briefly analyse female participation in various aspects of public and private life to provide a context for understanding women's involvement in entrepreneurship.

Women in Economy and Politics

The share of women in the population of Moldova has traditionally been greater than that of men. The highest share of women (i.e., 53.8 per cent) was at the end of 1950s, as a consequence of the World War II. During the post war period, women have become increasingly involved in economic activities, as they contributed to post-war recovery, representing approximately 51 per cent of industrial and office workers since about 1970 (Goskomstat SSSR, 1987). Since the late 1980s, the share of economically active women has been lower compared to men (43.3 per cent compared to 45.7 per cent men), despite the fact that women comprise the majority of the population. However, the low index of female economic activity may be partly explained by statistical inaccuracies. Women are more widely involved in economic activities that are likely to be under-reported. These include: informal household work, short hours or short week employment, or working as unpaid family help in a family business. Additionally, more women than men have emigrated and are working illegally in 'near' and 'far' foreign countries (according to unofficial data they comprise about 1 million persons) (Golea, 2004).

Economic activity For many years, women dominated in several types of activity and professions. For example, in 1986 58 per cent of engineers, 67 per cent of physicians, 87 per cent of economists, 89 per cent of accountants, and 91 per cent of librarians and bibliographers were women (CSU MSSR, 1984). Table 4.4 shows the distribution of female employees by types of activity in Moldova during the transition period. In 2002, women were mainly engaged in education, agriculture, industry and public health and social services. There are some 'female' types of activity where the women's share exceeds the one for men: in 2002 this applied to health protection and social services, hotels and restaurants, education, financial intermediation, and to a lesser extent also to public, social and personal utilities and trade. With regard to entrepreneurship, women are mainly concentrated in trade and services. According to a survey conducted by the Centre of Strategic Research and Reforms, women-owned enterprises are concentrated in activities such as hotels and restaurants (39 per cent), retail and wholesale trade (37 per cent), consumer services and recreation (30 per cent), social and cultural services (29 per cent) (CSIR, 2000).

Women often select economic activities, which are connected to their previous work, experiences and knowledge as well as to hobbies. It is rare that the choice of activity of women entrepreneurs is solely determined by thoughts connected to the future profitability of the potential business. As women rarely have a technical education, they can face difficulties in starting a business in sectors, such as construction, transport and some branches of industrial production. Furthermore, they also face difficulties assembling the financial resources needed for doing business in 'non-traditional female' activities.

Table 4.4 Female employment by types of activity

	Share of women in % to the total of Moldova		in % to the number of employees	
	1999	2002	1999	2002
Total	100.0	100.0	52.5	52.4
of which by types of activity:				
Agriculture, hunting and forestry	27.2	18.8	45.8	42.9
Industry	14.0	16.2	45.2	46.9
Construction	1.2	0.9	18.8	18.0
Wholesale and retail trade; repair of motor vehicles, motorcycles, household commodities and articles of personal consumption	4.6	5.0	60.0	53.8
Hotels and restaurants	1.2	1.4	78.1	77.3
Transport, storage facilities and communications	3.6	4.2	30.2	31.5
Financial activity	1.0	1.5	63.2	63.1
Real estate activities	2.6	2.7	41.0	36.8
Education	23.4	25.7	75.3	74.0
Public health and social services	14.1	14.8	80.2	79.4
Other public, social and personal services	2.7	2.8	58.1	57.4

Source: DASS (2001).

Unemployment Since the late 1990s, Moldova has seen a reduction in the share of registered unemployed women, from 65.5 per cent in 1995 to 61.9 per cent in 1999 and 50.8 per cent in 2001. Female unemployment is characterised by a high proportion of young women, between 16 and 24 years of age, partly due to inflows of school leavers (DASS, 2002). There are some gender differences with regard to reasons for loss of employment. Men more often leave on their own free will (31.1 per cent in 1999 and 35.2 per cent in 2001) compared to women (14.5 in 1999 and 19.8 per cent in 2001). Women are often dismissed from their jobs because enterprises are liquidated or reorganized. Women probably treat changes at the enterprises more patiently, hoping for somebody else to solve their problems, while men are quicker to leave, hoping to find an adequate job elsewhere (DASS, 2002).

Political representation Although women have been elected to government and local bodies for some time, during the Soviet period, the participation of women in power bodies has often seemed rather artificial, as the proportion of female deputies was usually planned before the elections. The share of female participation in political activity increased significantly during the transition period. In 1990, women accounted for 3.8 per cent of all parliament members, although by 2001, this had risen to 10.9 per cent in 2001 (Mindicanu, 2001). In fact, the speaker of the Parliament of Moldova is currently a woman. However, in government departments, few women work. There is only one female minister in the Government and no female vice-ministers. Among deputy ministers, women make 17.8 per cent. Women participate more actively in the Supreme Court's activity, where they account for 33.3 per cent of the total number of judges (1999) (Perchinskaya and Ekim, 2002).

General Characteristics of Female Entrepreneurs and Their Businesses

As official statistics do not provide much information on female entrepreneurship in Moldova, this section mainly is based on data obtained in an international research project (Welter et al., 2003a; Welter et al., 2003b). The data come from 218 interviews and 28 case studies, conducted in 2001-2002, as well as drawing on results from other surveys carried out in 1996-2001 (Smallbone et al., 1998; Smallbone et al., 1999; Welter et al., 2000).

Our data show that female business owners or managers account for about 37-38 per cent of all small firms in Moldova (Smallbone et al., 1998; Smallbone et al., 1999; Welter et al., 2000). Women entrepreneurs are concentrated in activities, such as trade and services; both of which are sectors where most employees also are females. Enterprises managed by women are usually small-sized, which partly reflects the sectoral orientation of women-owned businesses, but may also indicate restricted access to resources, especially at start-up stage, which hinders business growth.

Most of the female entrepreneurs in our survey (62 per cent) have higher education; in fact, a much higher proportion than the overall share of women with higher or secondary specialized education among all female employees (30 per cent) (DASS, 2002). The reasons suggest the existence of a 'glass ceiling', in terms of a lack of suitable employment possibilities for highly qualified women, but also an increase in professional know-how, business links and self-confidence. At the same time, less than a half of female entrepreneurs surveyed (48 per cent) had management experience before starting their own business; 19 per cent of them had previously worked in private businesses.

Women entrepreneurs in Moldova often need the support of spouses, fathers or boyfriends, especially when starting their business. Spouses often assist with financing, access to business partners and other important linkages, or general experiences with regard to business creation. Women value this support, and in line with general traditions concerning the role of women, appreciate it if spouses and family approve of their business activity. This is illustrated in that more than half of our surveyed women entrepreneurs emphasized that their spouses approved, which includes 49 per cent who render some kind of support and 37 per cent who were involved in the business with their partner. Types of support referred to included help with registering the firm, finance, overhauling the business premises, adjusting equipment, giving advice, or assisting with household work.

Interestingly, although 94 per cent of surveyed female entrepreneurs are involved in household work, the majority considers the distribution of household and family responsibilities between them and family members to be a fair one. This corresponds to the tradition of the Moldovan society to put most of the household responsibilities on women irrespective of their other activities. Moldovan women have always considered the attitudes of members of their families towards their activities to be very important, both during Soviet times and currently. Again, existing traditions and a widespread patriarchal attitude play an important role, as family happiness comes first, in the eyes of women, with their career second, which results in women voluntarily taking up household duties. During Soviet times, women spent three times more than men on household duties, although both had the same working hours (Goskomstat SSSR, 1987). This disparity continued during the transition period. As before, contemporary Moldovan women have a heavy workload at home, as well as being responsible for raising their children. This affects women-managers and female entrepreneurs, as well as other women.

Women Business Owners in Moldova: Entrepreneurship or Proprietorship?

The analysis presented in this section is based on a classification of business owners into proprietors and entrepreneurs, based on a concept developed by Richard Scase (1997). Indicators used to implement this concept empirically include entrepreneurial aptitudes, motivations for starting a business and business objectives, indicators for business performance and generally for the behaviour of the small business owners. The aim is to explore if the distinction made by Scase is appropriate in the Moldovan context.

The Classification of Business Owners: Key Literature

A long-standing debate in the entrepreneurship literature concerns the relationship between entrepreneurship and small business owner/management, which reflects differences in the way the term 'entrepreneurship' is used. Definitions range from broad ones, which point to the risks involved in any form of new venture or business ownership, to narrower definitions that typically focus on the qualities of entrepreneurship identified by Schumpeter. Richard Scase (1997) has contributed to the debate by distinguishing between entrepreneurship and proprietorship. The grouping is based on the orientation of business owners towards capital accumulation that determines the long-term perspectives of enterprise development. According to Scase, entrepreneurs re-invest accumulated capital into their business, while proprietors do not utilise the assets they own for longer-term purposes of capital accumulation and business growth. Proprietors are often pushed into business by economic necessity; and Scase considers proprietors to be more common than entrepreneurs in transition countries.

Smallbone and Welter (2003) applied the concept of Scase empirically, distinguishing between groups of entrepreneurs according to their main motives (push or pull factors) for setting up a business. However, they also concluded that in a transition context with low living standards and an unfavourable business environment, any classification solely based on motives is likely to be inadequate. It is suggested that entrepreneurial abilities as well as motives need to be considered in a Moldovan context.

Tihonova (1995) identifies 'willy-nilly' entrepreneurs, i.e. persons who had never before striven for entrepreneurship, only entering entrepreneurship after their living standards had been reduced or they became owners and managers following the privatization. Similar to Scase, Tihonova describes them as not aiming at capital consumption, preferring to spend any surplus on improving their personal well-being instead of reinvesting into their business. Sorokin (2001) develops a more detailed classification, distinguishing three types of business women: business ladies impelled by a desire to do their own business, and who entered a business of their own free will; entrepreneurs by chance, who were driven by situational and chance conditions; and willy-nilly entrepreneurs who were forced to start their own business due to unfavourable circumstances. This classification is based on the understanding that only some women would qualify as 'real entrepreneurs', because they start their own business out of interest, while others could best be described as necessity based entrepreneurs.

Classifying Female Business Owners in Moldova: The General Approach

Tichy and Devanna (1998) consider a manager's orientation towards changes to be a necessary and distinctive function of a leader. Such an entrepreneur does not only continually develop his/her own activity, but also initiates changes in people around him/her. Features of entrepreneurial activity, such as striving for innovation, atypical decision-making and searching for unusual possibilities are viewed as components of the definition of 'entrepreneurship' in a number of manuals of management (Gerchikova, 2002; Gorkinfel and Shvandar, 1997). In this context, innovative behaviour of an entrepreneur is associated with activities that (i) change dynamically, (ii) are orientated towards long-term business development, (iii) have an active influence on realising improvements within the enterprise such as creating new products and modifying existing ones, diversifying and entering new markets, introducing new equipment, technologies and management methods. Thus, in our understanding innovative behaviour refers to both activities and growth orientation. An innovative entrepreneur resembles a 'perpetual mover', who continually moves irrespective of any conditions. The innovative behaviour of an entrepreneur is of particular importance for a small business, since it offers the small enterprise flexibility, allowing it to adapt to changes in the external environment. This indicator is also of particular significance under conditions of frequent and unpredictable changes in the environment, which is a feature of transition economies.

Low wages and high unemployment in Moldova in the 1990s pushed a number of Moldovan women to seek for other income sources and opportunities for self-realization, including the creation of small enterprises. That is why we suggest that some female business owners cannot be considered as entrepreneurs in the classic sense, but rather as proprietors, who may not be able to run a business effectively. Nevertheless, in such a poor country as Moldova is, the activities of self-employed persons and micro enterprises (where the number of proprietors is relatively higher) is important, even if they just provide their families with employment and livelihood.

We have attempted to classify female entrepreneurs on the basis of different criteria and indicators. In attempting to distinguish between female business owners who possess entrepreneurial traits from those that do not, a number of indicators were used. Four indicators were used to estimate business traits, to assess firstly women's potential for entrepreneurship; and secondly, the realization of their entrepreneurial abilities. With respect to entrepreneurial traits, the first step was to classify women business owners on the basis of each of four indicators separately. These included motives for starting a business; entrepreneurial aptitudes; business performance and entrepreneurial behaviour. However, the results showed that on their own, these indicators were insufficient. As a result, the main indicator (i.e. entrepreneurial behaviour) was examined in combination with other indicators, through the use of correlation methods. The second stage involved classifying women entrepreneurs on the basis of all four characteristics. As a result, two groups of entrepreneurs were identified: one with a complex of entrepreneurial traits; the second with none at all. The classification was based mainly on survey results, although case studies were used to identify additional characteristics of chosen groups.

The Classification of Female Business Owners in Moldova: Empirical Results

Motives for starting a business Surveyed respondents were asked to name up to three reasons why they decided to start their own businesses, which were subsequently divided into three groups: push, pull and enabling factors. So-called push factors included: the intention to provide a basic income for living; to increase own welfare; and to escape unemployment. For the majority of respondents push factors were the most commonly reported reasons for starting one's own business (53.2 per cent), of which 'provide basic income' was the most commonly mentioned individual reason. Pull factors include: a desire for independence and self-realization; a desire to have one's own business; discontent with previous job; and social goals (e.g. satisfaction of society's needs). Such factors accounted for 27.1 per cent of female entrepreneurs deciding to start their own business, of which self-realization was the most frequently mentioned. So-called enabling factors included motives such as response to market opportunities and availability of resources (e.g. finance, equipment, skills, and contacts), which accounted for 17.4 per cent of surveyed entrepreneurs (Table 4.5).

Table 4.5 Main motives of women for starting a business*

Groups of motives	Number	Per cent
Pull	59	27.1%
Push	116	53.2%
Enabling factors	38	17.4%
Others	5	2.3%
Total	218	100.0%

*Respondents were asked to state their most important motive for entering entrepreneurship.

Source: Own survey.

Thus, on the basis of this analysis, more than half of surveyed respondents were 'pushed' into starting up their own businesses. This is not altogether surprising, since a large number of people were deprived of their livelihood after large state-owned enterprises were closed in the 1990s. At that time, according to Maslow's hierarchy of needs, the question of self-realization was not a real issue, until more urgent, basic needs were satisfied. At the same time, push factors resulting from unemployment and low living standards remain a major influence on the decision to start up businesses in Moldova in the contemporary period. Despite the growing small business sector, it is not easy to find employment in this sector, because most personnel are hired from the nearest milieu. Ethnic factors also affect one's opportunities for employment. For example, a significant proportion of the non-indigenous population, who does not know the official language of the state, cannot fill managerial post in any organization, and/or in the trade and service sectors, although this practically does not affect employment in small firms.

At the same time, it must be recognised that some women who entered business ownership because of push forces, may develop entrepreneurial abilities over time that they did not have before, particularly bearing in mind that during the Soviet period, neither personal or family experiences, nor the external environment favoured developing and showing entrepreneurial traits. Of course, the opposite situation is also possible, namely that a founder starts a business with great desire but subsequently entrepreneurial aptitudes are found to be missing or insufficient. For instance, a striving after professional or creative fulfilment may constitute evidence of personal goals and drive but does not necessarily mean the presence of business abilities.

Finally, the external environment is also of great significance. Running a business in Moldova, as in other transition countries, is always accompanied by shadow working, bribes and other infringements of legislation. Some citizens do not want to be involved in such methods for moral reasons. As a result, they either do not enter a business, or cannot bear to remain in it, so leave. Evidently, there is no simple relationship between motives for business start-up and entrepreneurial abilities.

The survey evidence also reveals small differences in the motives for business start-up given by men and women. Women more commonly referred to providing the income needed to survive, self-fulfilment and exiting unemployment. Men more commonly referred to trying to increase their income, having resources available, and entering entrepreneurship as a response to market opportunities/needs. Men were also more commonly driven by a desire for independence and discontentment with their previous job. It may be suggested, therefore, that women were more often driven by necessity, while men were more driven by a desire to improve something in their lives.

Business aptitude Entrepreneurship like any other type of activities requires certain personal qualities. Business owners participating in the survey were asked to evaluate five statements, based on a five point rating scale, which has been developed by Jerschina et al. (1996). Each statement characterized one of the business qualities of an entrepreneur. In the aggregate, they make it possible to evaluate the entrepreneurial potential of respondents on the basis of their self-appraisal. The statements were as follows:

- 'I like undertaking somewhat risky but profitable tasks',
- 'I often think about the future and plan various undertakings',
- 'I would rather work on my own account than for someone else',
- 'I am strong and competent enough to achieve the goals I aim for',
- 'I like difficult problems and I feel happy solving them successfully'.

Estimates of each of the listed statements show that women business owners feel themselves not completely ready to risk (median = 3), nor ready to solve difficult problems (median = 3). At the same time, the majority of them intends to arrange their own professional future by working for themselves (median = 5); they often plan and deliberate on future undertakings (median = 4); many feel themselves to be quite strong and competent to achieve the goals set (median = 4). Compared to men women are less inclined towards risk and more often prefer to plan their activity. The aspiration for independent work is exhibited to a smaller extent, they are less confident in themselves and their own ability to achieve their goals. Nevertheless, as Table 4.6 shows, more than three quarters of female respondents estimated their entrepreneurial aptitudes as 'very high' or 'high', although this was lower than the proportion of men.

Further analysis showed that respondents perceiving that they had high entrepreneurial aptitudes were typically those with previous management experience and/or those who had received management training. However, whether or not entrepreneurial aptitudes can be successfully exploited is likely to depend on the external environment, since in very hostile external conditions, some people with entrepreneurial potential may decide not to try to fulfil it, while other may try and become frustrated.

Table 4.6 Scale of business aptitude of entrepreneurs by gender

Ranking on the Scale of Business Aptitude	Women Per cent	Both gender Number	Both gender Per cent
very high	32.1%	99	35.2%
high	44.5%	123	43.8%
moderate	19.7%	51	18.1%
low	3.7%	8	2.8%
Total number of respondents	218	281	100.0%

Source: Own survey.

Goals and business performance As a consequence, business performance may be a more objective indicator for the level of development of a business owner's entrepreneurial abilities. A composite picture of enterprise performance, based on a number of indicators (e.g. the growth in income, sales, markets, types of activities and investment) may hint at the presence of entrepreneurial qualities and the achievement of goals. At the same time, individual indicators may point out particular attributes. For example, in terms of Scase's reference to reinvestment of profits as an indicator of entrepreneurship, almost one quarter of respondents use more than 75 per cent of their business income for family purposes; only 5.4 per cent do not direct any enterprise income into family income. According to Scase's concept, these results would raise the question of whether these business owners may be considered entrepreneurs. However, in a Moldovan environment, it is rather that their families have not reached a sufficient standard of living. Such indicators of business performance depend not only on abilities and behaviour of the business owners, but also on other factors, including the enterprise's potential and the external environment. It is difficult to separate the role of entrepreneur among them.

Innovative behaviour One of the most important characteristics of entrepreneurship is innovative behaviour. Specific indicators included in the survey referred to new product/service development and/or product/service improvement, although we limit our exploration to the former one as the main indicator. During the year preceding the survey, almost two thirds of respondents had introduced some form of innovation; nearly one quarter introduced at least one new product or service (Table 4.7). It should be noted, however, that most of this product/service innovation is modest by international standards. None of the surveyed enterprises used patented technologies. Only 1 in 6 of those business owners, who had introduced new or modifying products, used new technologies, methods and techniques, for the purpose. In other cases, an increase in the range of products, goods and services took place. However, in current conditions in Moldova, it is almost impossible for small businesses to engage in research and development, or make use of the latest scientific developments, since there are no centres for technology transfer to small enterprises in the country and the scientific budget is minimal.

Table 4.7 Introduction of new products/services during the previous year

Innovative Activity	Number	Per cent
no changes	84	38.5%
introduced at least 1 new product (service)	51	23.4%
modified at least 1 product (service)	18	8.3%
both	65	29.8%
Total number of female respondents	218	100.0%

Source: Own survey.

Do low values of indicators of product innovation in Moldovan women-owned enterprises mean that proprietors prevail among business owners? The short answer must be 'yes', since most small business owners do not understand sufficiently the need for continued renewal as a factor influencing competitiveness. Nevertheless, the behaviour of business owners is quite changeable in conditions of transition economy. Thus, in 1997 only 39 per cent of surveyed enterprises introduced new products (Smallbone et al., 1998), but in 2002 this had increased to 61 per cent. Moreover, factors such as access to financial resources needed, which is difficult to overcome in contemporary conditions in Moldova, also partly explain the low level of innovative behaviour. Scant and undifferentiated consumer demand caused by low living standard is another factor, with consumers being guided by prices and not higher quality or innovative products. It should also be noted that the over-regulation of the business sector and the unfavourable environment renders running a business a time-consuming and complicated type of activity, where little time is left to deal with business development, but most time is taken up with solving day-to-day problems.

Innovative behaviour of female business owners is strongly correlated with individual traits, such as the level of education, experience and management skills. For example, female entrepreneurs with higher or secondary vocational education introduce innovations more often than those in other groups: for example, among persons with secondary education 21.4 per cent were active in innovation; among those with secondary vocational education, it was 59.7 per cent; and among those with higher education, 61.2 per cent. Management experience and skills also favoured innovation. Among entrepreneurs who had no management experience, 53.6 per cent introduced some innovation, compared with 62.5 per cent of those without such experience. This also is reflected in differences across innovation behaviour and self-perceived business abilities: Among business owners with 'low' or 'moderate' business abilities, 37.5 per cent and 37.2 per cent of respondents correspondingly introduced some innovations. Among those who had 'high' or 'very high' business aptitudes, much more respondents made innovations: 61.8 per cent and 67.1 per cent respectively.

Comparing entrepreneurs and proprietors At the same time, an analysis based on correlating pairs of variables shows that most women cannot be allocated to either a proprietor or entrepreneur category, because most of them show some characteristics associated with entrepreneurial behaviour, whilst in other respect they appear proprietorial. As a result, a second stage of analysis was undertaken, which revealed that just 10.1 per cent of women surveyed had the whole complex of entrepreneurs' characteristics and 11.0 per cent could clearly be identified as proprietors. The rest of the respondents had traits associated with both categories.

A comparison of women from the 'entrepreneur' and 'proprietor' groups, using all indicators, revealed interesting distinctions between both groups (Table 4.8). Thus, entrepreneurs diversify their activity much more often: and also possess more resources for business development. Entrepreneurs were also characterised by having been educated to higher education level; having received management training; they have had management experience before starting their own business; and had previously worked in private business. Entrepreneurs actively used external sources of finance even at the start-up stage. They had also more often applied for a bank loan during the year preceding the interview and more frequently received a loan. Moreover, entrepreneurs allocated a smaller share of business income to the family budget; and the share of income going for business development is correspondingly higher. Only 4.5 per cent of entrepreneurs, but more than half of the proprietors put more than three quarters of their business income into family.

Entrepreneurs and proprietors can also be differentiated with regard to business premises and measures taken to improve the business. Nearly all entrepreneurs run their business from business premises, which they own or rent. By contrast, 42 per cent of the proprietors locate their businesses either entirely, or partly, at home, mainly because of the small scale of their activities, and/or to save money. In addition, entrepreneurs are more actively involved in developing their business. Both entrepreneurs (100.0 per cent) and proprietors (75 per cent) seek to improve the performance of their firms, but entrepreneurs are more frequently investing in order to do so. In addition, proprietors are less active than entrepreneurs in marketing their products and services. More than half of entrepreneurs, but none of the proprietors, use formal marketing methods, such as advertising in mass media, handing out brochures or have their own sales representative. Not surprisingly, it is mainly entrepreneurs, although a minor share, who export their goods and services, but none of the proprietors. Moreover, entrepreneurs are disposed to hire employees, while one fifth of the proprietors are self-employed.

A more pro-active behaviour of entrepreneurs is also reflected in that they more actively seek business contacts and maintain relations with partners, competitors, and support organizations. For example, entrepreneurs more often use assistance from consulting companies or private consultants and a chamber of commerce, than proprietors, and are also more frequently members of a business association. Furthermore, entrepreneurs more often cooperate with other businesses in ways other than selling or buying, compared to proprietors.

Table 4.8 Differences between entrepreneurs and proprietors (in per cent)

	Entrepreneurs	Proprietors
diversify into 2 activities	31.8	16.7
diversify into 3 activities	13.6	4.2
received management training	50.0	29.2
have management experience before starting own business	45.5	20.8
have worked in private business	31.8	16.7
manage the enterprise with:		
1-10 employees (micro)	50.0	83.3
11-50 employees (small)	50.0	16.7
received bank loans:		
at start-up stage	13.6	4.2
during the last year	13.6	0
seek to improve the performance of their businesses	100.0	75.0
export goods / services	9.0	0
had investments during the last year	54.5	16.7
use assistance from institutions of infrastructure, including:		
Consultants	31.8	4.2
Chamber of commerce	31.8	16.7
are members of business associations	13.6	0
are owners / co-owners of other enterprises	9.0	0
co-operate	50.0	20.8
Number of women	22	24

Source: Own survey.

Finally, entrepreneurs are less inclined to link business and gender. The share of entrepreneurs thinking their gender has an effect on their business activity is lower. For example, only 13.6 per cent of entrepreneurs compared to more than two fifths of proprietors consider the choice of their business activity was related to their gender. Entrepreneurs also do not attribute refusals for finance to gender, although one quarter of the proprietors does so.

All the differences mentioned above are related to the broad criteria chosen for classification. For example, according to the criterion of business abilities, proprietors are less inclined to risk. They are more cautious about investing their money into other activities, if they are unable to control expenses. So, these business owners rarely diversify their activity.

Case Study Evidence

Evidence from the case studies may be used to support the picture emerging from the survey. For example, many proprietors expressed a willingness to give up their entrepreneurial activity in favour of a wage job, if such an opportunity presented itself. One of the respondents reported that business was a heavy burden for her and she would feel a sense of relief if she found a job (Welter et al., 2003b). This reflects chiefly the character of this woman who was compelled to enter private business activity. The state-owned publishing house where she worked as an editor was gradually collapsing; there was not enough work, and wage payments were often delayed. The respondent started a business together with her former workmates. Later, the respondent faced many difficulties, which contributed to her thinking about leaving the business.

By contrast, women from the entrepreneur group flatly refused such possibilities. For example, a 28-year-old woman reported that she took a great interest in her business and could not imagine herself in any other role. She would never give up business even if she could find a job with higher income. The family even postponed bearing a child for the sake of establishing the enterprise (Welter et al., 2003b). In addition, other business owners in the entrepreneur group showed willingness and commitment to re-establishing a business after the bankruptcy of a previous one. For example, one entrepreneur, who created her own business in 1990, broadened it to three wedding salons and a shop subsequently, although she became insolvent in 1998. She considered her future for three years, but in 2001, bought a permit that gave the right to run individual business activity, to become involved in sewing on her own, with one sewing-machine at home. However, within two years she became an employer with 20 employees (Welter et al., 2003b).

The case studies provide a number of examples, which show how the external environment hindered business development, stifling entrepreneurial endeavour. For example, the owner of small trade enterprise enumerated a number of problems, which she faced (Welter et al., 2003b). The main problem she identified was complicated legislation, complaining that it was impossible to follow continual changes in it.

Other cases illustrate push-motives for starting a business, but also innovative behaviour of business owners. For example, one female respondent with children has moved to Chisinau, where her parents lived, from Belarus after her divorce. She was unemployed and needed income. When she decided to go into business, she began collecting information about different kinds of activity. She chose polygraphic manufacturing, considering she could manage this activity and also it did not require a lot of money at the inception stage. The business was growth orientated from inception, but the main problem was a lack of finance. However, as income increased, the respondent gradually bought additional equipment, which enabled her to expand the range of services and to improve the technological process. The respondent has recently purchased a computer. The entrepreneur intends to expand the business and to diversify the types of activity. She has already got accustomed to running her own enterprise, so now she wants to work only for herself.

It is important to stress that the classification offered in this chapter is based on characteristics at a single point in time, whereas an individual's entrepreneurial traits may evolve over time. This can be illustrated with reference to one of the case studies, who was a woman of 49 years old, who was a housewife, bringing up her children, while being married to a successful entrepreneur. However, after her husband's death she became the owner of his enterprise, initially deciding to retain it in memory of her spouse. In practice, she has managed not only to keep the business (with almost 50 employees), but also to broaden production. Nowadays she is very interested in running her own business and hopes to achieve ongoing success (Welter et al., 2003b).

Conclusions

Private enterprises originated in Moldova during the reforms of the 1990s, and small firms are predominant. They work with low productivity, concentrating on trade and low-level service activities, and make an insignificant contribution to the development of the country. The political environment does not favour the development of private business. The business infrastructure is insufficiently developed; access to most resources is limited; and legislative requirements are still too complicated, labour-intensive and expensive to meet. Although both men and women are actively involved in the economy, the share of economically active women has been decreasing. This is mainly due to a traditional view of women's role in society, as well as due to women's double burden, which was aggravated when family support systems collapsed during the post Soviet period. In this context, more and more Moldovan women are searching for new income sources, as they perceive new opportunities, but also because of low wages and high unemployment. Nowadays, female entrepreneurs account for one third of all small enterprises in Moldova.

Our empirical analysis has shown that with regard to the concept of entrepreneurs versus proprietors (Scase, 1997) very few women can be neatly classified as either entrepreneurs or proprietors, since a majority display characteristics from both groups. Nevertheless, this classification revealed interesting distinctions between both groups with possible implications for support policies. For example, while entrepreneurs more frequently consider their businesses need external support in terms of advice, consultancy or training, they also own larger businesses, possess more resources for business development and have higher qualification. Therefore, they are better able to realise what they need to fulfil their ambitious plans, while business owners from the proprietor group either do not possess sufficient information about what is available externally, they do not trust external advisers, or they consider themselves able to solve business problems on their own.

At the same time, the results from the classification exercise should be used with caution, as all of the chosen indicators may change over time. For instance, an individual's business abilities may develop as they gain skills and experience from working in a business; alternatively, aspects of the external environment may change. The low standard of living, which typically makes complete self-realisation impossible, contributes to the widespread influence of push motives for female entrepreneurs at business start-up. At the same time, this does not mean that people do not have entrepreneurial qualities. The business performance and behaviour of an entrepreneur may be connected not only with the business abilities of its business owners but also with external factors. Here, it is important to take into consideration the context in transition countries, where the environment is changeable and entrepreneurial aptitudes may be hidden at first, before they manifest themselves over time.

Note

1 'Female Entrepreneurship in Transition Economies: the Example of Ukraine, Moldova and Uzbekistan' (Intas-00-043).

References

Cara, E. and Patraşcu, I. (2001), 'Retrospectiva micului business în Republica Moldova', (Small Business Retrospective in The Republic of Moldova), *Economie şi finanţe*, no. 5, pp. 32-34.

CSIR (2000), *Maloe i srednee predprinimatel`stvo: Sociologicheskoe issledovanie, Moldova 2000 (po metodike issledovaniya, provedennogo Management Systems International v Ukraine v 1999 g.), (*Small and Medium-Sized Entrepreneurship: Sociological Survey), Otchet Centra Strategicheskih issledovanii I reform, Chisinau.

CSU MSSR (1984), *Narodnoe hozyaistvo MSSR v 1924-1984*: *Yubileinyi statisticheskii sbornik, (*National Economy of the Moldovan SSR in 1924-1984: Jubilee Statistical Review), Central'noe Statisticheskoe Upravlenie MSSR, Chisinau.

DASS (2001), *Anuarul statistic al Republicii Moldova 1999,* (Statistical Annual of The Republic of Moldova, 1999), Departamentul Analize Statistice si Sociologice al Republicii Moldova, Chisinau.

DASS (2002), *Anuarul statistic al Republicii Moldova 2002,* (Statistical Annual of The Republic of Moldova, 2002), Departamentul Analize Statistice si Sociologice al Republicii Moldova, Chisinau.

DSS (2003a), *Anuarul statistic al Republicii Moldova 2003,* (Statistical Annual of The Republic of Moldova), 2003, Departamentul Statistica si Sociologie al Republicii Moldova, Chisinau.

DSS (2003b), *Masurarea economiei neobservate in Republica Moldova, (*Measurement of The Non-Observed Economy in The Republic of Moldova), Departamentul Statistica si Sociologie al Republicii Moldova, Chisinau.

DSS (2003c), *Moldova in cifre: Culegere succinta de informatii statistice, 2003*, (Moldova in Figures: Short Statistical Book), Departamentul Statistica si Sociologie al Republicii Moldova, Chisinau.

DSS (2003d), *Ocuparea în economia informală în Republica Moldova*, (Employment in The Informal Economy in The Republic of Moldova), Departamentul Statistică şi Sociologie al Republicii Moldova, Chisinau.

DSS (2004), *Dezvoltarea social-economica a Republicii Moldova in anul 2003*, (Social and Economic Development of The Republic of Moldova in 2003), Departamentul Statistică şi Sociologie al Republicii Moldova, Chisinau.

Gerchikova, I. (2002), *Regulirovanie predprinimatelskoi deyatel'nosti: gosudarstvennoe i mejfirmenno* (The Entrepreneurial Activity Regulation: the State and Inter-firm ones), Konsaltbankir, Moscow.

Golea, A. (2004), 'Patriotism de ochii lumii', *(*Patriotism in World's Eyes), *Profit*, no. 5, pp. 4-5.

Gorkinfel, V. and Shvandar, V. (1997), *Kurs predprinimatel'stva,* (Entrepreneurship Course), Moscow: UNITI.

Goskomstat SSSR (1987), *Narodnoe hozyaistvo SSSR za 70 let*: *Yubileinyi statisticheskii ezhegodnik*, (National Economy of The USSR by 70 years: Jubilee Statistical Annual), Gosudarstvennyi Komitet Statistiki SSSR, Moskva.

Jerschina, J. et al. (1996), *Political Stabilisation and Foreign Investment Risk in Russia and 11 Countries of Eastern and Central Europe. A comparative analysis of political and economic attitudes on the basis of cross-national surveys*, paper presented to the Wapor Annual Conference, May.

Mindicanu, A. (2001), *Egalitatea genurilor in Republica Moldova, (*Gender Equality in The Republic of Moldova), Chisinau.

Perchinskaya, N. and Ekim, T. (2002), *Svoboda I razvitie zhenshiny kak lichnosti v sovremennom* obshestve, (Freedom and Development of A Woman as A Personality in A Modern Society), Chisinau.

Scase, R. (1997), 'The Role of Small Businesses in the Economic Transformation of Eastern Europe: Real but Relatively Unimportant?', *International Small Business Journal*, vol. 1, pp. 13-21.

Smallbone, D. and Welter, F. (2003), *Entrepreneurship in Transition Economies: Necessity or Opportunity Driven?*', paper presented to the Babson Conference, Glasgow.

Smallbone, D., Welter, F. and Aculai, E. (1999), *The Contribution of Small Businesses to Regional Economic Development in Ukraine, Belarus, Moldova (1997-1999),* National report for project INTAS-UA 95-266.

Smallbone, D., Welter, F., Aculai, E., Poliviannaya, T., Rodionova, N. (1998), *Identifying the support needs of small enterprises in Ukraine, Belarus and Moldova to develop an agenda for policy at the national and regional levels (1996-1998)*, National report for project TACIS T95-4139-R, CEEDR, Middlesex University, London.

Sorokin, E. (2001), *Osobennosti nacional`nogo zhenskogo predprinimatel`stva,* (Peculiarities of National Female Entrepreneurship), www.rokf.ru/articles/9572 (date of access:
2 May 2003).

Tichy, N. and Devanna, M. (1998), *The Transformational Leader* (translated into Russian), Economica, Moscow.

Tihonova, N. (1995), 'Predprinimateli ponevole', (Willy-nilly Entrepreneurs), *Maloe predprinimatelstvo v kontekste Rossi'skih reform i mirovogo opita*, pp. 170-181.

Welter, F., Smallbone, D., Aculai, E., Rodionova, N., Subashi, B., Dumitrashko, M. (2000), 'Employment, SMEs and the Labour Market in Moldova', in RWI (ed), *Employment,*

SMEs and the Labour Market in Russia and Moldova (1998-2000): National report for project INTAS 97-1805, RWI, Essen.

Welter, F., Smallbone, D., Aculai, E., Rodionova, N., Vinogradova, N. (2003a), 'Female entrepreneurship in the Ukraine, Moldova and Uzbekistan', in Welter, F. (ed), *Female Entrepreneurship in Transition Economies: the Example of Ukraine, Moldova and Uzbekistan (2001-2003): National Report on Survey Data for Moldova* (INTAS-2000-00843), RWI, Essen.

Welter, F., Smallbone, D., Aculai, E., Rodionova, N., Vinogradova, N. (2003b), 'Female entrepreneurship in the Ukraine, Moldova and Uzbekistan: Case Studies in Moldova', in Welter, F. (ed), *Female Entrepreneurship in Transition Economies: the Example of Ukraine, Moldova and Uzbekistan (2001-2003): National Report on Survey Data for Moldova* (INTAS-2000-00843), RWI, Essen.

Chapter 5

Djamila's Journey from Kolkhoz to Bazaar: Female Entrepreneurs in Kyrgyzstan[1]

Gül Berna Özcan

Introduction

Chingiz Aitmatov's novel 'Djamila' portrays tribal, communal and profound personal changes taking place for Kyrgyz women at the outset of the Second World War. The consolidation of Soviet power in Central Asia changed the lives of many Kyrgyz families and marked the beginning of massive transformation towards a command economy and society under Soviet rule. Thousands were removed from their nomadic yurts to agricultural kolkhoz life and to urban settlements to perform jobs in industrial establishments. Djamila's journey took her from the strictly delineated yet spiritually rich tribal life to the collective destitution of the kolkhoz. During the war years, the Soviet regime not only mobilised men to fight in trenches but also harnessed the remaining population to work for the production of army supplies. Djamila represents the many women who took charge of kolkhoz production, although she later attempted to shape her own destiny by abandoning the kolkhoz life for a new future. Djamila represents the spirit and hardworking character of Kyrgyz woman with her rich inner world and her strong determination and independence.

Still today, no matter what their ethic origin, the women of Kyrgyzstan are not passive to economic shocks. They work hard to preserve their dignity and to look after their families. Whether Kyrgyz, Uzbek, Uyghur or Russian (or one of the dozens of ethnic groups in Kyrgyzstan), women are all remarkably active and responsible in economic life. Thus, Djamila is an inspiration and a symbol for us as it is for them.[2]

Aitmatov leaves it to the reader to decide what ultimately happens to the hardworking and independent Djamila. This research exercises our imagination about women like Djamila as they respond to their social role in this and similar economies in transition. There is another story to be told about what happened to Djamila after she left her village. Before relating this we need to reflect on the transition era, that is the post Soviet life of an emerging state with a new mode of production and private ownership. What is evident is that a short period of prosperity under the Soviet regime during the 1960s and 1970s ended in a deep crisis and political, social and economic failure in the late 1980s. During the period of prosperity many Djamilas moved to factories, benefited from compulsory education, and took up professional jobs.

The industrial workers, engineers, and school teacher Djamilas of Soviet times are today trying to find new meaning and strength. One of the most striking elements of the collapse of the Soviet regime is personal insecurity. De-industrialisation, poverty and disorientation have forced women to seek new ways of surviving, supporting their families and preserving their dignity. The numbers of bazaars where women entrepreneurs predominate have become the only source of hope and income for thousands of families. Even for a casual observer, the bazaars appear to be a communal place and the incubation zones for businesswomen. This chapter analyses how women entrepreneurs shape their lives in these bazaars, to what extent their enterprise is generating income and job opportunities for their families and others, and how they cope with the risks and uncertainty of their business environment.

The research is based on 35 in-depth interviews with female entrepreneurs and numerous observations in various bazaars across the country, including the Dordoi Bazaar in Bishkek (formerly Frunze), the capital with 1.5 million inhabitants; Osh Bazaar (in Osh, the second largest city with 800,000 inhabitants); and AkTilek Bazaar in Karakol.[3] Other bazaars visited include the rapidly expanding Karasuu Bazaar, the Central Bazaar in Jalal-Abad, and the Osh and Medina Bazaars in Bishkek. This is part of a larger project that collected 135 interviews with business owners from all backgrounds and sectors in six cities (Bishkek, Karabalta, Karakol, Cholpon Ata, Osh, and Jalal-Abad). Our overall findings show rapid growth in the number of both female and male entrepreneurs in bazaars.

Bazaars provide the single most important commercial activity in the country. They are also increasingly evolving into entrepreneurial hubs with newly emerging business/entrepreneurial networks, providing the externalities of a capitalist market economy. The emergence of bazaars in the post Soviet economic landscape is a result of several factors. Firstly, the old and obsolete industrial complexes of the Soviet period were almost entirely dissolved, leading to complete de-industrialisation of the country. With a small and highly fragmented agricultural sector and no available financial capital for new investments and industrial re-structuring, commercial activities emerged as the major source of income generation and job creation. Secondly, highly fragmented and low working capital forced traders to seek externalities through local agglomeration, in which they lowered transaction costs and narrowed information gaps through networking and solidarity ties. Finally, with the dissolution of the USSR, network externalities and subsidies of the Soviet regime were no longer available to the Kyrgyz Republic and people were forced to supply many goods and services through markets filled by single traders.

While academic and policy studies on Eastern Europe have been rapidly increasing, there is very little empirically informed research on Central Asian development in general and Kyrgyzstan in particular. Central Asia deserves serious attention within the context of Eurasian development because understanding and helping the process of economic development in that region will be mutually beneficial for Europe and Asia. Since the economic role of women is so important there, it is crucial to analyse their entrepreneurial initiatives. Despite this, there is no informed research on bazaar activity in Kyrgyzstan (Bal, 2004). For gender studies, female entrepreneurship in Central Asia offers a very interesting case of the accommodation of pastoral nomadic traditions combined with Soviet ideals, Islam, nationalism and modernity. Modern Kyrgyzstan is a melting pot of different and sometimes competing identities of modern and secular Islam, as well as a reawakening of Islamic traditions. Yet, the nostalgia for Soviet order still prevails. At the same time, multi-ethnic Kyrgyzstan is striving to develop its own form of nation state beyond the old Russian domination and ethnic and tribal rivalries. Women face all these political and cultural undercurrents in their daily lives along with the pressing need to generate income for their households. While their country is going through fundamental economic and political changes, women's cognitive understanding of the world vis-à-vis their position is in deep turmoil. For them, the only fixed ground is their family and the struggle to survive in a highly volatile and insecure environment. Their battle is manifold and their story is yet to be narrated. This chapter is a modest attempt in trying to unravel this economic struggle.

The chapter is structured in the following five sections. The first section provides a background on the Kyrgyz state and economy with an emphasis on the economic reforms and macro-economic indicators. Small and medium-sized entrepreneurship and the role of women in this sector are illustrated in the second section. Due to a very high number of unofficial businesses, we are unable to provide an accurate estimate of the numbers of SMEs in the country. In the third section, we illustrate the role of bazaars in the evolution and growth of female entrepreneurship with detailed analyses of several bazaars. This is followed by our findings on female entrepreneurship and the business growth and survival patterns and on vertical and horizontal business growth. The conclusion summarises the research findings, emphasising the importance of institutions and the policy environment for sustainable and secure business growth, as well as capital accumulation to move away from the current situation of marginal and highly fragmented gains.

Kyrgyz State Building and Business

Kyrgyzstan[4] is a small land-locked country of 5 million people surrounded by Tajikistan, Uzbekistan, Kazakhstan and China. Since its independence from the former Soviet Union in 1991, the country has gone through dramatic economic and social transformations. Kyrgyzstan has a huge ethnic mix consisting of 65 per cent Kyrgyz, 14 per cent Uzbek, 12.5 per cent Russian, 1.8 per cent Ukrainian, 1.3 per cent Tatar and others (Korean, Kazakh, German, Tajik, Uyghur and Ahiska Turks). The country has been the deportation destination of many persecuted communities and despite the recent exodus of Germans and Russians and a history of ethic strife between Uzbeks and Kyrgyz in the south, Kyrgyzstan retains a remarkable ethnic diversity and harmony. The Ahiska Turks and Avars, Germans, Koreans and others were forcibly transported to Central Asia by Stalin as part of his assimilation and pacification policy. Tens of thousands of Uyghurs and Muslim Chinese, locally known as Dungans, escaped prosecution in China and established their communities in there.

The most important challenge for Kyrgyzstan today is to build an economy and state apparatus to sustain its population and maintain its viability. Independence came unexpectedly. Many Kyrgyz admit that they did not want to leave the Soviet Union but one day found themselves abandoned by it. The shift from being a satellite state in economic and political affairs to an independent and sovereign one required deep changes in social attitudes, as well as in economic development and state building. This is indeed the major challenge not only for Kyrgyzstan but for all former Soviet Republics in Central Asia. Potential dangers of ethnic and religious conflicts loom large in the process of modern state building and democratisation (Handran, 2001). In addition, there are currently many border issues to be resolved with Uzbekistan. The Soviet legacy of interlinked economic interests and artificially drawn borders and ethnic enclaves aimed to enhance the USSR regime is now causing trouble for the new states. Apart from divided communities, water resources and electricity and the use of gas are sources of deep anxiety and periodic tension between the Uzbek and Kyrgyz governments.

When the USSR collapsed, Kyrgyzstan had a small but diverse industrial base consisting of machine tools (the production of machine parts, weaponry, electrical machines, hay bailers, regulatory instruments and gauges, electric lamps), mining (extraction of mercury and antimony, rare-earth elements, gold, coal and oil), electric power, the production of industrial materials, furniture and consumer goods (textiles, shoes, cotton textiles, etc) and processed food products (meat and milk, bread, candy, alcoholic drinks). Agriculture was also diversified with products ranging from animal feed and commercial crops such as cotton, tobacco and sugar beets, grains and fruits. However, as the eminent Kyrgyz reformist Koichuev (2001) describes, the economy suffered the ills of the USSR pattern of economic development with extensive exploitation of resources and no emphasis on intensive development and technological advancement.

Soviet modernization policies were arbitrarily executed and territorially disintegrated and their legacy has led to the creation of a distorted industrial structure throughout Central Asia (Iwasaki, 2000). With its poor resource base, Kyrgyzstan especially needs urgently to overcome these distortions. The country could not maintain its fragments of Soviet industries that were interlinked to far-flung regions. When the USSR collapsed, these networked links of the former command economy were no longer economical or desirable for the new independent states. While some of these industrial complexes successfully transformed in countries with a larger industrial base such as Uzbekistan, in Kyrgyzstan most ceased to exist. This rapid downfall was also a function of the lack of any industrial policy or foresight of the political leadership for transition in the country (Özcan, 2004).

With no obvious natural resources like those of Turkmenistan or Kazakhstan, Gross Domestic Product (GDP) declined to 50 per cent of the 1990 level between 1991 and 1995. All economic indicators deteriorated. Hyperinflation, rising unemployment, and reduction of real incomes led to a dramatic increase in poverty. Despite the economic reforms of the mid 1990s, GNI per capita was $270 in 2000, and 51 per cent of the population live below the national poverty line (George, et al. 2002; Koichuev, 2001). However, there is a huge unregistered economy in the country, which many believe to be around 70 per cent of total activity.[5] While living standards have recently been improving in big cities like Bishkek and Osh, rural poverty is rampant in many oblasts coupled with poor public services such as health and education.[6]

Nevertheless, Kyrgyzstan has made significant macroeconomic progress since the comprehensive and rapid reform movement initiated in 1993. Important changes were made to the legal framework (in particular with business laws), most prices were liberalized, mass privatization began and the tax system was almost completely overhauled, with the introduction of a VAT and excise tax system. In 1993, a national currency, the Som, was introduced, permitting the authorities to assume full responsibility for monetary policy, and which allowed for international trade to be settled in convertible currencies. In 1994, the trade regime was liberalized as export and import licensing requirements were lifted. In 1997 the reform of the civil service began, which initially entailed reducing government employment and improving efficiency through the restructuring of public institutions. In 1998 Kyrgyzstan acceded to the WTO and remains the only republic of the CIS to do so thus far. Since 1996 the economy has begun to recover. Real GDP growth has averaged about 5 per cent per year since then and remained positive even during the regional financial crisis of 1998. The recovery in the agricultural sector, which accounts for over 35 per cent of GDP, after the privatization of land in 1998, together with yields from the Kumtor gold mine, account for most of this growth (Koichuev, 2001).

Despite these positive indicators, the Kyrgyz economy remains vulnerable to external shocks, as macroeconomic stability has not yet been fully achieved and foreign debt and debt service are now at worrisome levels. Moreover, there has been some slowdown in reform. At the micro level, the real problem lies in slow pace of enterprise creation and poor entrepreneurial development. While the leadership of President Akayev provides a stable and highly liberal regime, it is also entrenched and corrupt. Despite the wide range of international support and NGO presence, there is a lack of industrial and economic policy vision and no coherent plan for enterprise development. The level of corruption is deepening, representing an endemic problem at every level of society, in the public and private sectors alike (Çokgezen, 2004). Rumours of the massive wealth and power of the Akayev family are causing deep concern. All of these elements distort this fragile economy and damage income and job generation.

Despite this, in recent years liberal practices have allowed the country to become a hub of regional trade and commercial activities that seems now to be forming the backbone of income and job creation. The number of wholesale and retail bazaars is increasing and the sprawl of retail trading spaces is continuously growing in all cities. Goods from China, Russia and Turkey, and to a lesser extent from Kazakhstan and Uzbekistan are brought to and traded in Kyrgyzstan. Many wholesalers and some retailers from Russia, Uzbekistan and Kazakhstan obtain their goods from the Kyrgyz mega markets, Dordoi, Karasuu and Osh. Kyrgyzstan is becoming a gateway for Chinese products heading to Central Asia, Russia and Europe. The Chinese government has been boosting the economy of Urumchi, its westernmost urban centre, to take advantage of this emerging trade to Russia and the Central Asian states. While this form of international trade is currently generating jobs and income, its sustainability is linked to the economic political agenda. The lack of any productive base in the country and the marginal gains in transit trade might not lead to economic prosperity for small traders or economic growth since much of the trade remains unregistered.

Small and Medium-sized Enterprises and Female Entrepreneurship in Kyrgyzstan

Nomadic traditions that prevailed in Kyrgyzstan over the centuries were transformed by the Soviet command economy into collective farming in kolkhoz and urban centres were established based on heavy industries. Since Islamist social strictures are weak in Kyrgyz nomad traditions, Kyrgyz women quickly moved into new occupational positions. Even Uzbeks, who managed to maintain their traditions as well as Islam under communism, had to accommodate the command economy. Russian imperial adventures towards the end of the 19th century which created military-urban outposts, such as the town of Karakol[7] were later expanded into new settlement centres through Soviet planning. The notions of unity, grandeur, order and glory of mass industrial complexes reshaped the older centres of Bishkek and Osh. Thus, as was vividly illustrated by Aitmatov, Djamilas moved to kolkhoz and to industrial complexes from tightly knit nomadic families. Everybody had to work, share responsibility and came to expect to be allocated housing and other state provisions such as health and education. Women not only provided semi-skilled labour but through comprehensive compulsory education, new professional and lower middle range managerial positions opened up for them.

Small, mostly owner-operated business ventures replaced the former command economy with tiny amounts of investment capital and limited growth opportunities. Similarly, privatization in agriculture resulted in very small average farm size.[8] The share of manufacturing relative to agriculture within the GDP has been declining since 1985. In terms of the current factor cost, agriculture occupies 38.6 per cent of the output followed by 24.9 per cent for industry and 36.5 per cent for services in 2002. Trade has filled the economic vacuum left by the collapsed command economy. The survey by Proma and the International Business Council (2003) indicates the diminishing rates of employment and income creation measured by the declining number of businesses in agriculture (26.7 per cent) and manufacturing (5.5 per cent), while wholesale and retail trade accounted for almost 50 per cent of all businesses in the country. The Kyrgyz economy today relies heavily on its small and medium-sized trading businesses and the Kumtor gold mine, along with the financial support of international donors. Even for a casual observer the number of street traders and bazaar stalls that invade every corner is stunning, as if the entire population is on the move with trade. In 2003, there were 122,525 owner-operator small businesses in the country, mostly in retail and wholesale trade, indicating the very large number of micro-firms in a country of five million people.[9]

At the same time, private ownership and enterprise creation suffers from a whole set of legal, ideological and social handicaps. The individual habits of former command economy, such as a lack of personal initiatives, political involvement and interest representation still persist. Thus, ownership and enterprise rights are not well protected. While Kyrgyzstan may have adequate laws, enforcement is weak. Corruption and political influence over the judicial system are two other major handicaps that stand in the way of a well-functioning legal system. Our research indicates an overwhelming mistrust among business people towards public officers, in particular police and customs officials. Financial capital for enterprise creation is controlled by a few major banks which are politically manipulated by the Presidential Office. A weak securities market limits both borrowing and investment opportunities. Many Kyrgyz have never used banks to deposit their savings or borrow money. Indeed, modern banking is a new phenomenon and many services such as bank machines and credit cards are not yet offered. Businesses in need of credit often end up selling their assets or borrowing from loan sharks.

Our observations reinforce an analysis carried out by the National Business Opinion Survey[10] among over 3000 businesses in all oblasts and all sectors (Bishkek City, Chui, Issyk-Kul, Naryn, Talas, Osh, Jalal-Abad, Batken), which showed that there is widespread abuse of power by tax officials. Indeed, our research indicates that many old Soviet regulatory and monitoring bodies still survive as governmental agencies and their employees are reportedly harassing businesses for extra payments and taxes. This form of extensive inspection of businesses is also opening the door to further corruption and bribery by poorly paid state officials.[11] From the perspective of entrepreneurs, corruption makes lives difficult and drains resources, but also opens possibilities as long as companies pay a premium. In other words, bureaucratic procedures as well as illegal actions are often legitimized through bribery. This fosters a society with no concern for standards and law.

In Kyrgyzstan 43.9 per cent of the working population is self-employed, which is a high figure indicating the lack of alternative job opportunities (Hübner, 2000), rather than entrepreneurial choice for business. Many businessmen and women publicly admit that if they had had a stable job, as they did under the command economy, they would not run small businesses. Private business ownership is a way to survive where, as in many cases, there is no other income possibility. Such small business activities are in general outside the registered economy, tending to operate under pseudo-market conditions. Nevertheless, we will continue to use the term 'entrepreneur' for all small business owners due to their risk taking initiative and independent work.

Women occupy a significant part of this entrepreneurial activity, according to the Centre for Study of Public Opinion 2003 survey in Kazakhstan, Kyrgyzstan, Tajikistan, Turkmenistan and Uzbekistan, which shows that women entrepreneurs constitute almost one third of the all businesses in Kyrgyzstan, the highest percentage in the region (Table 5.1). However, as in other transition economies in the region, they tend to occupy the lower echelons of this spectrum: female entrepreneurs are in charge of enterprises, which are smaller in size and have lesser impact on the economy. Most of them are limited to small trade and services, but they nevertheless account for over 60 per cent of total retail and wholesale businesses.

Table 5.1 Gender distribution of entrepreneurs in Central Asia

	Gender of entrepreneurs				Total	
	Male		Female			
Kazakhstan	424	70.7%	176	29.3%	600	100.0%
Kyrgyzstan	351	70.2%	149	29.8%	500	100.0%
Uzbekistan	375	75.0%	125	25.0%	500	100.0%
Tajikistan	167	83.5%	33	16.5%	200	100.0%
Turkmenistan	159	79.5%	41	20.5%	200	100.0%
Total	1,476	73.8%	524	26.2%	2,000	100.0%

Source: Survey of the Center for Study of Public Opinion 2003.

There is almost no collective organization of entrepreneurs in Kyrgyzstan apart from a handful of associations promoted by donor agencies and the state.[12] Our survey shows that most of the female entrepreneurs in Kyrgyzstan are not part of any business association. Those who were involved in business associations prefer to use this affiliation for the promotion of their own individual interests, which leads to a common mistrust towards interest representation through collective action.[13] Indeed, as seen in Table 5.2, SMEs are not organized to pursue their common interests across Central Asia.

Business training is crucial for an emerging entrepreneurial class. This includes education of entrepreneurs and participation in drafting legislation. With no collective voice, women mainly rely on their family and kin contacts to arrange and solve business problems. They are also alienated from the political process of decision making since the current political structure is insulated from public participation in decision making. Despite the existence of 100 women NGOs registered on paper in the country, the gender divide in political power is widening with fewer and fewer women taking active political interest.[14] As pointed out by the Centre for Study of Public Opinion Survey (2003), the ability of the associations to influence the legislative and executive bodies in making decisions acceptable for the entrepreneurs reflects the actual power of the associations, their independence and effectiveness. Even in Uzbekistan where 37 per cent of entrepreneurs are members of business associations, only 31 per cent think that the associations are able to influence government organizations. In other countries this indicator is much lower: 20 per cent in Kazakhstan, 20 per cent in Kyrgyzstan, 17 per cent in Tajikistan and 8 per cent in Turkmenistan.

Table 5.2 Assessment of effectiveness of lobbying activities of associations in Central Asia

To what degree do associations render influence on central and local legislative and executive authorities with the view of adopting decisions acceptable for entrepreneurs?

	Fulfil		Rather fulfil		Rather do not fulfil		Do not fulfil at all		Don't know	
Kazakhstan	48	8.0%	70	11.7%	129	21.5%	97	16.2%	256	42.7%
Kyrgyzstan	36	7.2%	63	12.6%	122	24.4%	135	27.0%	144	28.8%
Uzbekistan	50	10.0%	107	21.4%	96	19.2%	85	17.0%	162	32.4%
Tajikistan	13	6.5%	21	10.5%	17	8.5%	26	13.0%	123	61.5%
Turkmenistan	3	1.5%	14	7.0%	50	25.0%	48	24.0%	85	42.5%
Total	150	7.5%	275	13.8%	414	20.7%	391	19.6%	770	38.5%

Source: Survey of the Center for Study of Public Opinion 2003.

Female Entrepreneurial Hubs: the Bazaars

A Kyrgyz proverb summarises the role of women in market place: 'Erkek kazanda, aial bazarda' (emphasising that women look after men through their bazaar activities). Bazaars are the biggest and most important sources of entrepreneurial talent and development for women, as well as men, in Kyrgyzstan. Our enterprise survey including 135 enterprises across the country indicates that many women learned and developed their business skills, and acquired a sense of market exchange and money in bazaars. Imitating and learning from the experience of family, friends and others opens new opportunities. In a country with no industrial base and inadequate backward and forward linkages to become an integrated economy, many individuals take up trade and delivery services. During the early years of economic crisis after independence, individuals were desperate to find a way to survive but very few understood how to operate trade and other private businesses because these were disgraced occupations in Soviet times. This changed as shuttle trade directed to China, Korea, Turkey, Germany and other countries in the region[15] made bazaars lively and businessmen and women gradually established better links with their suppliers abroad. With this came capital accumulation, external links and a great deal of learning. The success stories and rumours encouraged more men and women to travel and seek new opportunities through shuttle trade.

Economic and social lives overlap in often crowded alleys of bazaars. The bazaars are not only trading but also living spaces for women as well as men. As Dana et al. (2004) indicated, value creation in bazaars is greatly enhanced by relationships and networks, as the vendors and their customers forge a special and often long lasting relationships. This is rather different from single firm operation as well as internet based new economy. Our observations illustrate that prices are not fixed and bargaining on the selling price is a ritual that starts the bonding tie between customer and seller. Similarly, traders benefit from externalities of social and/or ethnic networks that reduce transaction costs and uncertainty for businesses as well as for individuals. For example, the prosperous male Uyghur traders of Medina daily pray in one of their designated containers. They have their Uyghur butcher and bakery nearby and stay overnight in their containers as they often travel by rented buses between Urumchi and Bishkek.[16] Similarly, many women in the Dordoi, Osh or Ak-Tilek markets eat, chat and live in their trading spaces all day long. They develop bonding, likes and dislikes with their fellow traders. This allows them to learn more about the business environment, whilst also contributing to intensifying competition, and providing new opportunities. It is their form of on-the-job training. Many female entrepreneurs claim that they developed their skills and learned more about doing business within this communal space of traders than from any formal education or business association.

The character of bazaars is also associated with post Soviet urban setting. First of all, bazaars provide commercial space that is scarce or unavailable in post Soviet urban structures for businesses. Under collectivized centralization, retail outlets were scarce and uncompetitive. Secondly, bazaars offer protection and solidarity in the unfamiliar territory of capitalist enterprise. Thirdly, in bazaars individuals learn the value of money and market exchange, new business ideas and how to survive with competition. Finally, bazaars have strong international connections through shuttle trade that many entrepreneurs cultivate, either directly, or through kinship links in urban areas. In short, bazaars are the breeding grounds for entrepreneurial activities and their social and economic dynamics are highly complicated. Not everybody prospers and businesses often suffer from the deep institutional and policy failings they have to function around. The biggest institutional challenge in Kyrgyzstan is the lack of any coherent industrial policy, coupled with the deep uncertainty caused by poorly defined property rights (Çokgezen et al., 2004).

Only a few commercial spaces for retailing existed during the Soviet times and new provisions for land ownership gradually generated privately owned bazaars or expanded the old ones in the major cities. Bishkek has several such big bazaars (Dordoi, Osh, and Medina). In Osh, there is a mile-long city bazaar along the Ak-Buura River which forms the heart of trade and is the single most important provider of employment after agriculture. Jalal-Abad has several smaller bazaars in addition to its central bazaar. In Karakol, Ak-Tilek, Makish and Bugu bazaars all form the core of trade. Most of the traders work with a patent system which is a form of tax registration. They also pay rent to owners of land for the stall or container used. Some of these bazaars are owned by local authorities and later privatised (Ak-Tilek) or newly established family enterprises (Dordoi).

A common characteristic of these bazaars is that they all have open stalls or semi-open simple stores, except for the Dordoi, Karasuu[17] and Medina Bazaars, which are formed out of cheap shipping containers arranged to establish commercial areas. Most of these trading spaces are only partially covered against rain and sunshine. Heat and cold affect traders badly and working conditions can be very harsh in extreme weather. Moving to a container or a small store is a significant upgrade for traders but even containers are very hard to heat in the winter.[18] These circumstances create very difficult work conditions for women bazaaries. Here we describe three major bazaars.

The Dordoi Bazaar This is by far the largest modern bazaar formed out of shipping containers, not only in the country but perhaps in the world. It was established in 1992 by the regional governor of Nayrn province and his brothers. The pioneers of the Dordoi market explain the reason for this initiative: 'Kyrgyzstan does not have an industrial base so we thought it could be a trade hub instead'.[19] Indeed, this vision proved to be successful as today it hosts 5000 containers (3000 owned by the Salymbekov family) and is visited daily by 80,000 people. Over 50 per cent of the goods sold in Dordoi go to neighbouring Central Asian countries and Russia. Dordoi is a gateway mainly for Chinese and to a much lesser extent Turkish and western goods of all kinds, including cars, to enter Central Asia and Russia through shuttle trade. The daily turnover is estimated to be around 18-25m US dollars (Bal, 2004).[20] Dordoi serves retailers, wholesalers and middlemen of all kinds. It also has a remarkable ethnic diversity of traders: Kyrgyz, Russian, Kazakh, Korean, Uyghur, Dungan, Dagistani, and Uzbek.

Osh Bazaar (Osh)[21] This is one of the old bazaars in a city where the history of trade goes back over 2000 years. Osh was also an important trading post on the Silk Road and benefited from being at the upper end of the fertile and legendary Fergana Valley.[22] Uzbeks (60 per cent) and Kyrgyz are the two main ethnic groups; and very few Russians remain. The Osh market grew in the 1990s. It is now is a mile long, 50 yards to 100 yards deep, consisting of shopping space with largely semi-open stalls rented out by various land owners and hosting around 10,000 traders every day. Uzbek and Tajik traders travelling from across the borders are among the customers. Textiles, clothing and foodstuffs occupy the largest areas in the market. But the diversity of other products includes construction materials, kitchen utensils, and second hand goods of all kinds. The market also hosts a gold trade carried out by women only. Around 60 to 80 women gather daily around a square to sell the popular gold jewellery common to women of Central Asia. A huge string of gold rings or earrings carried by a woman trader at first sight is a striking image of this intricate mobile gold trade.

The Ak-Tilek Bazaar (Karakol) This market was established during the last years of Soviet control, in 1987. During the 'perestroika' period several such markets were established as an intended panacea to combat increasing unemployment as many people were looking for new possibilities to earn money. However, at that time it was a small market of about 100 traders, whereas it now hosts over 1000 traders. The main goods sold are foodstuffs, clothes, cosmetics, shoes and small items. Every entrepreneur has to pay a fee to the bazaar's owner according to the space they rent. Karakol neither has the charm of Osh nor the power of Bishkek, and trade in this provincial town is much more regionally focused to its hinterland of small towns and villages.

A Case for Female Entrepreneurship through Vertical and Horizontal Expansion

A great majority of women surveyed are in their mid-thirties and forties; the youngest being 16 years old. Most have university degrees (only about 30 per cent have high school diplomas only). The Soviet system liberated women through education and employment but this also meant long working hours and hardship in state plants and workshops for many. The quality or relevance of this education is also questionable for an open society and market economy. Under communism, apart from medicine and some sciences, most social science education was dogmatic and backward. Today the situation is somewhat worse as, for example, Soviet criminal law is still being studied at law schools. Poverty reduced state spending on education, books and school maintenance and the mushrooming private education providers greatly vary in their quality. It is commonly known that high school and university diplomas can be gained through bribery. Thus, educational qualifications often mean little for the entrepreneurial development of women.

Women are very protective of their families and resist the temptation of using child labour in their businesses. The status of children in Kyrgyz society is, indeed, very different from other poor countries, as they are protected from work and economic exploitation. Women go out of their way to secure care for their children and usually avoid employing underage children in trade. They rely heavily on female solidarity within their close family and kinship, often developing partnerships with male members of their family. It is also increasingly common for men to look after the children while women work, although many regret not having enough time to spend with their children such as Çınara (Case 1).

Although there are commonly shared perceptions and stereotypes of each ethnic group in Kyrgyzstan; such as 'hard working Koreans and Ahiska Turks', 'canny Uzbek and Uyghur traders', 'laidback Kyrgyz' and 'trustworthy Russians'.[23] There is no observed ethnic difference in entrepreneurial talent; i.e. successful entrepreneurs typically come from a large pool of different ethnic groups. However, it is true that those who suffered from repression in China and Russia had to work harder to prove themselves and showed stronger solidarity and determination to survive, as is the case of ethnic Koreans and Uyghurs. Similarly, the settled life in the south that the majority Uzbeks enjoyed over the centuries, together with traditions of trade seems to foster a more business-adept environment. Russians long enjoyed the upper hand in education and intellectual life. With their calm and rather introvert character, Kyrgyz are tolerant and hospitable towards different peoples and ideas. As shown in Table 5.3, female entrepreneurship portrays distinct skills, motivations and business dynamics.

Table 5.3 A typology of female entrepreneurs in bazaars

Category	Characteristics	Exemplary Cases	Limitations
Qualities, skills	• canny • economical • fast adapter	All cases	Women's concern for the family livelihood limits risky and innovative ventures
Motivations	• single bread earner • partnership • income pooling	• Case 6 • Cases 3 and 4 • Cases 2 and 7	Poor business trust beyond family and friends inhibits institution building and company partnerships
Business growth and survival	• vertical expansion • horizontal spread • switching & skipping	• Cases 6 and 7 • Cases 1 and 5 • Case 4	Economic and political volatility as well as lack of external finance inhibits business growth

Source: Author.

Qualities and Skills

Women invariably state that their intuitive and communication skills are better suited for commercial activities, seeing themselves as more skilled and adept for trade. It is also astonishing to find men justifying female talent in commercial entrepreneurial activities while in other cultures this is not easily accepted or allowed to flourish (Özcan, 1995).[24] Along with the highly liberal Kyrgyz, even the more traditional and religious Uzbek families seem to accept that women are simply better at trade by nature. The observed superiority of female entrepreneurs, in this regard, is summarized below:

i) *Canny traders and communicators*: With no misgiving or regret, many men and women from all backgrounds believe that women are more talented in selling a product to a customer. This is commonly explained with the following expressions:

- 'women know how to talk and persuade'
- 'women can understand the desires of a customer better'
- 'women are more patient with an undecided customer'
- 'women are more stable and determined in trade'

ii) *Good money managers*: Women were considered to be better managers of business finances and more responsible members of their family. The laid-back manner of men is often referred to as an old Soviet attitude.

- 'women think of money for their families and children'
- 'women don't spend casually'
- 'women are more economical'
- 'women price products more carefully and they do not give lavish discounts'
- 'women know how to save for good and bad days'

iii) *Fast adapters*: The transformation to a market economy brought new thinking and principles. It has been very hard to run businesses and avoid unemployment, but women appear to be better equipped to adjust to these severe changes.

- 'women respond to changes faster'
- 'women make observations and generate ideas about their business faster'
- 'women are more rational about business change'
- 'women observe more carefully and understand trends'

The following cases illustrate these statements in more detail.

Çınara (Dordoi, Bishkek, case 1)[25] From selling small items on a street stall to her first trip to Turkey for shuttle trade, and then to Pakistan and Syria, Çınara managed to grow her business and now owns two containers in Dordoi. Now 32 years old, she has been involved in trade since she finished university. Over the years she has developed good contacts in Istanbul, taking advantage of her Kyrgyz and Turkish parentage and regularly sources merchandise through old established links. Most of her customers come from the newly independent states of Central Asia. She considers that she has learned a great deal from her trips abroad and feels toughened by stiff competition in Dordoi. Large numbers of traders in ready-made garments force entrepreneurs to look for new niche markets and Çınara admits that she often hides her ideas from others not to be imitated. Childcare that was available for working women during Soviet times is no longer there and she relies on her mother to look after her young child. As with many entrepreneurs interviewed, she expects the government to work harder to stabilise the economy and prevent corruption. She regrets not having enough time to spend at home with her child and family.

Şahanoza (Osh Bazaar, Osh, case 2) Şahanoza celebrated her 16th birthday on 8 September 2004 selling Uzbek 'atlas' textiles in her small stall. At the age of 15 she joined other female members of her family selling and trading. Her chatty, childish enthusiasm attracts many customers and she is a canny trader with a turnover around $150 per day, which is a considerable sum for the country. Seated between other fellow Uzbek silk traders she enjoys the jealousy as well as the support of her trading partners. The main pillar of the trade is her grandmother who despite old age weekly commutes to Uzbekistan to source 'atlas' from her contacts. Her mother organizes the work and joins Şahanoza in the stall as much as possible while her sister manages the household chores and cooking. Her father and brother both work in Russian Siberia in construction. In their tightly-knit Uzbek neighbourhood, the family enjoys the solidarity of their relatives in the absence of the male members of the family. Şahanoza is also being educated to be a devout Muslim by a neighbouring female preacher.

Motivations

The motivations pushing women to set up their own businesses are often linked to three issues of family circumstances. First, a sizeable number of single women work to support their children and sometimes extended family. Like Aisha (Case 6) many are the single bread earners for their family and often under pressure to generate employment and income opportunities for their children and close relatives. Secondly, women often work with their male partners, most commonly with husbands, in order to generate family income and share the multi-faceted responsibilities. Women often remain in charge of trade while their partner carries out the external tasks of purchasing and arranging daily chores. Finally, women take up trade while husbands or fathers are employed in other jobs. In most of these businesses, women rely on one or two casual workers along with their family members. As in the case of Şahanoza (Case 2), economic activities of family members contribute the family pool of resources. Many men travel abroad for trade or for seasonal jobs in construction and women generate income through trade to top up their family income. For example, in Osh, it is said that there is at least one male abroad in every household.

Women are motivated with a pursuit of economic opportunities in the market without any pre-set business plan. They tend to follow opportunities and imitate their competitors. Dana et al. (2004) argue that in the bazaar economy, competition implies a tension between buyer and seller rather than between sellers. This is only partly true. As bazaars are socially embedded economic spaces for traders, there is a certain degree of solidarity, but, they are also extremely competitive, ethically divised and full of built-in tension.[26] The bazaar's economic role is linked to the lack of information on new business areas, market, and technologies. This information gap makes bazaars most suitable for entrepreneurs with no access to political power and economic policy management in a highly blurred emerging market like Kyrgyzstan. Entrepreneurs often employ their intuitive skills to overcome imperfections of the emerging market economy through deepening social links and face-to-face contacts. As they imitate each other, secrecy in competition becomes the rule. This is often expresses as: 'I don't want to tell my business ideas because others would imitate immediately'. As is often pointed out, 'women with better social and communicative skills' find it easier to build these social networks that support business survival. Overall, women are social network builders in bazaars. However, some deepen these network externalities through ethnic and religious solidarity, as is common with Uyghur and Dungan traders with strong Islamic traditions.

Despite the good motivations and skills of female entrepreneurs, many traders would have liked to stay in their former government jobs instead of taking up trade (Case 6). This is because there are difficult working conditions (Case 5), high risk and volatility embedded in trade and only a small proportion of traders are prospering and managing to accumulate capital for business growth. Many traders survive on marginal gains and their savings are not enough to grow or upgrade their business. Many also lack the required know-how and ability to grow, as is often the case for micro and small firms in other parts of the world.

Aigula (Osh Bazaar, Osh, case 3) This 39 year old Tajik used to work for Kyrgyz Electricity Company as an accountant until she was laid off in 1991. She has been trading since then. Initially, she helped her husband, but later they were both convinced that because she was better in trade, she took over the management of the store while her husband dealt with the supply of merchandise from Bishkek-Dordoi (toys, lamps, clocks and other bric-a-brac). Her mother and sister are also involved in this trade and the family now owns two selling points. Despite their hard work they only barely manage to live and the current hardship makes them miss the Soviet times. She is very pessimistic about the management of the economy and 'bribery and corruption everywhere'.

Ainura (Dordoi, Bishkek, case 4) Ainura is a 42 year old Kyrgyz gynaecologist, who, like many of her colleagues, took up trade in order to supplement her poor salary. With her civil servant husband, she managed to expand the business to four containers in Dordoi selling leather bags and purses, later establishing a retail store in Dordoi Plaza, new shopping mall in central Bishkek, and also in Osh and Karakol. The business is controlled by the couple and four relatives. Ainura travelled extensively in 1997 across China as part of 'shuttle trade mania'[27] and later in Korea, and maintains regular contacts in Urumchi. Her travels shaped the current business and she also has many new business ideas, which includes setting up a private health clinic where she can practice her profession more rewardingly. Like many women, she regrets not having enough time to spend with her family and children.

Business Growth and Survival

This collection of business and personal accounts illustrate survival and growth trends in bazaars. Our observations and personal stories indicate three major patterns. Firstly, a common phenomenon is horizontal expansion through business growth and employment generation. Many traders wish to keep their businesses small and manageable by spreading new trading units (containers or stores) among family members (Case 1, 4 and 5). Thus, they share the management with their family and at the same time generate new job and income opportunities. The increased involvement of relatives is also linked to mistrust of strangers and of professional management, which is a totally new concept for the country. Equally important is the need to keep the business small (at least in appearance), in order to protect wealth from predators (tax officials, government inspectors and other extortionists.

Secondly, vertical integration is another way to reduce risk and uncertainty and to generate job opportunities for family members. In some instances, women are forced to develop their business with vertical expansion due to a lack of business linkages among small firms. This is partly due to unfilled gaps in the market by private businesses and partly to a mistrust of outsiders in business dealings. Like Anna (Case 7), who decided to sew her own towel dresses together with her family members, and Aisha (Case 6) whose sons produce pasta for her stall, some traders began to develop business ideas combining production and trade. This allows them to reduce costs and generate further income as well as new job opportunities for family members. This trend is visible in the clothing sector more than in foodstuffs, since food processing requires special technical skills and machinery. Indeed, food processing is now a very poorly developed sector in the country.[28] Thirdly, switching and skipping between businesses is an opportunistic activity among women who recognize new avenues of trade and services (Case 4). Business failures and/or capital accumulation leads to new business investments in other sectors. In recent years, the number of restaurants and cafes, hair dressing salons, and private medical services has been increasing and areas of highly crowded trade in bazaars are also feeding new business ideas. For new business opportunities, entrepreneurs rely on imitation and there are changing cycles of popular businesses.

Economic and political insecurity as well as widespread corruption negatively effect business growth and survival. Female entrepreneurs are outspoken about these shortcomings and they often emphasize the unfair and arbitrary treatment of taxmen, state inspectors and customs officials. They also seem to be tougher in dealing with these officials than their male partners (Cases 3 and 5).

Kim (Dordoi, Bishkek, case 5) Kim is a 41 year old ethnic Korean who has been engaged in wholesale trade in Dordoi since 1997. She learned the business through buying and selling in small quantities with her family members. She used to work as an engineer in a Soviet factory and now has two containers selling ready-made trousers from China to small retailers and wholesalers coming from Tajikistan, Russia, Ukraine and Uzbekistan. Her grandparents escaped from Chinese oppression to Russia only to be deported by Stalin to Kyrgyzstan where she says they found peace. She still has an aunt living in China and hopes to find her someday. Ms Kim's sister is also a trader in the same market and her husband runs four small stores in the city. She thinks women are better negotiators and more successful in coping with customs and tax inspectors. She says, 'we don't trust the government, they don't think of the people. There has to be reforms easing customs regulations, as well as bureaucracy and bribery at the borders. But having said that, we are happy to live here and it is a much freer country than its neighbours, better than China, Kazakhstan and Russia'. Kim complains about the cold and difficult working conditions, especially in winter, when 'we just keep drinking cognac to keep warm.'

Aisha (Ak-Tilek, Karakol, case 6) Aisha is a tired-looking 51 year old Uyghur whose family escaped from China for a better life. She started working in a Soviet state canteen in 1969 and has been in Ak-Tilek since 1990. On a damp and cold day, standing around the open stalls of the bazaar is a real hardship and throughout her life Aisha has just managed to keep her head above water. Her two teenage sons are unemployed and produce Uyghur pasta at home for her to sell. She deals with small quantities of rice, soap, biscuits and other foodstuffs brought from Bishkek, and most of her customers are urban dwellers, as well as impoverished peasants travelling from nearby villages. Aisha complains about her work circumstances as it is uncomfortable and unhealthy 'for a woman', but she sees no other income opportunity for herself and her children in the sleepy town of Karakol. On the contrary, life is getting harder and harder for her with high taxes and 'bad economic management'.

Anna (Dordoi, Bishkek, case 7) At the age of 43, Anna is a successful Russian entrepreneur selling towel dresses and other textile products. She did various forms of trade with China and Turkey for many years. She was selling Turkish garments and towel products and eventually decided to set up her own sewing workshop in order to reduce prices and diversify products. She normally brings designs from Istanbul and replicates them at one third the cost of original item. The business grew rapidly and she currently employs 30 people in her sewing workshop. She runs the business together with her daughter, father and husband, each sharing a different task under her coordination.

Conclusions

The tale of Djamila dramatises the determination and free will of Kyrgyz women and we can see how today's Djamilas work and how they think within the context of today's Kyrgyz economy. The evidence presented has shown that bazaars play a crucial role in income and job generation as well as in entrepreneurial development. Women from different ethnic backgrounds take advantage of these hubs and shape their businesses along with changing market opportunities. Both horizontal and vertical expansion and capital accumulation are used to move to new sectors as three effects of bazaar activities. Female entrepreneurship is often regarded as a segment of a larger pool of family enterprises that are shared most commonly by married couples. However, unlike other family businesses in societies where women have a secondary and less managerial role, female entrepreneurs and business partners in Kyrgyzstan play a strong managerial role and often hold the upper hand in businesses. This is seen in our survey by common perceptions about women's superior qualities in trade and money management.

Bazaars have been identified as an intermediary operational level between the firm and the market in this study. Bazaars are also socially embedded economic spaces for traders. While solidarity is shared among friends and relatives, they are also extremely competitive, ethnically divisive and full of built-in tension. Thus, bazaars host socially embedded network relations and inherent tension between rival businesses. Competition through imitation is the main driving force behind business creation, entrepreneurial innovations and tension in bazaars. The built-in tension in bazaars has many layers; between retailer and wholesalers; customers and sellers; between state officials/inspectors and businesses; between different ethnic and/or social groups. Women entrepreneurs in these economic spaces not only manage to develop their businesses but also provide a crucial social asset, in the form of their communication and social skills in building relations within networks of customers and suppliers as well as neighbouring traders. Networks and relations built by friends and relatives of women reduce transaction costs, uncertainty and fill the information gap. Thus, these networks enhance the survival and growth of businesses. However, women's deep preoccupation with their family livelihood and future of their children make them act in a less risky manner in their financial dealings for new business ventures.

While bazaars are endowed with inter-personal trust in social networks against the shortcomings of the market and poor institutional structures, the lack of institutions and a stable policy framework negatively affects the formation of companies beyond family and social ties. This lack of impersonal trust beyond family and friends appears to be a limiting factor for business growth in bazaars, as well as in the business community in general. Similarly, collective action through interest representation and business associations is not yet part of the economic activities and behaviours of bazaar traders.

While a free market economy is slowly emerging out of the Communist Party and state control, the emerging post Soviet state power impinges upon the business environment as an unaccountable distributor of largess rather than an even-handed arbiter. The superior, hard working character of women in Kyrgyzstan cannot overcome the institutional and macro challenges. The biggest institutional challenge is a deep sense of uncertainty and poorly defined property rights. The regulatory system in Kyrgyzstan is not transparent and rules are applied inconsistently. Within this institutional context, despite the presence of numerous international donor agencies and aid programmes, small businesses often fail to benefit from initiatives to promote entrepreneurship and business creation (see also Khodov, 2003; Dadasev et al., 2003). Hard work needs an institutional umbrella of law and order, protection of private gains and property, and stability. None of these are fully secure in Kyrgyzstan.[29]

Acknowledgements

I am grateful for the help of the EBRD micro-finance programme managers and consultants in Bishkek, Karakol, Karabalta, Osh and Jalal-Abad (in particular Heike Nonnenberg and Margarita Cherikbaeva) and Eamon Doren of the USAID. I greatly appreciate the logistical support of the Kyrgyz-Turkish Manas University. My special thanks go to my research assistant Aybek Aytbaev for his patient and considerate support. Many Djamilas I met inspired and impressed me with their charm, hard work and inner strength. Without their warm hospitality and support this research would have not been possible. I am deeply indebted to them. Nevertheless, I am solely responsible from the views, omissions and opinions expressed in this chapter.

Notes

1 This research is funded by the Nuffield Foundation.

2 Today Kyrgyz people pay tribute to their 19th century leader Kurmanjan Datka, the women chief who negotiated a peace settlement with the advancing Russian powers, thus changed the destiny of the nation.

3 Kyrgyzstan is divided into seven administrative provinces – oblasts – identified with their main cities. Batken province (Batken), Osh province (Osh), Naryn province (Naryn), Jalal-Abad province (Jalal-Abad), Issyk-Kul province (Karakol), Talas province (Talas), Chui region (Bishkek).

4 Although the name has been officially changed to the Kyrgyz Republic, we use both terms interchangeably.

5 Many observers and experts in the country reckon the size of informal economy ranging from 50 per cent to 70 per cent.

6 See World Bank (2002).

7 Soon after a Russian military post was established nearby, the grid city of Karakol, meaning military post in Turkish, was founded in 1869. It was then called 'Przhevalsky' after the Russian explorer Nikolai Przhevalsky who provided crucial intelligence on the geography and peoples of Central Asia for Russian imperial expansion in the region.

8 After the privatization, agricultural land was divided into very small, economically inefficient units. Now the typical farm size is around 1.1 and 1.5 hectares and this is creating many problems (interview with Scott Wallace, Kyrgyz Agro-input enterprise Development, USAID, Osh, September 2004).

9 Many of these are individual patent (tax code) owners involved in small-scale trading activities. See Proma and International Business Council (2003).

10 See Proma and International Business Council (2003).

11 An average state employee earns around $19 (800 som) per month while a parliamentarian is paid $350 per month.

12 Forming associations is another new way of thinking for Kyrgyz people and donor agencies have been trying to help to initiate this public participation. Proma and International Business Council lists the following associations as partners: Chambers of Commerce and Industry of Kyrgyzstan, Entrepreneurs' Union of Karakol, Kyrgyz Exporters' Association, Small Business Development Centres in Bishkek and Narn, Women Entrepreneurs Support Association, Congress of Business Associations and the Centre for Public Opinion Survey and Forecasts.

13 A skilled female entrepreneur who was active in the Entrepreneurs Union of Karakol was quick to take advantage of privatization of a former Soviet factory and free zone initiative by utilising the Union solely for her own business interest. My visit to her flour factory, whose site was grabbed from the state, illustrated the grand opportunities delivered to a small well-connected group of business people.

14 Cf. Tabyshalieva (1999) on the political power of women.

15 An ethnic Uzbek trader's telling story about travelling across Turkey for five years working and undertaking small trade and later flying to Japan together with other small traders from CIS illustrates incredible courage and capacity of individuals.

16 Uyghur traders bring goods from their autonomous region in China to sell in Bishkek despite great hardship. They are not granted passports by the Chinese authorities and only travel with an issued ID paper. They often spend many nights in containers in between their trips.

17 The Karasuu Bazaar is newly established near to the old city bazaar in small city of Karasuu and is modelled after Dordoi bazaar in Bishkek. The Chinese border market set up near Doostuk is the main source of goods to Karasuu along with Dordoi.

18 To purchase a container or obtain a licence for a convenience store in Bishkek costs on average $2,500, which is a significant sum for small traders working on small margins.

19 Interview with Ulugbek Salymbekov, Chairman of the Dordoi Plaza, April 2004, Bishkek.

20 The lowest turnover is estimated to be around $4-7 million. The range between the low and high figures is huge and this is due to fact that most of the trade remains to be unregistered. The container rents vary between $600-700 per month and purchasing a container in Dordoi can be as expensive as $20,000 (Bal, 2004).

21 This market should not be confused with the bazaar in Bishkek of the same name.

22 The founder of the Mogul Empire, Babur, provides a vivid account of the Fergana Valley, its Turkic peoples, prosperous cities, and unmatchable fruits, in his personal accounts, known as the Baburname (see The Baburname, 2002). He is believed to have visited Suleiman too, the holy mountain in the centre of Osh, prior to his successful campaign in India and to have built a monument there.

23 These are expressions commonly used about different ethnic groups in cross reference.

24 An extensive survey on Turkish SMEs indicates that there is a clear gender bias against female employment and entrepreneurship. Women entrepreneurs are accepted more if they are outsiders and/or have higher educational qualifications.

25 To keep the respondents identity confidential, pseudo names are given to each case.

26 Deliberate fires and mafia type activities happen in bazaars. The former Uyghur Turbaza bazaar was completely burned down in 2002 and a bus full of them were robbed and killed by a group of bandits in 2003 near Narn.

27 Following the independence of the country and the fall of the communism, many people wanted to discover the world that they were not allowed to endeavour before. Partly as a response to travel restrictions and partly due to high expectations from shuttle trade, thousands of people left for China, Turkey and other western European countries. Individuals also want to imitate success stories. In recent years, for example, travelling

to Germany and bringing a second hand car loaded with second hand goods has been highly popular among men.

28 Seasonal fruit and tomato produce is often conserved by household and the remaining is wasted due to the small number of largely backward processing industries in the country.

29 In 1999, Transparency International ranked Kyrgyzstan 87th out of 99 countries.

References

Bal, H. (2004), 'Corruption and unregistered economy in transition countries: The case of shuttle trade in Kyrgyzstan', *Proceedings of the First International Conference on the Fiscal Policies in Transition Economies*, April, Bishkek, pp. 169-195.

Center for Study of Public Opinion (2003), *2003 Survey*, conducted in Kazakhstan, Kyrgyzstan, Tajikistan, Turkmenistan and Uzbekistan, USAID.

Çokgezen, M. (2004), 'Corruption in Kyrgyzstan: the facts, causes and consequences', *Central Asian Survey*, vol. 23, pp. 79-94.

Çokgezen, M. et al. (2004), 'Sources of uncertainty in Kyrgyzstan', (in Russian and Turkish), *Proceedings of the First International Conference on the Fiscal Policies in Transition Economies*, April, Bishkek, pp. 189-195.

Çolak, Y. (2002), 'Nationalism and Islam in Central Asia: Truths or Fantasies on Nation', in E. Eefegil (ed), *Geopolitics of Central Asia in the Post-Cold War Era*, Research Centre for Turkestan and Azerbaijan, Haarlem.

Dadasev, A. et al. (2003), 'The effectiveness of support for small business', *Problems of Economic Transition*, vol. 45, p. 69.

Dana, L.P., Etemad, H. and Wright, R. (2004), *Networking as a means of value creation*, Paper at the Rencontre-de-St. Gall, Appenzell, Switzerland.

George, C. et al. (2002), *Structural Adjustment in the Transition: Case Studies from Albania, Azerbaijan, Kyrgyz Republic, and Moldova*, World Bank, Washington D.C.

Handran, L. M. (2001), 'Gender and ethnicity in the transitional democracy of Kyrgystan', *Central Asian Survey*, vol. 20, pp. 467-496.

Hübner, W. (2000), *SME Development in Countries of Central Asia (Kazakstan, Kyrgyzstan and Uzbekistan): Constraints, cultural aspects, and role of international assistance*, UNIDO, Vienna.

Iwasaki, I. (2000), 'Industrial structure and regional development in Central Asia: a microdata analysis on spatial allocation of industry', *Central Asian Survey*, vol. 19, pp. 157-183.

Khodov, L. (2003), 'The structure of small business and distinctive features of its motivation', *Problems of Economic Transition*, vol. 45, p. 84.

Koichuev, T. (2001), *The Economy of Kyrgyz Republic on the Way of Reforms*, Public Society Economists for Reforms, Bishkek.

Özcan, G.B. (1995), *Small Firms and Local Economic Development: Entrepreneurship in Southern Europe and Turkey*, Aldershot: Avebury Press.

Özcan, G.B. (2004), *Industrial policy for transition and small and medium-sized enterprises*, paper to the Conference on Reform in Public Sector Finance, Manas University, Bishkek, April.

Özcan, G.B. and Çokgezen, M. (2003), 'Limits to alternative forms of capitalisation: the case of Anatolian holding companies', *World Development*, vol. 31, pp. 2061-2084.

Proma and International Business Council Survey (2003), *National Business Opinion Survey in Kyrgyzstan*, Bishkek.

The Baburname (2002), Translated, edited and annotated by W.M. Thackston, New York: The Modern Library.

Tabyshalieva, A. (1999), *Women of Kyrgyzstan: Access to Political Power*, Gender in Development Bureau, Diamond Association, unpublished report, Bishkek.

Transparency International (TI) (1999), *Corruption Perceptions Index, 1999*, http://www.gwdg.de/~uwvw/1999Data.html.

Winiecki, J. (2003), 'The role of the new entrepreneurial private sector in transition and economic performance in light of the successes in Poland, Czech Republic, and Hungary', *Problems of Economic Transition*, vol. 45, p. 6.

World Bank (2002), *World Development Indicators*, World Bank, Washington D.C.

Part 3
Women's Entrepreneurship in Central Europe

Chapter 6

From Business Ownership to Informal Market Traders: The Characteristics of Female Entrepreneurship in Lithuania

Ruta Aidis

Introduction

In 1997, as part of my research on female entrepreneurs, I met with different governmental and non-governmental officials. In one unforgettable meeting with the then director of the governmentally funded agency supporting small and medium-sized enterprises (SMEs), I expressed my interest in studying female entrepreneurs. The director flatly responded that I would have nothing to study since there were no female entrepreneurs in Lithuania. In 2004, I doubt if anyone would share that view. Female entrepreneurs have become more visible and there are now even governmentally sponsored programmes developed to assist them. Although more still needs to be done, some positive steps have been made in the right direction. However, female traders in informal markets are still a blind spot. In general, informal market traders seem to occupy a vague unnamed category, though the majority of them hold official business licenses and as such are officially considered SMEs.[1] But in terms of support or information programmes, business license holders are a neglected group. One of the main aims of this chapter is to provide a further understanding and insight into this category of female SMEs. The other aim of this chapter is to provide an introduction to the situation for women in Lithuania in general and specific information on SME owners.

This chapter is structured as follows: section one presents a description of the status of women in Lithuania highlighting the Soviet and post Soviet situation. In section two the characteristics of SME growth during the transition period in Lithuania are presented and the recent governmental initiatives and programmes for SMEs are also described. This section includes a specific look at female entrepreneurs in Lithuania. Section three presents the similarities and differences between male and female SME owners in Lithuania. In section four, we turn our attention to informal open air market traders. The traders at Gariunai, the largest open air market in the Baltic States are highlighted. In addition to presenting the characteristics of male and female traders at Gariunai, the specific motivations of female traders are categorized. Related issues such as the large numbers of female traders and the classification of these traders as entrepreneurs are discussed. Section five presents policy recommendations and a conclusion.

Women in Lithuania

Since the beginning of the 20th century, men and women in Lithuania have been 'equal' according to the law.[2] However, informal norms of behaviour already in place in independent Lithuania emphasized different role expectations for men and women. Men were expected to be the main 'breadwinner' and to be active in the public sphere whereas women were expected to be homemakers and to prefer the domestic sphere.

Under Soviet occupation, formal rights between men and women were further substantiated and Lithuanian women and men were legally considered 'equal'.[3] However, prevailing attitudes under the Soviet regime introduced the new expectation for women to participate in the paid labour force without bringing about any significant changes to the unpaid role fulfilled by women in the domestic sphere. In some limited instances women benefited from differential treatment: they were entitled to paid maternity leave, exempt from compulsory military service and enjoyed early retirement.

Soviet rule implemented quota systems that allowed women access to some of the higher levels in decision-making structures; but these position were largely 'symbolic' in nature. Both male and female Party members were represented in the Supreme Soviet but this was due to the quota system and not necessarily based on merit. Though the Supreme Soviet was formally recognized as an important decision-making organ, in reality, the Supreme Soviet's powers were limited. In the entire history of the Soviet Union, only one woman (Mrs. Furtseva) ever served as a full member of the Politburo, which was the centre of political power in the Soviet Union and the main de facto decision-making body. As Hesli and Miller (1993, p. 509) comment: 'The fact remains that Soviet society was constructed and directed by men, with very little opportunity for a woman's voice to be heard'.

Though women were highly represented in the Lithuanian labour force (in 1989, 53 per cent of the labour force was female[4]), their overall position in the labour force vis-à-vis men was not 'equal'. Females were under-represented in managerial and supervisory positions. Though women had increased access to professional positions under state socialism, there was a continuing gender segregation of the rest of the labour force (Einhorn, 1993, p. 125). Also even though women had access to higher education and professional jobs, their salaries were significantly less than their male counterparts. On average, Soviet salaries for women were one third less than those of Soviet men (Rimashevskaia, 1992, p. 15). Furthermore, many women were underemployed, working in a position below their educational or skill level (Hesli and Miller, 1993, p. 509).

In the Soviet labour force women were concentrated in certain job categories such as trade and public catering, health care, physical culture, social security, education and culture (Hesli and Miller, p. 509). Strikingly, even within female-dominated professions, such as light industry and textiles, the managers still tended to be male (Einhorn, 1993, p. 125).

In addition, Anastasia Posadskaya argues that 'equality' between the sexes was generated more from an economic standpoint, than a gender-equality standpoint. She writes: 'Women's labour power was a means, a resource used to solve the problem of economic growth: the authorities alternately introduce the ideology of sex equality and the ideology of women's 'natural mission', depending on what suits them at that time.' (1994, p. 9).

Furthermore, the so-called equality of women in the paid labour force did little to change the division of unpaid labour in the home. The majority of unpaid labour in the family continued to be seen as the duty of the Soviet woman (Posadskaya, 1994). In essence, a woman's right to paid labour inevitably became a requirement (i.e. duty) to engage in paid labour (Juceviciene, 1998, p. 20). The triple task of paid labour, domestic unpaid labour and the time and energy spent in the acquisition of household needs[5] (including standing in queues) negatively influenced many women's career choices.[6]

Even though the transition period from 1989 onwards brought about dramatic changes to the lives of both Lithuanian men and women, gender roles have tended to remain surprisingly stable. Embedded gender roles have had negative consequences for both Lithuanian women and men. As other researchers have indicated, women as a group, have suffered disproportionately from job loss, increased labour market discrimination and domestic violence (Molyneux, 1994; Unicef, 1999). Furthermore, independence brought a re-emergence of support for the traditional roles for men and women (Grapard, 1997). For men this resulted in added pressure to become the sole 'breadwinner' and for women this has meant a glorification of the 'housewife role'. Ironically, the benefits enjoyed by women under the Soviet system have become handicaps. In Lithuania, many private businesses will refuse to hire women of childbearing age for fear that they will have to extend the generous maternity benefits[7] inherited from the Soviet system. In addition, given the low level of Lithuanian state pensions, early retirement for women is becoming synonymous with female pensioner poverty.[8]

In spite of the fact that the official political system in Lithuania has changed dramatically, old networks still exist between the former Communist elite and their focus has shifted from party-related privileges to the direct attainment of financial rewards through private business activities (both legal and illegal) as well as continued political involvement. In practice, the old male dominated networks are still intact and assist in obtaining benefits in either of these endeavours. The percentage of men and women in decision-making positions in governmental bodies and in private and public enterprises seem to reflect the influence of male-dominated networks. In addition, the removal of mandatory quotas for women in elected positions seems to have had a negative influence on female representation in political bodies. In many transition countries, the number of women in decision-making positions has declined (Einhorn, 1993; Grapard, 1997; Lakhova, 1998; Medvedev, 1998). In Lithuania, the percentage of women in the Lithuanian parliament and other elected offices has decreased since 1996 (Table 6.1).

Table 6.1 Lithuanian election results for parliament (Seimas) and municipalities councils (election year in parenthesis)

	Total	Female	%	Male	%
VIII Seimas (1996)	138	25	18.0	113	82.0
IX Seimas (2000)	141	15	10.6	126	89.3
Members on local gov't councils (1997)	1,484	326	22.0	1,158	78.0
Members on local gov't councils (2000)	1,562	275	17.6	1,287	82.4
Mayors (2000)	56	3	5.4	53	94.6

Source: Lithuanian Department of Statistics (2001).

In terms of unemployment, the raw figures in Table 6.2 show little difference between the levels of male and female unemployment. However, these figures conceal a more alarming reality. A study conducted by Kanopienė (2000) indicates that the largest percentage of unemployed women in Lithuania is between the ages of 31-54, whilst for male labourers, unemployment numbers are greater only in the 'under 18' age group. Furthermore, the figures conceal a relatively high percentage of the underemployed. Given the fact that more women are represented in the low wage state sectors experiencing severe budget constraints, it seems that women, even if they are employed, are at greater risk of underemployment. Privatization of state-owned enterprises has also resulted in reduced employment opportunities for women since many women find it difficult to obtain employment in the private sector, partly due to discrimination and lack of contacts (Spevacek, 2001).

Table 6.2 Unemployment rate based on the Lithuanian Labour Exchange 1994-2003 (in per cent)

	'94	'95	'96	'97	'98	'99	'00	'01	'02	'03
Total	3.8	6.1	7.1	5.9	13.2	14.6	16.4	17.4	13.8	12.4
Women	3.8	6.4	7.7	6.3	11.6	13.0	13.9	14.7	12.9	12.2
Men	3.8	5.8	6.6	5.6	14.7	16.2	18.8	19.9	14.6	12.7

Source: Lithuanian Department of Statistics (2004).

Given the existing findings, a form of gendered role 'lock in' and path dependence in Lithuania seems evident. Even within the new social, political and economic structures, the expectations of women's domestic responsibilities is higher than for men while the valuation of women's paid labour is generally lower.

Characteristics of SME Growth in Lithuania

Lithuania was a part of the Soviet Union until 11 March 1990 when it became the first Soviet republic to declare its independence. As in other formerly Soviet countries, very few forms of private business ownership were previously allowed in Soviet Lithuania until the mid 1980s.[9] In 1987 limited forms of cooperative style enterprises were permitted.[10] A year after regaining independence in 1991, Lithuania embarked on an ambitious stabilization and reform program supported by the International Monetary Fund and the World Bank, which allowed for all forms of private enterprises. Lithuania has made tremendous progress in establishing a democratic and western oriented market economy. Though this process is by no means complete, Lithuania's membership to the European Union (EU) in May 2004 has provided official international recognition of this accomplishment.

In Lithuania, as in many other transition countries, private enterprise mushroomed during the initial transition period in the early 1990s. From 1993-1995 there was a steadily increasing trend in the number of enterprises in Lithuania in all size categories (of registered businesses). As Table 6.3 shows, the most rapid growth took place in the smallest size category (less than 5 employees and 5-19 workers) in 1993 and 1994. Enterprises with less than 5 employees increased by 48 per cent and enterprises with 5-19 workers increased by 39 per cent from 1993-1994. Since we can safely assume that the vast majority of the small-sized enterprises (up to 19 workers) are private businesses, this table provides a good indication of the changes in growth patterns of small enterprises. Based on this data, however, we cannot say whether increased enterprise exits or decreased number of business start-ups was the main factor for the changes in growth.

Table 6.3 Number of functioning enterprises in Lithuania

	1993	1994	1995
Functioning enterprises	33,067	47,650	63,241
Less than 5 workers	24,214	35,865	48,321
5-19 workers	5,123	7,100	9,151
20 – 199 workers	3,348	4,225	5,192
200 + workers	382	460	577

Source: UNDP (1997).

Figure 6.1 illustrates a slightly different trend for newly created private enterprises. According to the World Bank (1998), the number of newly registered private enterprises has been stable with a dramatic decline occurring in 1995.

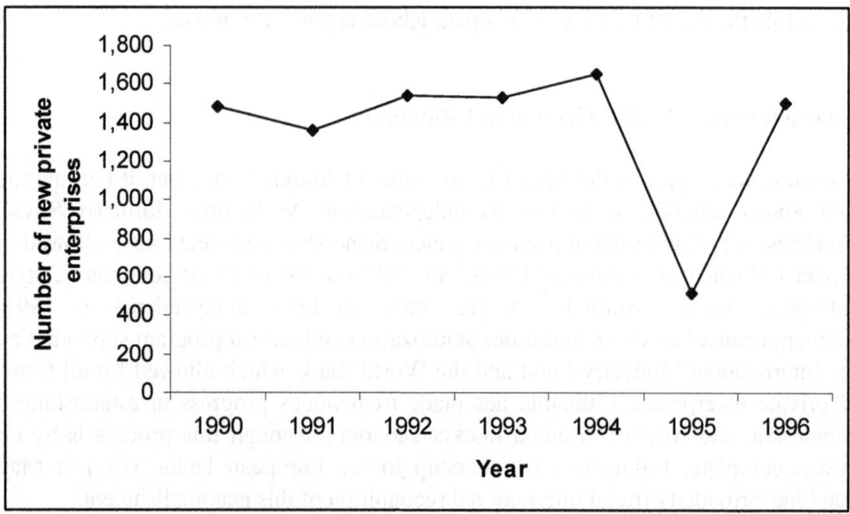

Source: World Bank (1998, p. 201).

Figure 6.1 Number of newly created private enterprises by year of registration

The lack of increasing numbers of SMEs is of concern, having been most likely caused by both micro- and macro- level conditions. The combination of increasing regulations (in the form of requirements, taxation, etc.) coupled with decreasing business opportunities (due to increasing competition[11]) seem to have resulted in decreasing numbers of new private enterprises.[12]

The period from 1999-2000 has also seen a decrease in registered SMEs. At the beginning of 1999 there were 81,600 registered[13] SMEs, but by the end of 2000 this had dropped to 52,000 (SMEDA,[14] 2004). The main factors influencing this rapid decrease seem to be both internal changes and external economic shocks. Internal changes included increased labour costs (for hiring employees), additional taxation, additional bureaucratic barriers, increased competition from large chain stores (especially for trade related businesses) and low consumer demand. External shocks included both the Russian rouble crisis (August 1998) and an increasingly unfavourable Litas-Euro exchange rate. The Lithuanian Human Development Report (UNDP, 1999) noted that the Russian crisis was hardest for small businesses that were involved in trade with Russia. Since the Litas was tied to the US dollar, the increasing value of the latter and the decreasing value of the Euro resulted in Lithuania's exports being less competitive and made it more difficult for Lithuanian SMEs to engage in profitable export activities. In addition, a simplification of the regulations for de-registering inactive businesses in 2000 may have influenced the apparently large decline in private businesses from 1999 to 2000.

Although little was being done to promote SME development at the beginning of transition, the Lithuanian government is currently undertaking a number of measures to foster SMEs. The most important development was the creation of the Lithuanian Development Agency for Small and Medium Sized Enterprises (SMEDA) in 1996. The five main aims of the SMEDA are (1) to stimulate the development of new SMEs, (2) to increase the competitiveness of SMEs, (3) to promote the creation of new jobs, (4) to increase the survival rate of SMEs, and (5) to increase information technology (IT) literacy of SMEs. Furthermore, SMEDA is responsible for analyzing the economic and legal environment for SME development, updating and disseminating information about financing possibilities and providing publications on SMEs. It is involved with initiating and administering the provision of subsidized consulting services for SMEs and participation in international SME programmes and projects. SMEDA currently subsidizes business advice and consultancy at various business centres throughout Lithuania. In 2002, under government mandate, SMEDA created government supported guarantee funds through the agency INVEGA to assist SMEs in accessing bank loans. In July 2002, the SMEDA received a government subsidy in order to implement a project that provides support for starters. As a part of this project, subsidized consulting services are provided to starters in six regions of Lithuania. The services are intended to be accessible by both rural and urban starters. Special attention will be paid to female starters and young starters (ages 20-29). In addition, SMEDA already supports the development of business incubators in seven Lithuanian cities.

EU membership has had a further positive impact on drawing governmental attention and resources to the SME sector in Lithuania. In April 2002, Lithuania along with the other candidate countries signed 'The Maribor Declaration' which acknowledges the importance of the principles of the European Charter for Small Enterprises.[15] The European Charter for Small Enterprises was adopted by the General Affairs Council of the EU on June 13, 2000 as the basis for EU action to support and develop small enterprises. The main elements of this charter focus on training, education, information for SMEs on EU enlargement, improvement and simplification of SME legislation and regulation, SME financing, technology improvements for SMEs and the development of business advisory councils. In a report submitted to the EU in September 2002, Lithuania outlined all the ways in which it was complying with the European Charter for Small Enterprises.[16] Even though the initiatives undertaken are impressive, much still has to be done. A report presented by the European Commission in January 2003, describing the state of SMEs in EU candidate countries found many issues that still needed to be addressed.[17]

Some new programmes have been developed specifically directed towards female entrepreneurs. In addition to targeting female business start-ups, SMEDA now includes a separate rubric containing information about female entrepreneurs in Lithuania on its website. This is a refreshingly positive development compared to the complete lack of information or interest in female entrepreneurs in the mid 1990s. Their website includes a number of success stories highlighting female entrepreneurship as well some general statistical information regarding female employment and private business involvement. Furthermore, it is likely that support for female entrepreneurs will continue to increase as a result of harmonization with EU directives.

Though progress is being made in greater recognition of the SME sector as a whole, license traders such as the ones selling goods at open air markets continue to be neglected by policymakers.

Female Entrepreneurs in Lithuania[18]

As Figure 6.2 indicates, the percentage of female business owners in Lithuania has been increasing since the late 1990s and in 2002 reached 43.3 per cent.

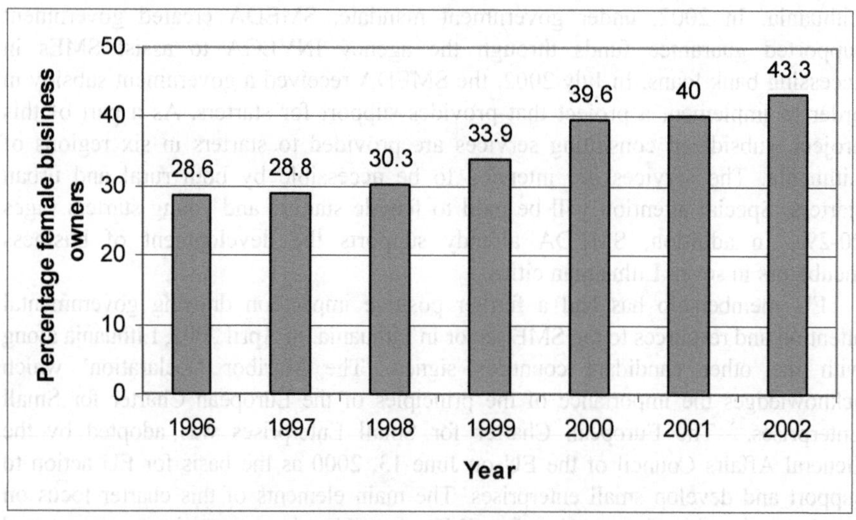

Source: Lithuanian Statistical Office (2004).

Figure 6.2 Percentage of female business owners in Lithuania (1996-2002)

A survey of male and female SME owners in Lithuania conducted in 2000 highlighted a number of similarities and differences between male and female SME owners.[19] With regard to personal characteristics, female and male business owners are similar in terms of age, education and native language. Also, in terms of education, the majority of male and female SME owners have a university or higher degree. Most male and female business owners were married, but male business owners were significantly more likely to be married than female business owners. Most male and female business owners were between 30-45 years of age. Female business owners tend to have less prior work-related management experience and less prior business experience (in the form of another private business) than male business owners. Only a few male or female business owners had been employed in the private sector before starting their business (17 per cent).

In terms of business characteristics, female business owners tend to more often start sole-proprietorships while the majority of male SME owners have corporations (Table 6.4). In general, female SME owners work fewer hours and have a lower turnover than male SME owners. Also female business owners employed fewer workers: the average number of employees for male SME owners was 14 while the average number of employees for female SME owners was only 10. In addition, female entrepreneurs had less full-time employees, or employees with either permanent or temporary work contracts. In terms of business sector, the majority of female SME owners were operating in retail trade or the services sector. However, just under half of all male business owners were also operating in these sectors. There were no differences between male and female SME owners in terms of exporting goods and/or services but more male SME owners were importing goods and/or services than female SME owners. There were no significant differences found between male and female SME owners in terms of location of business, family members as employees or home-based business. For both male and female business owners, more than 85 per cent responded that their business is their main source of income.

In terms of motivation to start a business, both male and female SME owners indicated pull factors such as 'always wanted to have my own business' and push factors such as 'economic reasons' as the main reasons for starting a business. More female SME owners also chose 'easier to combine home/work responsibilities' than male SME owners but this was not statistically significant. Very few Lithuanian female SME owners chose 'dissatisfied with present (past) employment' (8 per cent).[20]

When asked if they were earning enough income to cover their living expenses, female SME owners replied more often that their business earnings were not sufficient or completely insufficient, while the majority of male SME owners responded that they earned sufficient or more than sufficient income from their businesses (Table 6.4). Although the majority of both female and male SME owners felt that the general economic situation in Lithuania will improve, more female SME owners responded that they did not know (20 per cent versus 12 per cent for male business owners). Small-scale studies conducted in Lithuania have indicated that women encounter discrimination in the transitional business environment. Unfortunately, information about discrimination remains scant. Interviews with twenty-one female business owners in 1997 indicated that the majority of business owners interviewed felt discriminated against as female entrepreneurs (Aidis, 1998). In addition, a survey of business administration students in 1998 at the Kaunas Polytechnical University revealed that the students have an acute awareness of gender prejudice in the current business environment (Juceviciene, 1998, p. 30).

Table 6.4 Characteristics of male and female SME owners in Lithuania (in per cent)

Issue	Female business owners	Male business owners
University education	71	69
Age (30 - 45 years)	68	58
Civil status: married	70	89
Prior work-related management experience	41	53
Prior business experience	36	54
Hours worked at business: 35 or less per week	22	12.5
Annual business turnover (1999) no more than USD 125,000	69	38
Business type: sole proprietorship	52	39
Business size: 10 or less employees	63	51
Business with full-time employees*	69	84
Business with employees on permanent contract*	70	77
Business with employees on temporary contract*	19	26
Business sector: services or retail trade	56	49
Importing goods and/or services	26	45
Business location: urban areas	92	96
Employment of family member	52	51
Home-based business	17	10
Business main source of income	82	87
Business earnings sufficient or more than sufficient to cover living expenses	49	67
General economic situation in Lithuania will improve	52	63

*Percentage calculated based on those with employees.

Source: Adapted from Aidis (2003c, p. 194).

Female and Male Traders in Informal Open Air Markets[21]

Under Lithuanian law, there exists yet another form of SME business owner that does not usually appear in general statistical results on SMEs namely, license holders. A business license[22] allows an individual to legally engage in a number of market activities and according to Lithuanian law a license holder qualifies as an SME owner. A license can be obtained for a flexible time period ranging from one day or a number of days or months to an entire year. The cost of the license is generally low and varies depending on the type of activity. Licenses are obtained through the tax office. A license holder can employ family members and are expected to keep a record of the goods they sell but they do not have to officially declare these sales or pay tax on them. As a result, all the goods that are sold with a license are not recorded officially.

Most traders at informal open air markets have a business license. It is difficult to obtain a clear idea of how many license traders there are in Lithuania since the period of registration and use is more flexible than a more formal business registration process. Nevertheless, the Lithuanian Statistical Office provided the following data which indicates that the total number of individuals using a business license has decreased from the period 2000 to 2003 (Figure 6.3). Nevertheless, despite this decrease, the number of license holders exceeds the total number of registered SMEs for 2000.[23]

Traders at open air markets (OAMs) in Lithuania are especially interesting from a gender point of view because in many cases, women make up the majority of traders. Below, we will focus on the characteristics of female traders at Gariunai, the largest OAM in the Baltic States.

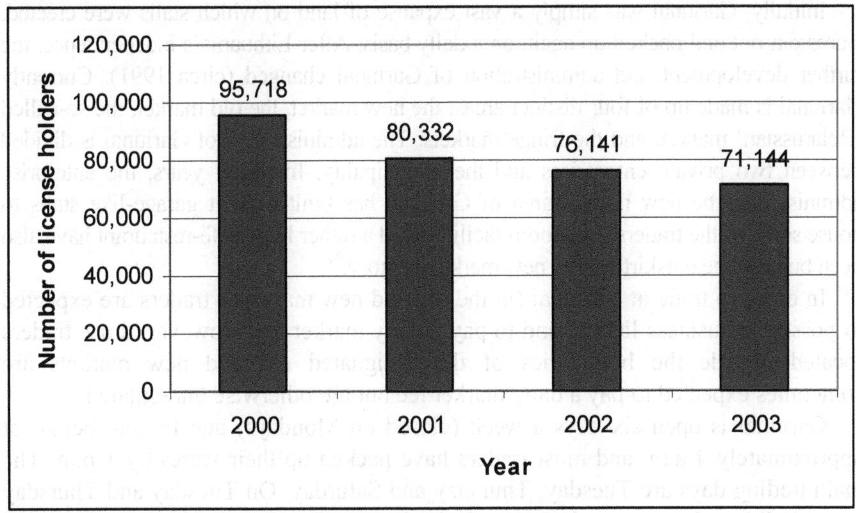

Source: SMEDA (2004).

Figure 6.3 Total number of license holders (2000-2003)

The Gariunai Market

Under the Soviet system, 'private' trading was limited to basic goods such as handmade clothing and food products (berries, mushrooms, honey, homemade jam, etc.) and was permitted in designated market areas. These market areas were usually located in the centre of cities. In Lithuania's capital city, Vilnius, the number of buyers and sellers outgrew the market areas within city limits and so in the mid 1980s local officials created a new market in an area called 'Gariunai' located about 10 km outside of Vilnius proper. The Gariunai market has been in existence for over 15 years.

Gariunai has gone through many changes. As with many informal markets, most individuals associate a level of criminality with Gariunai. This association is reasonably substantiated given Gariunai's history. In the early 1990s, during the initial 'transition' chaos in Lithuania, Gariunai exploded into a massive market where a wide range of legal and illegal goods was sold. In those days, one could come to Gariunai to buy a new winter coat, a used western-made car or an automatic pistol. Racketeering was prevalent as were incredible profits. According to one trader, after a day of good trading, you could buy yourself a used car, and in a week, you had earned enough money to buy a house.

Initially, Gariunai was simply a vast expanse of land on which stalls were erected, wares put out and packed up again on a daily basis. After Lithuania's independence, the further development and administration of Gariunai changed (circa 1991). Currently Gariunai is made up of four distinct areas: the new market, the old market, the so-called 'Belarussian' market, and the fringe markets. The administration of Gariunai is divided between two private enterprises and the municipality. In recent years, the enterprise administering the new market area of Gariunai has built cement garage-like stalls to house some of the traders. Restroom facilities and a rather large café-restaurant have also been built on the outskirts of the new market territory.[24]

In order to trade at Gariunai (in the old and new markets), traders are expected to possess a business license and to pay a daily market fee. However, those traders located outside the boundaries of the designated old and new markets are sometimes expected to pay a daily market fee but are otherwise unregulated.

Gariunai is open six days a week (closed on Mondays) and trading begins at approximately 4 a.m. and most traders have packed up their wares by 1 p.m. The main trading days are Tuesday, Thursday and Saturday. On Tuesday and Thursday most 'bulk' trades are conducted early in the morning whereas on Saturday most buyers are individual buyers from Lithuania. The number of traders is constantly shifting and varies due to the day of the week and seasonal influences. There are no official statistics regarding the number of traders at Gariunai.[25] A rough count of traders on a busy day (Tuesday, Thursday and Saturday) is approximately 4,000 stalls. On the less busy days (Wednesday, Friday and Sunday) there are approximately 1,000 to 2,000 stalls. Many traders work in teams of two individuals (often husband-wife teams) so on a busy day we could expect approximately 8,000 traders and on a slow day 2,000 to 4,000 traders to be working at the market.

Characteristics of Female and Male Traders

Both personal and business characteristics of 65 traders at Gariunai were collected based on semi-structured interviews[26] (see Table 6.5). The majority of traders did not consider Lithuanian to be their native language. We used this question as a proxy for identity. Moreover, only a slight majority of traders possessed a reasonable command of the Lithuanian language. The rest either did not speak Lithuanian well or did not speak it at all. This is surprising given the fact that officially less than 20 per cent of the population of Lithuania are non-Lithuanians.[27] Most of the non-Lithuanians trading at Gariunai were Russian, Polish, Belarussian or other Slavic-language speakers. Some traders were ethnically Azerbaijanis although they had been living and working in Lithuania for many years. In addition, a small number of Vietnamese traders have moved to Lithuania mainly from Russia[28] in order to trade at Gariunai.

Given the 'sinister' and 'dangerous' stereotypes of the Gariunai market, one would expect a 'masculine' environment to prevail. This was probably the case in the past, but not now. The majority of the traders interviewed were women and this was a reflection of the general composition of traders at Gariunai. In twenty per cent of the cases, couples were working together in a 'family business' often with a clear division of labour: the husband helped with setting up and taking down the stall while the wife's primary duty was sales.

The traders interviewed ranged in age from 23 to 65 years of age. The average trader's age was 42 years. Almost all the traders had previous work experience in a state-owned enterprise and less than a fourth of the traders had previous trade experience. In terms of education, nearly a fourth of the traders had university education. Table 6.5 provides some further characteristics of Gariunai traders. Most traders owned their businesses and less than a fourth were hired employees. The vast majority had not set up an official business structure (such as a sole proprietorship or corporation) but traded using a renewable trading license. The individual trading operations tended to be small, with the average number of employees being less than one. Though most traders did not legally employ family members, our observations confirm that a large number of traders do not work alone and are most likely assisted by family members on an unofficial basis. For the majority of traders interviewed, their trading activities were not temporary in nature and the 'average' trader had been trading for approximately five years. Close to sixty per cent of the traders stated economic reasons as their main motivation for starting trading activities at Gariunai. Only two per cent stated that they were motivated by the desire to have their own business. This is in strong contrast to the responses of non-license trading SME owners where 42 per cent of the SME owners started their businesses because 'they always wanted to have their own business' and only 34 per cent had started their business due to 'economic reasons' (i.e. they needed money).[29]

Table 6.5 General characteristics of Gariunai traders

Characteristics	Category	Per cent	N
Native language	Lithuanian	32	65
	Non-Lithuanian	68	
Command of the Lithuanian language	Good	54	65
	Poor	17	
	Not at all	29	
Sex	Male	39	65
	Female	61	
Husband – Wife teams (co-preneurs)	Yes	20	65
	No	80	
Education	University or equivalent	23	62
	Other	77	
Previous work experience	State-owned sector	84	62
	Unemployed	5	
	Other	11	
Business ownership	Yes	77	65
	No – hired employee	23	
Business type	Trading license	82	61
	Other	18	
Do you employ family members?	Yes	40	65
	No	60	
Business motivation	Economic reasons	59	49
	Always wanted my own business	2	
	Other	39	
Where do you acquire your merchandise? Primary source			59
	Lithuania	44	
	Poland	25	
	Other	31	
Gariunai as main source of income	Yes	95	64
	No	5	
Would you stop trading at Gariunai if you were offered a better paying job?	Yes	76	50
	No	24	
Main barriers: First choice	Low purchasing power	*40*	*60*
	Too few customers	*20*	*60*
Main barriers: Second choice	Customs	18	45
	Mean	**SD**	
Age of trader	42.74	10.32	65
Number of employees	0.48	0.77	65
Year started trading at Gariunai	1994	2.79	54

N = total number of responses; SD = standard deviation.

Source: Aidis (2003c, p. 90).

In general, most of the merchandise sold at Gariunai does not originate from Lithuania but is brought in from elsewhere, most notably Poland but also Turkey, Greece and even China. Many traders interviewed are travelling to other countries to buy merchandise that they then resell at Gariunai. In this sense, Gariunai seems to play a significant role in international trade activities.

For the vast majority of interviewees, trading at Gariunai was their main source of income. Most others cited additional economic reasons such as no jobs available or lack of job availability with reasonable salaries and the need for supplemental income in addition to meagre disability or pension payments.[30] Three-fourths of the respondents said they would stop trading if they were offered a decent job elsewhere.

Our own assessment of the situation indicates another underlying motivation. It is likely that the majority of traders are selling at Gariunai because their command of the state language (Lithuanian) is too weak to obtain reasonable employment in the formal labour market. In addition, a number of traders work at Gariunai because they make a good living off their sales, better than if they worked elsewhere. Finally a smaller number have become traders due to family ties and established cross-border networks engaged in trade activities.

In response to the main barriers encountered by the traders interviewed, low purchasing power and too few customers was the most frequent response and primary concern. Low purchasing power results in fewer customers. According to long-time traders at Gariunai, there has been a rapid decline of customers at the market. One trader commented that several years ago, he was not able to see the traders on the other side of the walkway because of the thick crowd of customers. This is definitely not the case anymore. In this regard, the situation for traders at Gariunai and SME owners in Lithuania is similar. SME owners in Lithuania identified low purchasing power as a primary barrier to their business operations (Aidis, 2003c). Furthermore, the traders indicated customs and high OAM costs as barriers. Customs is a barrier that affects traders at Gariunai for two reasons. Firstly, it affects the seemingly large number of traders that bring in their merchandise from other countries and secondly, it affects sales to foreign customers who buy goods at Gariunai with the intent of bringing them back to their home country. If customs regulations change, as they have in the past, such as by increasing customs duties and restricting quantities of tax-free import/export, sales and supply at Gariunai can be drastically reduced. High OAM costs refers to costs such as the unofficial 'rental cost' of specific stall locations at Gariunai, daily market fees and automobile entrance fees as well as the threat of fines issued during random checks by inspection officials.[31]

Female Trader: What motivates them to trade?

When we compare our female respondents to our male respondents we find that a significantly higher percentage of female traders started trading at Gariunai because they had lost their jobs. Male traders were more frequently motivated to trade at Gariunai because it was more profitable than other activities. However, there were also other motivations given for trading at Gariunai by female traders that indicated a rather more positive motivation for trading. In this section, we will discuss the variety of motivations expressed by the 43 female traders interviewed at Gariunai. The diversity of responses is illustrated in figure 6.4.

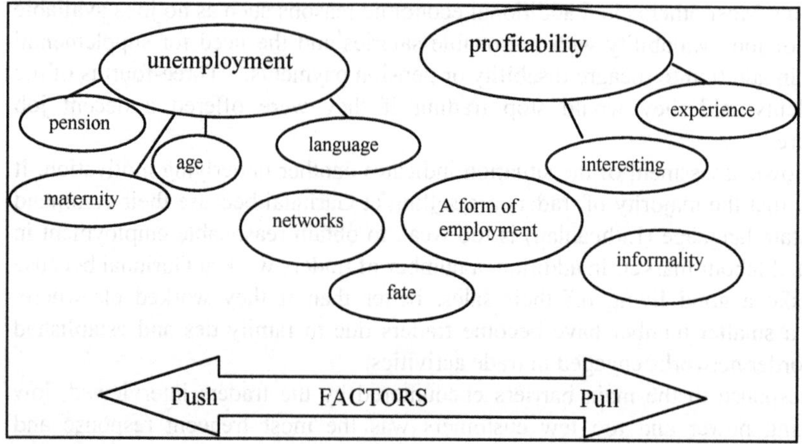

Source: Author.

Figure 6.4 Factors affecting the motivation to become a female trader

The most extreme push factor is clearly unemployment. Within this category, most female traders stated that they had lost their jobs and several explicitly said that their previous state-owned employer had gone bankrupt. Two respondents specifically stressed that their age (50 and 54 years) was a barrier to obtaining formal employment elsewhere. Two other women (aged 28 and 35) lost their jobs while on maternity leave and began trading as a way to make a 'decent' income. Given the low levels of minimum pensions in Lithuania (approximately $ 34.50 USD per month)[32] many pensioners must seek employment to supplement their monthly pensions and two female traders fell into this category. Finally, limited Lithuanian language skills that restrict further employment possibilities, was the explicitly stated motivation for two native Russian speaking women. But as previously discussed, this motivation most likely played an influential role for many other traders at Gariunai.

On the push/pull spectrum of motivations, the more neutral space is occupied by three different types of female traders: those who began trading because of informal networks, due to fate, and as a form of 'official employment'. In the network group, we encountered three female traders who all began trading at Gariunai because they had either family or friends trading there. Even though they may have lost their jobs or have limited job opportunities elsewhere, through their informal networks they were able to secure an income through trading. One female trader remarked that 'fate' was the reason she was trading at Gariunai. This response illustrates a general sentiment shared by many Lithuanians that feel a lack of control over their livelihoods during the transition process. Interestingly enough, for two of our respondents, trading at Gariunai was their official formal job that they had obtained by responding to an employment advertisement in the newspaper. Neither of them realized that their employment would entail trading at an OAM and not behind a sales counter in one of the many shops located downtown.

Moving towards the other end of our spectrum, we encountered four other types of female traders motivated by pull factors. The main type of female trader here is motivated by profitability. Five of our respondents stated specifically that they were trading for profit. One respondent had already been trading at Gariunai even during the Soviet period and for her, the continuation of trading was the further application of her previous experience. At the beginning, her trading at Gariunai was an informal undertaking in addition to official state employment. But when she lost her official job in a state-owned enterprise, she switched to full-time trading. The motive of informality was highlighted by one female respondent, a native Russian speaker in her sixties. She was not a Lithuanian citizen but had come to live with her daughter (who was legally residing in Lithuania). Trading at Gariunai allowed her to make an informal additional income for herself. Finally, one of our respondents specifically stated that she was trading at Gariunai because it was more interesting and more socially engaging than her official profession as a seamstress. This respondent decided very consciously to quit her formal job to become a trader at Gariunai.

At first glance, female traders at Gariunai may seem like a homogenous category but by exploring their motivations, we reveal a broad range of reasons for trading ranging from push to pull factors. A large portion of the female traders are at Gariunai in order to make ends meet for themselves and for their families. It provides an important source of income. For others, it provides more than just an income opportunity: it allows them to apply their skills in an interesting and profitable way. Though these categorizations may seem static, they should be viewed as dynamic and prone to change over time. A woman who feels she has been pushed into entrepreneurship may feel the pull of entrepreneurship under certain conditions such as increasing profitability. It is therefore of importance not only to focus on an entrepreneur's motivation for starting their business venture but on other external factors that can affect business success including governmental policies.

Before we explore the role of government policies, a few additional issues regarding female traders such as the magnitude of female trading and the categorization of female traders as entrepreneurs are discussed.

Why are there so many Female Traders?

We found that the majority of traders at Gariunai were female. Since women are traditionally highly represented in retail trade and petty trading activities, this does not come as a complete surprise. However, this counters the observations made by Czako and Sik (1999), that most traders in Hungarian OAMs are male. There may be several reasons for the higher proportion of female traders at Gariunai. Firstly, it may be a consequence of the large decline in female employment in Lithuania, reflecting the difficulty many unemployed women have in finding new employment especially in the private sector. Having said this, all individuals who lost their previous jobs and are middle aged have a difficult time finding employment in Lithuania and it is for this reason why we probably encountered traders who were for the most part in their forties. Secondly, women in general seem to have better developed communication skills and this may lead to better sales and greater trading success for female rather than male traders. Thirdly, our interviewees suggest that Gariunai has become less profitable and the reduced potential earnings of traders at Gariunai could be another reason why we encounter fewer male traders. Although respective statistics are not available, anecdotal evidence indicates that the Gariunai market was dominated by male traders in the early to mid 1990s but the presence of male traders diminished in the late 1990s. This change coincides with several external factors such as the Russian rouble crisis in 1998 and the tightening of borders limiting the access for customers from Russia. Both of these factors significantly contributed to diminishing the profitability of trading at Gariunai. As a result, it seems that female traders are more prevalently represented in areas where profitability is lower than in areas where male traders are more dominant. It may be possible that this is the core reason for the greater male trader presence at Hungarian OAMs than at Gariunai.

Are Female Traders likely to continue Trading?

In the previous discussion we have established that female traders make up the majority of traders at Gariunai and we have discussed the possible reasons for this situation. The next important question is whether market trading will remain attractive for female traders. A number of factors play a role in this development. Most importantly, however, is the persistence of barriers to obtain reasonable employment in the formal labour market faced by many women. As long as these barriers continue, one can expect women to be pushed into trading as one of the few viable options for making a decent income.

Another related issue is the continued viability of OAMs in the Lithuanian context. Some OAMs seem to be decreasing in size and scope as they encounter increasing competitive pressures from the 'indoor' sector. Yet, despite of these pressures, well-established OAMs such as Gariunai seem to continue to attract large numbers of customers. In spite of a boom in hypermarkets in and around Vilnius, trading at Gariunai continues to survive. An important influence is Gariunai's reputation for low prices. This is especially important for buyers coming from other regions or countries. These foreign buyers know what they can expect at Gariunai while they do not know what they can expect from one of the nearby hypermarkets. Though the traders themselves feel that they do not build relationships with their clients, the clients seem to build a relationship with the market. Since the Gariunai market is known, it reduces uncertainty and transaction costs even though other alternatives are present.

In 2004, the further institutionalization of the Gariunai market took place with the increasing number of solid concrete trading stalls and the transparent overhead covering for the walkways to protect foot traffic from inclement weather that have been built. In addition, construction is underway in the surrounding area of the Gariunai market. More permanent stalls and storage spaces are being built. Two banks have set up branch offices and cash machines near the market entrance. Given these new developments, it seems Gariunai will not disappear any time soon.

Lithuania's recent EU membership presents a number of opportunities and threats for OAMs like Gariunai. In terms of opportunities, OAMs may be able to further develop their strengths such as the ability to respond rapidly to changing customer demands (due in part to their low stock investments) and by providing low cost alternatives to 'indoor' shop goods. In this way, traders may continue to capitalize on the OAM's reputation as an 'inexpensive' market tailoring to customer tastes. However, there are also a number of threats that may affect OAM traders as a result of EU membership. It is highly likely that the Lithuanian government will emphasize the formalization of SME structures squeezing out less formalized SME types such as license traders. In addition, increasing competition from hypermarkets competing for increased market share through price wars could conceivably exert a heavy blow to OAM traders since they tend to have less price flexibility due to their relatively low profit margins on a smaller range of goods. Lower profitability would result in reduced income for OAM traders and more difficulty in deriving a 'decent income' from their trading activities.

Are Female OAM Traders Entrepreneurs?

The exact classification of what constitutes entrepreneurial behaviour and who exactly can be classified as an entrepreneur in the transition setting is a highly contested issue. On the one hand there are authors such as Scase (2000) who argue that, in general, OAM traders do not constitute a form of entrepreneurship. According to Scase, entrepreneurs are interested in growing their businesses and as such save their earned profits to reinvest in their venture. While female OAM traders tend to consume their profits. On the other hand, authors such as Aidis (2003a, 2003c) have argued that OAM traders constitute a form of entrepreneurship. These traders have been able to adapt their activities not only to the changing demand of extremely price sensitive customers, but also to the ever-changing regulatory environment that characterizes Lithuania's transitional process. Their activities are further productive to the extent that they provide a decent income for themselves and their families. Although it is unclear to what extent traders engage in bribery and corruption in order to bring their goods to market, in general we find OAM traders activities to be a form of 'productive entrepreneurship'. However, a precise classification remains difficult since entrepreneurship constitutes a dynamic process. It is likely that a majority of traders who are now motivated by profit (pull factors) began their trading activities out of necessity (push factors). Similarly, a number of the interviewed traders who are trading out of necessity now, may become more opportunity oriented later. It seems that a more important question to ask is how can the productive entrepreneurial qualities of OAM trading be further enhanced and supported through governmental policy.

Conclusions

The transition from a Soviet republic to an independent market-oriented country brought dramatic changes to the lives of both Lithuanian men and women. One of the most fundamental changes has been the legalization of all forms of private business ownership. In Lithuania, as in many other transition countries, private enterprise mushroomed during the initial transition period in the early 1990s. The combination of increasing regulations coupled with decreasing business opportunities due to increasing competition seem to have resulted in the declining numbers of new private enterprises in the late 1990s. As a result, there is an increasing need for governmental support for the SME sector. In recent years, the Lithuanian government has been implementing new programmes and projects for SMEs. Lithuania's EU membership will facilitate this process through the harmonization of legislation and programmes directed at SMEs.

There is also increasing attention being directed towards female entrepreneurs. Although the total number of new private enterprises is decreasing, the percentage of female business owners is increasing to more than 43 per cent in 2002. However, in Lithuania as in many other countries, there exists a gap between policy development and actual implementation of these policies. In the past, implementation has been weak. There is an increased need for policymakers to actively engage with entrepreneurs and seek out the actual policy impact through interactions with non-governmental organizations representing entrepreneurs. Furthermore it is important for governmental officials to specifically engage in dialogue with representatives of different types of SME owners including license holding traders in order to obtain a clearer understanding on how existing policies or policy changes affect or potentially will affect these SME owners. Finally, the increased visibility of female entrepreneurs through more balanced and broader press coverage is crucial in order to raise public awareness of the economic and social contribution of female entrepreneurs to Lithuania's national development. Some efforts have been made but given the importance of stimulating and supporting the growth of female entrepreneurship, additional attention needs to be paid to this issue.

This chapter drew special attention to the characteristics and motivations of female license traders at OAMs. Interviews with female traders at the OAM in Gariunai indicates that for many people trading is an activity of last resort in order to make an income when only few other options are available, though some of our other respondents were trading because it was profitable. Could these individuals go on to expand and grow their activities to lead to viable businesses? It is hard to answer this question due to lack of available data. Anecdotal information does point out that a number of traders have moved on to start up formal businesses in town. The further development of entrepreneurship is clearly influenced by its environment and this is an area where the Lithuanian government has played little attention. Though, the Lithuanian government has begun to provide services for SMEs, traders seem to remain a blind spot in their policies. Given the important role that OAMs like Gariunai play in terms of employment of disadvantaged groups such as older women, Russian speaking Lithuanian residents, supplementing pensions, and providing a starting point for entrepreneurship, it may be of interest for the government to further enhance trading at Gariunai. This can be done by improving the working conditions at Gariunai and by actively promoting the further formal business development of traders through targeted programmes and information.

Notes

1 Although the term 'small and medium-sized enterprises' (SME) is widely used, its definition varies greatly from country to country. The official Lithuanian definition for SMEs (harmonized to European Union legislation and in effect since January 2003) includes all registered businesses (or license holders) which have less than 250 employees. Prior to this new definition, registered businesses with less than 50 employees were officially considered SMEs. In practice, policies are still focused on SMEs that have less than 50 employees. In this chapter, we use the de facto definition of SMEs as businesses with less than 50 employees.

2 In December 1905, the Great Parliament of Vilnius acknowledged the principles of equality between women and men which should be put into practice in an Independent Lithuania. In 1922, women's right to vote and legal gender equality was confirmed in the Lithuanian Constitution.

3 New evidence is emerging that illustrates the legislative inequalities that occurred within the so-called egalitarian Soviet system. For example, in the Soviet Union, females applying for a driver's license were required to pass a gynaecological exam! Male applicants were expected to pass a medical exam. Apparently, the rationale was to enforce a mandatory and random health check. This law was finally revoked by the Lithuanian parliament in January 2002 (almost 12 years after independence). This rather bizarre example illustrates the contradictory practices of Soviet laws. The fact that it took almost twelve years for the independent government of Lithuania to revoke this discriminatory law indicates the resilience of Soviet practices.

4 Rai et al. (1992, p. 12).

5 Difficult and time consuming in the USSR where goods were scarce (see also Juceviciene, 1998, p. 20).

6 However, it is important to remember that the individual experience for both men and women may diverge from general group experiences. Therefore, though women as a group are discriminated against, for some women, constraints may fall away as if they never existed. Also, some constraints may be individually negotiated, while others need political or social control. Age, education, ethnic identity, marital status and number (and age) of children are some of the main factors that help explain differences in women's experiences.

7 Although illegal, anecdotal evidence indicates that private businesses are known to require a signed letter of resignation to be submitted upon hiring new female employees, which are then used in the event the employee becomes pregnant. For further discussion of how maternity leave acts against women seeking employment see Medvedev (1998).

8 In 1995, the Lithuanian policy of early retirement for women was changed and a slow increase of male and female retirement ages was initiated. By 2009 women's retirement age will have increased to 60 years and men's retirement age will reach 62.5 years. On average, women in Lithuania outlive men by 10 years and if retired at age 55 (the legal female retirement age prior to 1995), will on average, live almost 22 years on a pension (based on 1998 figures). Due to their earlier retirement age, longer life expectancy and generally lower pensions (due to lower wages) more elderly women are at risk of poverty. Furthermore given their duties as grandmothers (filling the gaps of lack of childcare facilities), pensioned women are less likely to seek re-employment (Einhorn, 1993, p. 66).

9 Such as sale of produce grown on private garden plots and the sale of handicrafts.

10 Under the Perestroika program propagated by the then Soviet leader M. Gorbachev.

11 A similar trend has been observed in Latvia (UNDP, 1998).

12 We focus our study here on legally registered private enterprises though in doing so, we are probably underestimating the true size of Lithuania's private sector. A study carried out by the Economic Research Center of Lithuania estimates that the 'underground' or informal economy accounts for 36 per cent of GDP in 1994 and 41 per cent of GDP in 1995 (World Bank, 1998). A study carried out by the Lithuanian Department of Statistics estimates that in 1995 the informal economy accounted for 23.4 per cent of GDP (Lithuanian Department of Statistics, 1997). However, using the Russian case as an example, Kontovorich (1999) argues that the preferred strategy of informal activity is to register a business but hide earnings and employment. In this case, the distortion would more greatly affect the size and profitability of reported businesses than their actual number.

13 The number of registered SMEs is likely to include a significant percentage of inactive SMEs.

14 Lithuanian Development Agency for Small and Medium-sized Enterprises.

15 For further information see: http://europa.eu.int/comm/enterprise/enterprisepolicy/charter/

16 European Charter for Small Enterprises Report – Lithuania (September 30, 2002).

17 See Commission of the European Communities (2003).

18 For a more detailed comparison see Aidis (2003b).

19 A survey was carried out by the author from September to December 2000. Questionnaires were sent out to private business owners throughout Lithuania, most of who were members of an entrepreneurship organization. Of the total respondents, 332 were SME owners (241 men and 91 women). A fifty- per cent response rate was received. Though the survey was not based on a random sample, most addresses were obtained through the membership lists of various entrepreneurship organizations in Lithuania. A SME owner met the following criteria: they had their own business, it was still in operation, they had less than 50 employees and their main business activity was not in the agricultural sector.

20 For further discussion see Chapter 7 in Aidis (2003c).

21 For a more detailed discussion see Aidis (2003a).

22 Also referred to as a business certificate.

23 This may also be true for 2001 to 2003. However, data on the total number of SMEs for these years are not yet available.

24 More recently, a hotel has been built near Gariunai.

25 The old and new markets take market fees from traders every day but the administrators of these two areas would not disclose the total number of traders.

26 From October to December 2000, ten visits were made to Gariunai and a total of 65 semi-structured interviews were carried out on a random basis with traders at the market. The interviews occurred on different days of the week and at different times of day in order to obtain a more balanced sample. The semi-structured interviews were

conducted in either Lithuanian or Russian by the author and a hired assistant who spoke Lithuanian and Russian fluently. All respondents were able to communicate freely in one of the two languages.

27 Official statistics only provide an indication of Lithuanian citizens and nationality and not language speaking ability (Lithuanian Department of Statistics, 2000). In Lithuania, citizenship and nationality can be distinctly different categories. For example, an individual can be a Lithuanian citizen but have Russian nationality. In 2001, approximately 55 per cent of the residents of the Vilnius region were of Lithuanian nationality while 42 per cent were of Polish, Russian, Belarussian, or Ukrainian nationality (Lithuanian Department of Statistics, 2002).

28 Many Vietnamese nationals found themselves far from home and without income and means of livelihood as a result of the collapse of the Soviet Union. Relying on their networks and access to cheap imports from Vietnam, many have become traders at various OAMs throughout the former Soviet Union and Eastern Europe countries.

29 For further discussion see Aidis (2003c).

30 The minimum state pension in 1999 was 138 Lt per month (approximately $ 34.50 USD) (UNDP, 2000). In April 2002, the minimum state pension was increased to 142 Lt per month.

31 In the old and new markets at Gariunai, the traders rent out segments of the market for a fee that varies depending on market location. In addition, if the traders drive their cars onto the market grounds they must pay a daily automobile fee. Also traders pay a daily market fee. Numerous inspection agencies can randomly check traders for unlawful activities such as illegal employees, selling in US dollars instead of the national currency, trading without a valid license, etc. If traders are caught breaching the regulations, they are fined.

32 See UNDP (2002).

References

Aidis, R. (1998), *Women and entrepreneurship in Lithuania: research results and recommendations*, Report, Vilnius.

Aidis, R. (2003a), 'Officially despised yet tolerated: Open-air markets and entrepreneurship in post-socialist countries', *Post-Communist Economies*, vol. 15, pp. 461-473.

Aidis, R. (2003b), 'Female small and medium-sized enterprise ownership in Lithuania: A comparison', *Journal of Baltic Studies*, vol. 14, pp. 332-353.

Aidis, R. (2003c), *By law and by custom: Factors affecting small and medium-sized enterprise development during the transition in Lithuania*, Thela Thesis, Amsterdam.

Commission of the European Communities (2003), *Report on the implementation of the European Charter for Small Enterprises in the Candidate Countries for Accession to the European Union*, Commission Staff Working Paper, SEC(2003)57, Brussels, http://europa.eu.int/comm/enterprise/enlargement/charter/.

Czako, A. and Sik, E. (1999), 'Characteristics and Origins of the Comecon Open-Air Market in Hungary', *International Journal of Urban and Regional Research*, vol. 23, pp. 607-714.

Einhorn, B. (1993), *Cinderella goes to the market: Citizenship, gender and women's movements in East Central Europe*, Routledge, London.

Grapard, U. (1997), 'Theoretical Issues of Gender in the Transition from Socialist Regimes', *Journal of Economic Issues*, vol. 21, pp. 665-686.

Hesli, V. and Miller, A. (1993), 'The gender base of institutional support in Lithuania, Ukraine and Russia', *Europe-Asia Studies*, vol. 45, pp. 505-533.

Juceviciene, P. (1998), 'Lithuanian women today: social attitudes, gender and the new economy', *Journal of Baltic Studies*, vol. 19, pp. 19-34.

Kanopienė, V. (2000), 'Lietuvos Moterų Padėtis Darbo Rinkoje' in G. Purvaneckienė and J. Šeduikienė (eds), *Moterys Lietuvoje*, Danielius, Vilnius, pp. 66-81.

Kontovorich, V. (1999), 'Has New Business Creation in Russia come to a halt?', *Journal of Business Venturing*, vol. 14, pp. 451-60.

Lakhova, Y. (1998), 'Transition - a mixed blessing for women', *Transition*, pp. 25-26.

Lithuanian Development Agency for Small and Medium-sized Enterprises (SMEDA) (2004), 'Lietuvos smulkaus ir vidutinio verslo būklė', http://www.svv.lt.

Lithuanian Department of Statistics (1997), *Neapskaitoma Ekonomika: Sampratos, Tyrimai, Problemos*, Vilnius.

Lithuanian Department of Statistics (2000), *Statistical Yearbook of Lithuania 2000*, Vilnius.

Lithuanian Department of Statistics (2001), *Statistical Yearbook of Lithuania 2001*, Vilnius.

Lithuanian Department of Statistics (2002), *Vilniaus Apskrities Gyventojai pagal lyti amziu, tautybe ir tikyba*, Vilnius.

Lithuanian Department of Statistics (2004), 'Aktyvumo, užimtumo ir nedarbo lygis' http://www.std.lt.

Medvedev, K. (1998), 'A review of women's emancipation in Hungary: Limited successes offer some hope', *Transition*, p. 26.

Molyneux, M. (1994), 'Women's rights and the international context: Some reflections on the post-Communist states', *Millennium: Journal of International Studies*, vol. 23, pp. 287-313.

Posadskaya, A. (1994), *Women in Russia: a new era of Russian feminism*, Verso, London.

Rai, S., Pilkington H., and Phizacklea A. (eds) (1992), *Women in the face of change: the Soviet Union, Eastern Europe, and China*, Routledge, London.

Rimashevskaia, N. (1992), 'Perestroika and the status of women in the Soviet Union.', in S. Rai, H. Pilkington and A. Phizacklea (eds), *Women in the face of change: the Soviet Union, Eastern Europe and China*, Routledge, London, pp. 11-19.

Scase, R. (2000), *Entrepreneurship and Proprietorship in Transition: Policy Implications for the Small- and Medium-size Enterprise Sector*, United Nations University World Institute for Development Economics Research, Helsinki.

Spevacek, A.M. (2001), 'Lithuanian Women Bear the Brunt of Transition', *Transition*, April-May-June, p. 20.

United Nations Development Programme (UNDP) (1997), *Lithuanian Human Development Report*, Vilnius.

United National Development Program (UNDP) (1998), *Latvian Human Development Report*, Riga.

United Nations Development Programme (UNDP) (1999), *Lithuanian Human Development Report*, Vilnius.

United Nations Development Programme (UNDP) (2000), *Lithuanian Human Development Report*, Vilnius.

United Nations Development Programme (UNDP) (2002), *Lithuanian Human Development Report*, Vilnius.

United Nations Children's Fund (Unicef) (1999), *Women in Transition*, Florence.

World Bank (1998), *Lithuania: An Opportunity for Economic Success*, World Bank, Washington D.C.

Chapter 7

Women Entrepreneurs in Slovenia: By Fits and Starts

Mateja Drnovšek and Miroslav Glas

Introduction

Slovenian women played an active role in the first entrepreneurial wave during the early 1990s. Two important factors played a significant role in employment decision-making: a) the economic crisis during transition threatened women with a greater psychological threat of unemployment; and b) the emergence of hidden discrimination in Slovenia, which frustrated women employed in large self-managed, or socially owned, companies, Such organizations represented a distinctive types of self management in the former Yugoslavia during the socialist period, although they were subject to political influence. A widespread belief among the population was that, as an independent entrepreneur, an individual would have a higher degree of control over their destiny. It may be argued that the participation of women in economic activities has not only resulted in the productive use of labour, but also may have improved the quality of business practices because of hypothesized differences in male and female entrepreneurs and managers in terms of women's holistic approach to problem-solving and the special care they take with customers and employees.

There are two key groups of motives in the entrepreneurship literature that trigger an individual's decision to start up their own business. Some entrepreneurs are pushed by negative circumstances (e.g. unemployment), while others are pulled by positive opportunities. Prior research in Slovenia shows that both groups of motives were at work during the transition period, although the push motives were relatively stronger than in some other countries, especially for female entrepreneurs. Further, this very specific combination of start-up motives contributes to some other recognizable aspects of female entrepreneurship. Practitioners in the field have characterized women entrepreneurs as having a different approach to men. It is suggested that they are better communicators, can manage more tasks at any given time and work well with other members of staff. The projection theory offers insights into the way women treat their employees. The basic premise is that people provide order to events consistent with their own needs, fears, desires, and ways of perceiving and responding

(Cohen, Swerdlik and Philips, 1996). If a woman starts a private business due to a feeling that she was discriminated against, or for a need for greater flexibility to better balance work and her family, she will do everything possible to offer her employees a sense of autonomy and flexible work schedules so they can also plan their private lives better.

Recently, the legislative framework in Slovenia has further enhanced equal gender job opportunities. Although gender equality is protected by several acts such as: the Act on Equal Possibilities of Women and Men, the Act on Employment Relationships, and the Act on Parental Custody and Family Allowance, the Global Entrepreneurship Monitor Report for Slovenia 2003 recently reported a sharp fall in nascent entrepreneurship among Slovenian women. However, current estimations based on sample data and interviews with key entrepreneurship experts call for a more systematic approach.

Recognizing the gap in studies on female entrepreneurship studies in Slovenia and drawing from projection theory, this research aims to answer the following questions:

- What is the contribution of women-managed businesses to gross output and employment growth in Slovenia?
- What are the overall characteristics of companies managed by women entrepreneurs in Slovenia compared to their male counterparts?
- What kind of strategies and related business challenges do Slovenian women entrepreneurs undertake?
- What are the gender-specific characteristics of managing a growing business?

To shed light on these questions we have used qualitative and quantitative research methods combined with several statistical sources. First, the present state of the development of female entrepreneurship in Slovenia is assessed through a univariate analysis of an economy-wide database of incorporated and sole-proprietor companies. Second, in order to gain an insight into the business and strategic characteristics of women-managed companies we conducted a questionnaire-based survey on a sample of the 500 fastest-growing companies in Slovenia in 2003, which was extended by a random selection of companies from Slovenia's private business sector. The survey instrument was carefully designed to cover basic demographic characteristics, entrepreneurial motives, the problems most often faced and growth aspirations, career satisfaction, performance and certain other strategy-related questions. The financial data of respondents was amended in line with their qualitative data.

In so doing, we offer implications to different readers: academic researchers, policy-makers, entrepreneurs, managers and business students. For local academic researchers this study makes important theoretical and empirical contributions to the changing role of women in our society. In relation to policy-makers, this study brings useful insights on how to design policy measures to foster dynamic entrepreneurship and entrepreneurs.

Overview of Past Research on Women's Entrepreneurship in Slovenia

As in the rest of the world, Slovenia experienced an increase in the share of female entrepreneurs in the 1990s, following the transition from a socialist to a market economy. The reasons for this are partly the same as in other developed countries, e.g. the trend towards service sectors that opened up more opportunities for women in areas where specialized labour skills were not required, and global trends increasingly favouring conditions which foster female entrepreneurship (Brush, 1990). In addition, the specific transition process removed many administrative barriers to the entry of new firms and also opened up opportunities for women.

Why was owning a business such an attractive option for women in the past? Considering the role of women in Slovenian society and business in particular, we might find controversial issues involving contradicting general views and objective facts. The socialist era proclaimed strict gender equality but, in reality, the traditional roles of women were still deeply rooted in society. The Human Development Report: Slovenia 1998 best illustrates this situation by examining the participation of women in several aspects of the public sphere.

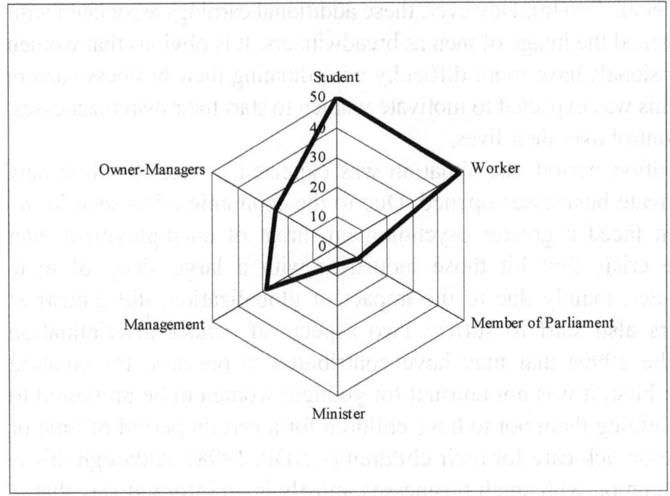

Source: UNDP (1998, p. 59); for owner-managers Glas and Drnovsek (2000, p. 11).

Figure 7.1 Women's participation in the public sphere in Slovenia, 1998

During the socialist period, Slovenian women achieved high levels of both education and employment participation. Further, women of a childbearing age did not leave the labour force and used to work full-time in paid employment until retirement age (35 years of work for women, 40 years for men), if they did not retire earlier due to poor health. However, women have never had an important share of participation in the political arena and only a few held high paid managerial jobs. In addition, the strong feminization of some sectors emerged. For example, the share of women was 81.9 per cent in health, 67.3 per cent in education and culture and women had high levels of employment in some industries encompassing many unskilled and relatively poorly paid occupations (76.6 per cent in leather and shoes, 61.4 per cent in textile), while they also occupied positions of service workers. Still, the male-female wage differentials were lower than in Western countries in the 1980s (Petrin and Humphries, 1980; Glas, 1986), on average by 20-24 per cent. However, when some differences due to work in shifts and overtime payments were excluded, in 1986 there was only 16 per cent wage differential (Kanjou, 1996).

The high level of women's participation in full-time employment also contributed to women's dual burden. Research on the quality of life in Slovenia in the 1980s found that women on average spent 28.5 hours per week doing housework and men only 7 hours, while women spent a further 23.7 hours on child-raising activities and men 17.9 hours. Men actually spent more hours in the grey economy (Glas, 1986) that was then quite extensive, with a 25 per cent share in GDP according to some estimates (Rebernik et al., 2004a). However, these additional earnings associated with this activity, strengthened the image of men as breadwinners. It is obvious that women managers and professionals have more difficulty co-ordinating their business careers and family life and this was expected to motivate women to start their own businesses, so as to gain more control over their lives.

During the transition period, the situation was expected to worsen while new opportunities for private businesses opened. Due to the economic crisis seen in the early 1990s, women faced a greater psychological threat of unemployment than men. However, the crisis first hit those industries with a large share of male workers and only later, mainly due to the impact of globalization, did industries with female workers also start to suffer. Two aspects of gender discrimination developed during the 1990s that may have contributed to pressure for creating one's own business. First, it was not unusual for younger women to be pressured to sign job contracts obliging them not to have children for a certain period of time or to organize day-care or sick-care for their children (UNDP, 1998). Although this is illegal, it is not uncommon with small businesses, mostly in an informal way that is impossible to sanction. Second, there is increased awareness of sexual harassment due to the strong social power of employers, in a situation of increased unemployment and also in fragmented micro-businesses where it is more difficult to provide any formal evidence.

Women's participation in the entrepreneurial wave received more research attention in the mid-1990s, initially with a focus on an analysis of their motives. A brief synthesis of the early research was published by Glas and Petrin (1998). Novak (1994) found the drive for autonomy, providing jobs for one's children and higher income to be the prevailing motives. According to Hribar (1997), the main reasons to start one's own business were frustration with working in larger companies (41 per cent), an identified and challenging business opportunity (32 per cent), unemployment or expected job loss (17 per cent), carrying on the family business (16 per cent) and an unsatisfactory salary (10 per cent) However, in general, women's motives did not differ from their male colleagues: the most important motive was independence, followed by the need for achievement, higher earnings, better career options (Glas and Drnovsek, 2000).

Other research compared the performance of women- and mal-managed businesses, based on financial and other criteria.. In 1995, 24.4 per cent of small incorporated businesses were managed by women; however they employed only 18.4 per cent of all workers: male-managed businesses employed 3.3 employees on average, while female-managed ones only employed 2.3 employees per firm. Women were significantly more likely to establish businesses in 'feminised' sectors (Glas and Petrin, 1998). On average, female-managed businesses had lower revenues (by 28 per cent) than those managed by men; they earned lower profits; but they also had fewer losses; fewer assets (44 per cent less); and were slightly less export-oriented. However, the liabilities/equity ratio did not suggest that female-managed businesses would have greater difficulty obtaining external finance. Similar research in 1997 shed some new light. Of the 34,791 businesses incorporated in Slovenia 23.2 per cent were managed by women, employing 17.6 per cent of all workers; while a further 4.1 per cent had joint male-female management. Again, female-managed businesses were smaller in the number of their employees, had lower revenues (68 per cent of the level of male-managed businesses), had significantly lower assets (49 per cent), less exports (56 per cent) and less profit (61 per cent); they only had fewer losses. This weaker financial performance was partly due to stronger competition in activities in which the majority of female-managed businesses are involved and generally worse financial results. In addition, women were less profit-focused; they cared more for employment and a also positive organizational culture (Glas and Drnovsek, 1998). The structure of management changed further in 1998. Of 34,620 small incorporated businesses, 17.4 per cent were female-managed, 65.7 per cent were male-managed and the share of joint management had risen to 16.9 per cent.

In Slovenia's small business and entrepreneurship development strategies, in both 1996 and 2001 women were considered a target group as an expanding source of new businesses, and a new quality of these businesses was expected:

- entrepreneurship would open up a window of opportunity for women to better exploit their abilities and ambitions in the relatively conservative social environment;
- it involves a form of economic emancipation and avoidance of gender discrimination; and
- new opportunities would open in the expanding non-profit sector (education, culture).

However, the period of relatively 'stalled' SME development early in the first decade of this new century contributed to a pessimistic picture of women's entrepreneurship drawn by GEM research in Slovenia in 2002 and 2003 (Figure 7.2). While the ratio of male to female entrepreneurs was 1.8 to 1 for all countries in the 2002 survey, this ratio was 2.2 to 1 for Slovenia, with less women planning to establish a new venture (Rebernik et al., 2004a). In 2003, this ratio increased up to 3.8 to 1 for Slovenia, thereby achieving the worst ratio among all 31 countries; the only countries close were Ireland, Japan and Denmark (Rebernik et al., 2004b).

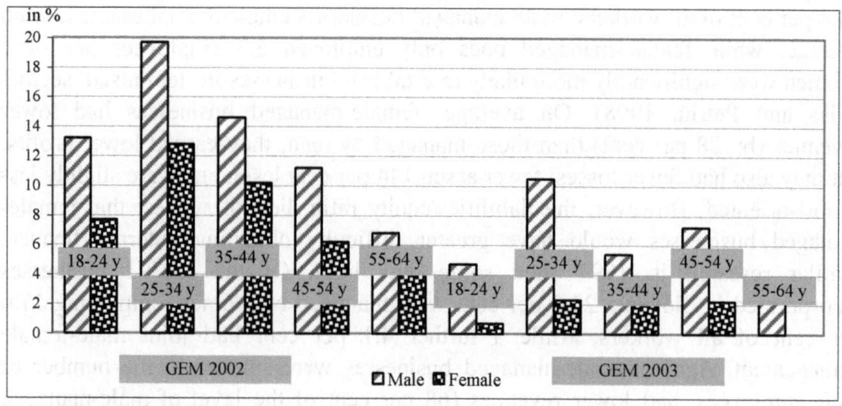

Source: Adapted from Rebernik et al. (2004a); Rebernik et al. (2004b).

Figure 7.2 Total entrepreneurship activity index for Slovenia, men and women for different age groups

The TEA (Total Entrepreneurial Activity) index shows the proportion of the adult population (18-64 years) actually engaged in setting up a new business (nascent entrepreneurs) or which already has a new business no older than 42 months (new entrepreneurs). This index is already fairly low in Slovenia, reaching 4.63 in 2002 (25th place among 37 countries) and as low as 4.05 in 2003 (24th place among 31 countries). In 2003, this index was 6.36 for men and just 1.66 for women, a sharp drop from 2002.

Overall, there is not a feeling of evident gender discrimination in Slovenia. Slovenian experts, selected from the academic, business, political and other professional communities evaluated the general climate for women entrepreneurs as favourable: their evaluation ranked Slovenia 12th in 2002 and 14th in 2003. However, the results from GEM show a rather poor participation of women in entrepreneurship. It seems that experts identify some differences that influence women participation in entrepreneurship. While experts think that starting one's own business was a socially acceptable career for women, women themselves were less positive about their access to such opportunities (Rebernik et al., 2004c). Also, the government did not undertake some specific measures to target women entrepreneurs and only for the period from 1999 to 2003 Turk (2002) noted that the government accepted the idea of supporting women through business support services. A group of women's entrepreneurship promoters were trained by a consortium in order to build a network of such experts. The Small Business Development Centre in currently supporting further activities but the impact of these measures does not look like producing a statistically recordable impact. The experts interviewed in the GEM research maintained that women have the same access as men to good business opportunities for setting up a new firm and motivation. However, women themselves were less positive about their access to such opportunities (Rebernik et al., 2004c). It is interesting though that women did not differ from men in necessity-based entrepreneurship, but mostly in opportunity-based entrepreneurship for both 2002 and 2003. Will this trend be maintained in the new century? This study seeks to answer this question.

Assessing the Business Performance of Female Entrepreneurs in Slovenia: the Present Study

Methodology and Data Sources

Women entrepreneurs are the fastest-growing group in developed countries. In Canada, for example, their number has increased by 200 per cent in the past 20 years. Women are creating three times as many businesses as men, contributing over USD 14 billion to the Canadian economy (Domeisen, 2003). To assess the economic role of women entrepreneurs in Slovenia, the financial results of incorporated businesses and private individual entrepreneurs in Slovenia in 2002 were analysed. The financial results of incorporated and sole-proprietorship companies that had the status of a registered active company in 2002 were compared with the Directory of Businesspeople in order to segregate them according to gender. Similar analyses have been previously conducted by Glas and Drnovsek (1998). Using this approach, three groups of companies were identified:

- 'women-managed companies' where all company owners were women;
- 'men-managed companies' where all company owners were men; and
- 'mixed-managed companies' where there were male and female owners of the company.

Additionally, to overview the engagement of women in the Slovenian economy, two additional perspectives have to be accounted for. First, the role women play in family businesses (which are very often registered as 'man' managed company. Second, there is an also supplementary business activity in the grey economy and households (which is estimated at some 25 per cent of gross domestic product). Unfortunately, there are no official statistical records to reliably estimate the female engagements in those roles. Moreover, the advantage of the 2004 analysis is that it covers the whole formal business (except for agricultural farms) while early research was primarily based on reported financial data of incorporated businesses. Still, there exists a considerable grey economy in Slovenia, which has been estimated to contribute 24 per cent of the official GDP: While former research pointed to significantly lower participation of women in the grey economy, due to their (unpaid) family and household activities, to our knowledge there has not been any gender related research lately.

This kind of methodological approach is novel in Slovenia since there is no established data on company results by gender that includes both sectors: incorporated and private individual entrepreneurs. Yet, this approach raises the question of the gender definition of a company. To define women and men companies, the equity shares of owners could have been used but not enough archival data was available. Instead, the gender of the managing director (in the case of incorporated businesses), or the founder of the company (in the case of private entrepreneurs), was evaluated. Finally, records from statistical (official) sources that were included in our database had to correspond with certain criteria including equity ownership and operating status. Correspondingly, all companies reporting state or private-state mixed equity were excluded. All companies registered in the financial sector (i.e. banks, insurance companies) were excluded. Duplicitous occurrences of companies were cleaned. Firms that did not realize at least 100 EUR in sales in 2002 were excluded. The process of cleaning the database yielded 30,862 useful records out of 38,052 companies in the source database (1 per cent of records was excluded). Companies that did not have data on gender (61 occurrences) were classified as 'mixed'.

The Overview of Economic Contribution of Slovenian Firms

The following section summarizes the economic contribution of Slovenian firms classified by size and gender. We calculated several economic indicators to overview and structure relative and absolute impact by types of firms.

The overall results revealed that some 17 per cent of all incorporated firms were women-managed (Table 7.1), while there were 28 per cent of women sole-proprietors (Table 7.2). The results show a significant fall in the number of incorporated women-managed businesses compared to the results of earlier studies in Slovenia (i.e. in 1995 approximately 24 per cent of all businesses were women-managed). Women-managed businesses were smaller than their male counterparts; they realized EUR 350,095 in sales per firm per year and on average employed 4 workers. Their contribution to gross sales of incorporated businesses was 9 per cent and their contribution to total employment was 10 per cent.

Within sole-proprietors, the share of women-managed businesses is considerably higher – 28 per cent with a relatively higher contribution to gross sales and gross employment (21 per cent and 27 per cent, respectively). The aggregate data

Table 7.1 Incorporated business sector by gender, 2002

Gender	No. of firms	Share of firms, %	Av. sales per firm (EUR)	Total sales (EUR)	Share of sales, %
Female	5,279	17	350,095	1,848,152,057	9
Male	19,681	64	759,162	14,941,061,974	70
Mixed	5,902	19	790,749	4,667,003,265	22
Total	30,862	100	695,231	21,456,217,296	100
Gender	**No. of employees**	**Share of employees %**	**Average employment**	**Average sales per employee (EUR)**	
Female	21,444	10	4.06	75,576	
Male	156,102	69	7.93	94,507	
Mixed	48,080	21	8.15	90,507	
Total	225,626	100	7.31	86,864	

Source: Own calculations based on IPIS-AJPES databases 2002.

Table 7.2 Private individual entrepreneurs sector by gender, 2002

Gender	No. of firms	Share of firms, %	Av. sales per firm (EUR)	Total sales (EUR)	Share of sales, %
Female	15,532	28	49,385	600,419,457	21
Male	40,719	72	63,285	2,197,502,826	79
Total	56,251	100	112,670	2,797,922,283	100
Gender	**No. of employees**	**Share of employees %**	**Average Employment**	**Average sales per employee (EUR)**	
Female	23,515	27	1.51	25,533	
Male	65,188	73	1.6	33,710	
Total	88,703	100	1.58	31,543	

Source: Own calculations based on IPIS-AJPES databases 2002.

on incorporated and sole-proprietorship firms show that 24 per cent of firms, which are women-managed contribute some 14 per cent of total employment and some 10 per cent of total sales. The gender-size structure of companies reveals a falling share of women companies as company size increases (Table 7.3). Slovenian companies are small – 98 per cent of all companies have less than 49 employees and contribute 53 per cent to total employment. There is a large share of micro businesses in the Slovenian business sector: 21 per cent of all firms had no full-time employees and 67 per cent had between 1 and 9 employees. The share of women-managed business is highest in the class size of micro businesses (1-9 employees).

Among medium and large sized Slovenian companies only 0.2 per cent are women-managed. The best represented size class is between 1-9 employees (67 per cent of all companies).

Table 7.3 Distribution of small-sized firms by size classes and gender in Slovenia, 2002

	Share of firms, %			Share of employment, %		
Size	**Female**	**Male**	**F+M**	**Female**	**Male**	**F+M**
0	4.1	12.7	4.0	-	-	-
1-9	11.9	42.1	13.0	4.1	15.9	4.9
10-24	0.8	5.5	1.4	1.5	10.9	2.8
25-49	0.2	2.0	0.5	0.9	9.4	2.3
50-99	0.1	0.9	0.2	0.6	8.3	1.5
100-249	0.1	0.5	0.1	1.1	10.7	1.8
250 +	0.0	0.2	0.1	1.3	13.9	7.9

Source: Own calculations based on IPIS-AJPES databases 2002.

Table 7.4 Distribution of firms by industry and gender in Slovenia, 2002 (in per cent)

	Share of firms (%)			Share of employment (%)			Average sales per worker in 1000 EUR		
Industry	**F**	**M**	**F+M**	**F**	**M**	**F+M**	**F**	**M**	**F+M**
Primary	0	1	0	0	2	1	51.8	106.5	54.2
Manufacturing	2	11	3	3	29	9	61.2	72.8	65.4
Construction	1	6	2	1	7	1	87.5	63.9	57.1
Trade	7	23	8	3	17	6	102.5	128.2	114.5
Transportation	1	3	1	0	3	1	114.8	96.6	93.9
Intermediation	0	2	0	0	1	0	66.4	76.1	86.1
Services	5	14	4	2	9	3	47.3	75.6	89.4
Education	0	1	0	0	0	0	45.4	36.7	33.4
Personal	0	1	0	0	0	0	35.4	49.7	60.6
Other	1	21	0	0	2	0	29.9	85.1	45.8

Companies classified according to industry sector (NACE activities: a) A-C ('primary': agriculture, hunting, forestry, fishing and mining); b) D-E ('manufacturing': manufacturing and electricity); c) F ('construction'), d) G-H ('trade': wholesale trade and retail distribution, catering), I ('transportation': transport, storage and communication); e) J ('intermediation': financial intermediation); f) K-L ('services': renting, business services, real estate); g) M ('education'); h) N-O ('personal': health and social security, personal services). – F: women-managed; M: male managed; M + F: mixed ownership.

Source: Own calculations based on IPIS-AJPES databases 2002.

The literature says that due to constraints of financial and technical skills, women-managed businesses tend to concentrate in certain sectors. Data was structured according to gender and sector. The share of women-managed companies was particularly low in the primary sector, financial intermediation, education, and personal services. Women-managed businesses concentrate in wholesale trade, retail distribution, and catering (40 per cent of all women-managed businesses, 7 per cent of all businesses) and renting, business services and real estate (28 per cent of all women-managed businesses, 5 per cent of all businesses). A considerable share of women-managed businesses (12 per cent) was also found in manufacturing.

Table 7.5 Distribution of small-sized firms by size classes and gender in the period 1998-2002

Gender	Share of firms 02	Share of firms 98	Share of employ. 02	Share of employ. 98
Female	17	17	12	13
Male	64	66	69	73
Mixed	19	17	19	14
All*	30,862	34,820	119,043	144,693
	No. of employees per firm		**Index: 1998=100**	
Gender	**2002**	**1998**	**Firms**	**Employment**	**employees per firm**
Female	2.8	2.4	87	100	117
Male	4.3	3.7	84	98	116
Mixed	3.9	2.8	99	139	139
All	3.7	3.0	89	82	124

Small firms: 0-49 employees. Share in %.
*The number of active incorporated small firms in 2002.

Source: Own calculations based on IPIS-AJPES databases 2002.

Since several empirical studies on women's entrepreneurship have been undertaken in the past, we compared the present results with the latest previous study by Glas and Drnovsek (1998). The relative data comparison does not reveal any dramatic changes or different trends in the development of female entrepreneurship in Slovenia (Table 7.5), which is not so surprising since major structural changes usually happen over a longer period than five years. The absolute number of registered small-sized companies has decreased over the period, although the employment share in the small-firm sector has been sustained. In fact, the data exhibit a positive trend of an increase in the average firm's size.

Overall conclusions can be drawn from the aggregate statistical analysis of Slovenian incorporated and sole-proprietor sector companies in order to answer our first **research question** concerning the *specific contribution of women-managed businesses to gross output and employment* in Slovenia. There were 17 per cent of incorporated women-managed businesses in Slovenia in 2002, which contributed 9 per cent of total sales and employed 10 per cent of total employment in the incorporated sector. The share of women-managed businesses in the non-incorporated sector is higher: 28 per cent of women managed businesses contributed 21 per cent of total sales and 27 per cent of total employment. Overall, 20 per cent of women managed businesses realized 17 per cent of total sales and employed 22 per cent of total employment in business sector on average in Slovenia in 2002.

Every sixth newly incorporated company in Slovenia was woman-managed while the same was true of every fourth new sole proprietorship in 2002. Women-managed companies are much smaller than men-managed companies. The size difference between women- and men-managed incorporated businesses is a bit less than double in terms of employment and a bit more than double in terms of sales, which implies that performance in terms of sales per worker is relatively higher in women-managed firms than in men-managed firms. The difference between women- and men-managed businesses is smaller in the sole-proprietor sector, implying less variance in the growth ambitions and goals of that group of entrepreneurs. Moreover, a bivariate statistical analysis of the aggregate data on women's entrepreneurship in Slovenia further supports the finding that women-managed firms are smaller than men-managed firms in both groups: incorporated and sole-proprietor sector (Chi Sq = 491.7; $\alpha = 0.00$; DF = 7). Men-managed companies are 1.3 times bigger in terms of sales and 1.05 times bigger in terms of the number in full-time employment. However, those results were not controlled by the age of firm in the year of calculation, since data had not been available. Correspondingly, one may speculate that those differences partly reflect differences in age of firms.

Women-managed Companies: Sporadic Progress

Survey Design and Sample Characteristics

In order to gain a good understanding of entrepreneurship processes in women-managed businesses we collected data survey on a stratified sample of Slovenian companies. For these purposes, the survey instrument incorporated specific questions referring to the following characteristics in order to answer the second research question of this study, which refers to strategic characteristics of women-managed companies in Slovenia. Survey questions incorporated the following topics:

- Present operations of a firm;
- Entrepreneurial leadership;
- Competitive advantages;
- Objective and subjective performance measures;
- Management competencies;
- Personal characteristics of entrepreneurs.

Our initial ambition was to acquire in-depth survey data on dynamic Slovenian companies. The sample consisted of all companies that in 2003 were listed as the 500 fastest-growing companies in Slovenia; 50 companies on this list were women-managed. Unfortunately, in the first round only 6 per cent of companies from the list (19 men-managed and 8 women-managed) answered our postal questionnaire. That is why the initial sample had to be extended. We created an additional random sample of 200 companies; half of them being man-managed and half of them being women-managed. We personally contacted the companies in the sample to ensure a satisfactory response rate. Our final sample thus included 109 dynamic and typical Slovenian companies with an approximately equal representation of companies according to gender (57 firms in the sample are man-managed and 52 companies are women-managed). The sample is thus stratified since it does not reflect the real picture of Slovenian firm distribution by gender. The average age of a sample company is 11 years; 10 per cent of companies started before Slovenia's transition (1989), 59 per cent of companies started between 1990 and 1994, 24 per cent between 1995 and 1999 and 7 per cent in 2000 or later. There were no gender-specific significant differences. The sample structure according to industry sector was representative economy-wise and was the following: 3 per cent of companies were in the primary sector, 33 per cent in manufacturing, 5 per cent in construction, 34 per cent in trade, 3 per cent in transport, 20 per cent in real estate and business services and 2 per cent were classified as other.

The General Characteristics of Firms

The following section exhibits survey findings in terms of: a) start up and business gestation process characteristics; b) the nature of business making, and c) socio-demographic characteristics of firms.

Start up and business gestation process The majority of entrepreneurs financed the start-up using their own savings (69 per cent), or saving from their families, relatives, and friends (9.4 per cent). Other sources of *initial capital* included: banks (2.8 per cent), government support (1.8 percent), suppliers (4.7 per cent), customers (2.8 per cent) and other. There are no statistically significant differences by gender; however 72 per cent of female founders used their own savings in comparison to 66 per cent of their male counterparts. Correspondingly, 73 per cent of entrepreneurs hold the majority of *ownership*, 2 per cent of respondents said they only have up to 5 per cent of the company ownership, 17 per cent of respondents has up to 10 per cent of ownership and some 13 per cent between one-tenth and one-third of ownership. Before starting the present company 33 per cent of them had between 11 and 19 years of *work experience*; 21 per cent had 1 to 10 years of prior experience, while 7 per cent did not have any work experience at all. The majority of entrepreneurship projects are *team projects*: 26 per cent per cent of respondents manage their firms by themselves, while 74 per cent have at least one partner. In most cases, there are two founders (41 per cent) or between 3 to 5 founders (18 per cent). This opens opportunities of ownership in other projects: 27 per cent of respondents acknowledged they were owners in other companies and with significant gender differences. 35 per cent of male respondents are owners in other companies, while only 18 per cent of female respondents said they owned other projects (Chi Sq.=3.9, α=0.05, DF=1).

Nature of business making Businesses in our sample mostly sell to other businesses, accounting for more than 50 per cent of their sales, followed by retailers and direct sales to end customers, only some 10 per cent of business is with public institutions. Women tend to have businesses that sell a larger number of services and products, probably reflecting their larger share of trade and service businesses. Interestingly enough, women think that a larger share of staff is doing research and development tasks, although it is not significantly larger. Men- and women-managed businesses do not differ significantly in the perception of their prices and quality as compared to their competition, although more men-managed businesses think their prices are lower than the competitors'. Both types business consider their quality as superior to the competition, with this view being stronger with women. Generally, about 40 per cent of both men and women managers think their businesses would suffer if they left the firm, while one-third consider they have good prospective successors. While it is generally assumed that women are better organized, almost exactly the same share of businesses, 66 per cent, are used to writing annual business plans, which is above what one would expect from consultants' experience with Slovenian SMEs. It is interesting though that 73 per cent of women and 66 per cent of men admit the firm has already experienced a crisis in its business. The difference in the character of firms is shown by the 33 per cent of men- and 25 per cent of women-managed businesses that were created in order to exploit the advantages of new technology.

Socio-demographic characteristics of entrepreneurs When socio-demographic characteristics of entrepreneurs are examined, 73 per cent of respondents were *married*, 8 per cent divorced, 5 per cent widowed and the others were single. The majority of respondents (60 per cent) had two *children*. The sampled entrepreneurs have an above-average *education* since the majority has a university education (71 per cent), with an additional 2 per cent holding a postgraduate degree, while just 22 per cent has a high school education and 4 per cent has finished vocational school or less. Nevertheless, a good majority of the respondents (70 per cent) plan to continue their education. Indeed, half of the respondents actually spend between 20-29 additional working days per year attending seminars. This corresponds to the common sense notion that the more highly educated someone is the stronger is their need for additional knowledge improvements. Moreover, the majority of respondents (38 per cent) are seasoned business people with 25 years of work experience on average, while an additional 21 per cent of them have more than 30 years of experience. A good tenth of them have less than 10 years of experience. Their work experience is mixed: marketing (16 per cent), development and technology (2 per cent), production

(3 per cent), finance (10 per cent), human resource management (3 per cent), while a large majority of respondents list a more general profile of practical experience involving at least two specialized areas, for example, finance and human resource management (7 per cent) or marketing, production and technology (7 per cent). However, most respondents with experience (76 per cent) gained their experience as job-takers rather than job-makers. Women entrepreneurs are more likely to have family members or friends who are entrepreneurs: 45 per cent of female respondents said they have family members with entrepreneurship experience in comparison to 33 per cent of their male counterparts. There were no gender-specific differences on the sources of initial capital, ownership, work experience and selected socio-demographic characteristics.

Gender-Specific Characteristics of Entrepreneurs

Drawing from projection theory we identified key business aspects where women entrepreneurs are most likely to differ from their male counterparts:

- Financing and relationships with professional partners;
- Support through strong ties (family);
- Start up motives and goal-setting;
- Business strategy characteristics.

Financing and relationships with professional partners This aspect comes from the many instances showing that female entrepreneurs have found their gender to be a barrier when finding sources of formal financing. While *financing* is a problem for every entrepreneur, for women entrepreneurs the problem is often more acute (Hisrich and Brush, 1986). Sexton and Bowman-Upton (1990) listed the most important reasons for the barriers women experience in finding finance. Women generally possess fewer personal funds due to their previous experience of being in a less qualified position; women tend to go into retail trade or services, which are less capital-demanding; and they prefer to rely mostly on their own or relatives' savings rather than going into debt. The second bias is also supported in the literature on marriage and family, which indicates that women are more likely than men to have domestic responsibilities. Women entrepreneurs are more inclined to divide their time between their families and jobs than to spend time for themselves and recreational activities (Hisrich and Brush, 1986). Ram (1996) found that, although entrepreneurship was a fulfilment of women entrepreneurs' needs for autonomy, they gave maximum importance to their husband, children, and relationships with them, while their careers only came later in priority.

In our research data, there were gender-specific differences seen between men and women in the *relationships* they keep with banks and local authorities. There were no other statistically significant differences; the majority of respondents thought that their gender did not affect business-making in terms of getting finance and relationship management. However, it is evident (Table 7.6) that women respondents thought that the fact they were women many times actually helped them in business-making, with the exception of dealing with officials.

Table 7.6 Gender-related effects on the ease of business-making (in per cent)

Does your gender matter?	Relationship with banks		Relationships with bus. partners		Relationships with customers	
	Male	Female	Male	Female	Male	Female
Doesn't affect	59	62	50	35	41	37
Help	13	10	32	39	36	39
Hinder	0	4	4	8	4	6
Can't say	9	6	5	8	5	18
Not relevant	19	18	9	10	14	8
Does your gender matter?	**Relationships with suppliers**		**Subordinates**		**Local authorities**	
	Male	**Female**	**Male**	**Female**	**Male**	**Female**
Doesn't affect	48	48	43	30	54	42
Help	29	34	34	36	14	12
Hinder	2	4	2	8	0	8
Can't say	3	8	7	12	13	18
Not relevant	18	6	14	14	19	20

Source: Survey on gender entrepreneurship in Slovenia, 2004.

Further, there are statistically significant differences by gender in the average number of working hours that entrepreneurs spend in their companies (Table 7.7). Male entrepreneurs tend to spend more working hours than their women counterparts due to the abovementioned household obligations the latter still have.

It is not only the number of hours physically spent in the company by which entrepreneurs differ; there are also significant differences in the number of hours per week entrepreneurs dedicate to talking and discussing business issues with: family members (7.7 hrs); friends (3.8 hrs); members of different informal clubs (1.4 hrs); business partners (13.8 hrs); potential new customers (6.1 hrs); professional consultants (1.6 hrs); members of government organizations (1 hr); members of business associations (0.8 hr); and lawyers and solicitors (1.4 hrs). There are meaningful differences by gender and the number of hours entrepreneurs spend in dealing with government officials, with women entrepreneurs tending to spend fewer hours dealing with government officials than their male counterparts.

Table 7.7 Number of hours spent in the company per week (in per cent)

Weekly hours at work	Male	Female
Less than 40 hours	2	2
40 - 50 hours	32	56
50 - 80 hours	55	33
More than 80 hours	11	9
Significance	Chi Sq.=6.6, α=0.09, DF=3	

Source: Survey on gender entrepreneurship in Slovenia, 2004.

Support through strong ties We found some gender-specific differences in the relationship that entrepreneurs maintain with their families (Figure 7.3). The support an entrepreneur receives from his or her family is crucial. Half of the respondents (50 per cent) said their families supported and approved of them being entrepreneurs. Some 39 per cent of female respondents said their partners were actively involved in the firm's management.

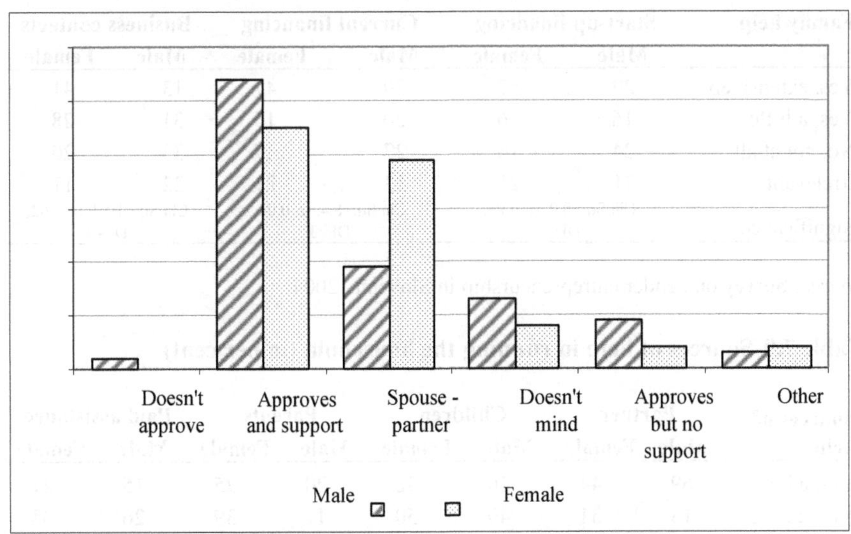

Source: Survey on gender entrepreneurship in Slovenia, 2004.

Figure 7.3 Family attitude to (support of) the business venture

Family members are an important source of providing tangible and intangible help needed by a newly founded firm, such as financing, both at start-up and of current operations; offering emotional support; mentoring and counselling; and help with premises and business contacts through social capital and personal networks.

Indeed, the survey revealed significant gender differences when the family's role in start-up and current operations financing and business contacts through social capital and personal networks were considered.

Family help in start-up financing was crucial for 57 per cent of women-managed business, but significantly less for male-managed businesses (Table 7.8). Likewise, family help is crucial in financing current operations for 47 per cent of women-managed business, which is significantly higher than for their male counterparts. The most significant gender difference is the role the family plays in providing business contacts, where 41 per cent of female respondents assign the importance of family business contacts in comparison to 13 per cent of their male counterparts. Moreover, help and support from family members is not only crucial in managing the venture but also in managing the household. Unsurprisingly, there are statistically significant differences by gender and the help that a respondent can expect from his or her marital partner and parents.

Table 7.8 Types of support in business-making offered by family by gender (in per cent)

Family help	Start-up financing		Current financing		Business contacts	
	Male	Female	Male	Female	Male	Female
Yes, extensively	29	57	20	47	13	41
Yes, a little	16	6	20	15	31	28
No, not at all	24	16	27	17	33	20
Irrelevant	31	21	33	21	22	11
Significance	Chi Sq.=8.9, α=0.03, DF=3		Chi Sq.=8.4, α=0.04, DF=3		Chi Sq.=10.2, α=0.02, DF=3	

Source: Survey on gender entrepreneurship in Slovenia, 2004.

Table 7.9 Sources of help in running the household (in per cent)

Sources of help	Partner		Children		Parents		Paid assistance	
	Male	Female	Male	Female	Male	Female	Male	Female
Yes, a lot	69	44	20	32	20	25	15	21
Yes, a little	13	31	49	50	17	39	26	35
No, not at all	9	21	20	12	52	30	41	36
Irrelevant	9	4	11	6	11	7	18	8
Significance	Chi Sq.=10.3 α=0.02, DF=3				Chi Sq.=8.02, α=0.05, DF=3			

Source: Survey on gender entrepreneurship in Slovenia, 2004.

The data in Table 7.9 support the common notion related to gender equality that male entrepreneurs do not undertake many household-related activities, while women entrepreneurs are not excused from their traditional obligation of running the household and are, as such, actually taking on two forms of employment. Most of the help they can expect comes from their parents; for example their mothers usually help by taking care of their children, cooking and other household duties.

Nevertheless, the sampled entrepreneurs also obtain help from sources other than informal circles, such as entrepreneurship counsellors from regional development agencies, business consultants, and other professionals (Figure 7.4). A recent evaluation of the voucher system of consulting in Slovenia (Drnovsek, 2003) demonstrated that entrepreneurs most often searched for help in quality management (10 per cent); with finance (9 per cent); and business plan preparation (7 per cent).

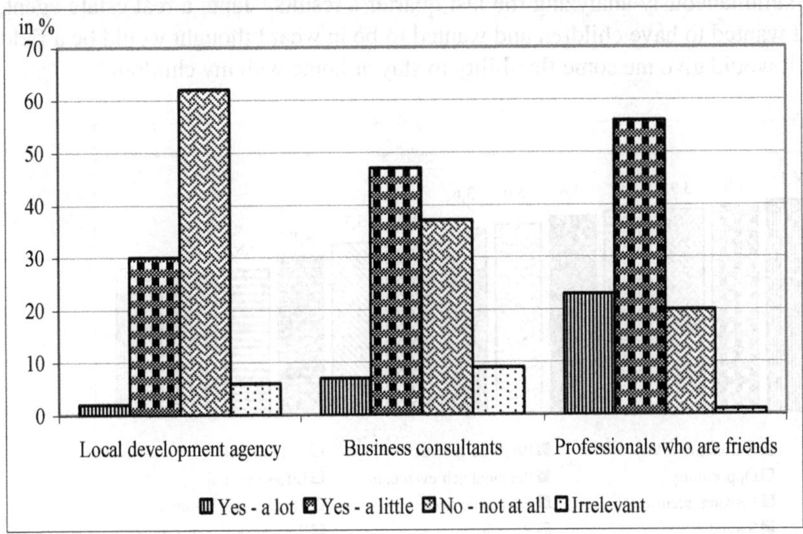

Source: Survey on gender entrepreneurship in Slovenia, 2004.

Figure 7.4 Sources of help in managing the venture

Start up motives There are two main groups of motives that trigger venture creation decisions. Some entrepreneurs are pushed by negative circumstances, such as unemployment), while others are pulled by positive opportunities, or some combination of the two, since both motives can operate as contextual, as well as specific triggers. The reasons for start-up that are most often cited by women entrepreneurs are greater career advancement, increased economic rewards, and flexibility. The decision to become an entrepreneur is the net result of circumstantial factors coming together, such as preferences for work, parental, and partner roles (Goffee and Scase, 1985; Wilkens, 1987). Entrepreneurship provides an additional work alternative when job opportunities are unavailable or do not fulfil a person's needs (Tigges and Green, 1994). A key reason women start up their own business in developed economies is to gain accessibility and flexibility that are not provided by the jobs currently available (NFWBO), since women are expected to take care of the home and children even if they have a full-time job.

Many researchers in female entrepreneurship have come to the same conclusion that the trigger for a woman to start a business is flexibility and autonomy in time-management. Unsurprisingly, this reason came out as a gender-differentiating factor in the present research. Two women entrepreneurs shared with us a practical perspective on their search for flexibility. Marija, a business consultant, stated: 'I believe that the need for flexibility in SMEs is an area where women managers can really excel – one minute answering the phone, the next minute greeting customers, whilst simultaneously analyzing the last quarter's results.' Jane, a real estate agent, said: 'I wanted to have children and wanted to be in what I thought would be a field where it would give me some flexibility to stay at home with my children.'

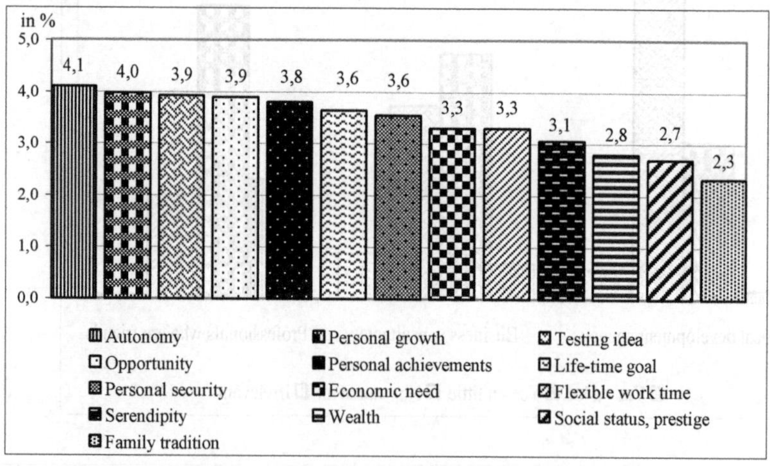

Source: Survey on gender entrepreneurship in Slovenia, 2004.

Figure 7.5 Distribution of start-up reasons by importance

The most important start-up reasons (assessed on a Likert scale with 1 'not important' and 5 'very important') are autonomy; personal growth; testing an innovative idea; opportunity recognition; personal achievements; life-time goals; personal security; economic need; flexible working time; serendipity; wealth; social status; prestige; and continuance of the family tradition (Figure 7.5).

Goal-setting theory assumes that entrepreneurs engage in tasks in pursuit of desired goals (Frese and Rauch, 2001; Markman, Balkin and Baron, 2003). Correspondingly, the level of goals people set, determines what they will do and how well they will perform in the future. We asked respondents to use a Likert-type scale (1 – not important; 5 – very important) to list the importance of the goals they have for their business-making in the forthcoming year. Interestingly, sales (Mean = 4.18) and profits (Mean = 3.95) are not the most important reported goals and only come after new knowledge acquisition (Mean = 4.28) and an increase of market share (Mean = 4.23). Other goals included: increased employment (Mean = 2.68); internationalization (Mean = 3.32); development of new products/services (Mean = 3.86); finding new financing (Mean = 3.34); termination of operations (Mean = 2.39); and shrinking the business scope (Mean = 1.67). There were gender-specific differences in the goals of increased sales and increased employment. The salience of knowledge in a company is additionally strengthened through business measures and activities undertaken to improve the company's competitive position. The most important activities undertaken in this direction were investments in the entrepreneur's own knowledge and knowledge of the employees, followed by quality improvements, marketing and distribution channel improvements. This is expressed by Helena, a hairdresser: 'Continuous improvement is important for me. I believe that constantly wanting to improve and being open to new ideas is the key to being prepared for management!'

Table 7.10 Importance of goals (in per cent)

	Sales increase		**Employment increase**		**Quality**	
Goal importance	**Male**	**Female**	**Male**	**Female**	**Male**	**Female**
Not important	2	6	17	14	2	0
Somewhat important	4	2	30	19	6	0
Important	20	10	41	45	22	10
Very important	37	19	13	10	39	29
Extremely important	37	63	0	12	31	61
Significance	Chi Sq.=9.6, α=0.05, DF=4		Chi Sq.=8.3, α=0.08, DF=4		Chi Sq.=12.3, α=0.02, DF=4	

Source: Survey on gender entrepreneurship in Slovenia, 2004.

Women entrepreneurs tend to assign greater importance to future sales expansion and employment expansion than their male counterparts (Table 7.10). This could imply that they experience greater market pressure to expand their business in order to keep up. They are also more likely to think that striving for quality services and products (M = 4.22) bring important competitive advantages. Other competitive advantages (on a Likert scale with 1 'Small advantage' and 5 'Great advantage') include: controlling a unique market niche (M = 3.49); geographical location (M = 3.30); unique technology (M = 3.14); lower price range than the competition (M = 3.25); a wide assortment of products (M = 3.56); after-sales support (M = 3.81); skilled employed (M = 4.21); access to financial sources (M = 3.43); access to critical information (M = 3.94); control over cash flow; and costs (M = 3.92), human resource management (M = 4.05), and personal contacts and networks (M = 4.05). Successful goal attainment comes through self-regulation (M = 4.07); the need for achievement (M = 4.02); dynamics (M = 3.96); social skills (M = 2.8); and autonomy (M = 3.8). Other skills have less importance.

Business strategy characteristics Traditional economic models in entrepreneurship research assumed money or profit generation to be the primary motive of entrepreneurial activity; as such, they are by far the most common measures of entrepreneurship performance. For classical economists, the entrepreneur assembled the factors of production and took on the risk of producing a product that would sell for more than the cost of production (Douglas and Shepherd, 1999). Recently, Amit et al. (2000) gave evidence counteracting the common perception that money is the only, or even the most important, motive for an entrepreneurial decision to start up a new venture. Wealth attainment turned out to be a less salient motive than other non-monetary motives such as power, lifestyle, leadership, independence and ego. Hence, there is a strong argument that, along with objective financial measures, subjective measures of venture performance should also be incorporated within performance measurement and this is how performance was measured in the present study.

Subjective *measures of performance* included: the entrepreneur's personal satisfaction with the venture's financial results (sales growth, profitability, and growth potential), the entrepreneur's satisfaction with 'soft measures' of venture performance (organizational culture, quality) and the entrepreneur's satisfaction with the achievement of his or her personal goals (autonomy, time flexibility, personal growth). Objective measures of performance included: sales volume; sales orientation (domestic-foreign); an index of sales growth; an index of export growth; an index of employment growth; the DaBeg index (David Birch employment growth index); share of capital in financing; return on equity; return on assets; sales per worker; profit per worker; and value added per worker. We first report results on the subjective measures of performance (Table 7.11) and then continue with the objective performance measures.

Table 7.11 Satisfaction with subjective measures of performance (in per cent)

Satisfaction level	Growth potential		Product quality	
	Male	Female	Male	Female
Not satisfied at all	0	0	0	0
Somewhat satisfied	11	18	5	0
Satisfied	28	41	32	20
Very satisfied	49	27	51	47
Completely satisfied	12	14	12	33
Significance	Chi Sq.=5.9, α=0.11, DF=3		Chi Sq.=9.6, α=0.02, DF=3	

Source: Survey on gender entrepreneurship in Slovenia, 2004.

There are meaningful differences in satisfaction levels experienced by the two groups of entrepreneurs. Women entrepreneurs tend on average to be less satisfied with the performance results related to the venture's future growth potential, whereas their male counterparts are less satisfied with the quality of products and services.

Table 7.12 Distribution of firms by gender and type of sales (in per cent)

Sales percentage	Domestic market		Foreign market	
	Male	Female	Male	Female
0	13	2	24	48
1 – 10	15	4	22	20
11 – 50	8	20	29	12
51 – 99	38	26	16	20
100	26	48	9	0
Significance	Chi Sq.=14.7, α=0.05, DF=4		Chi Sq.=13.1, α<0.001, DF=4	

Source: Survey on gender entrepreneurship in Slovenia, 2004.

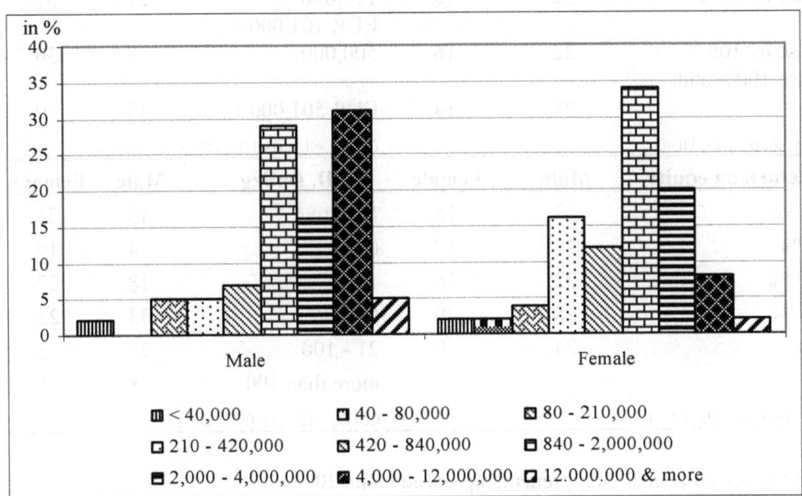

Source: Survey on gender entrepreneurship in Slovenia, 2004.

Figure 7.6 Distribution of firms by sales and gender

The objective financial ratios of the sampled companies are high. Since the sample structure includes one-third of fast-growing companies, the average results are positively biased. If we exclude dynamic entrepreneurs from the sample, the average results based on business volume decrease by some 5 to 10 per cent. The distribution of financial results by gender shows significant differences. Women-managed firms tend to be smaller and less export-oriented. Moreover, there are significant gender differences in the distribution of sales realized in local markets and foreign markets. The majority of women-managed firms (48 per cent) predominantly sell in local markets and there was no fully internationalized women-managed firm (Figure 7.6., Table 7.12).

Other significant gender differences included: index of sales growth, return on equity, employment growth, sales per worker, and the DaBeg index. The general observation is that women-managed businesses on average scored lower, since a higher number of women businesses (as compared to men) tended to be in lower performance classes.

Table 7.13 Distribution of firms by gender and performance measures (in per cent)

A. Employment growth 1999 - 02	Male	Female	B. Sales per employee	Male	Female
Contracting	18	37	EUR 0 - 20,000	10	4
Increase by 50%	32	33	EUR 21,000 - 100,000	27	57
Increase by 100 %	22	16	EUR 101,000 - 500,000	50	30
Increase 100% and more	28	14	EUR 501,000 +	13	9
Chi Sq.=5.6, α=0.13, DF=3			Chi Sq.=8.9, α=0.03, DF=3		
C. Return on equity	**Male**	**Female**	**D. DaBeg**	**Male**	**Female**
Negative	2	18	Negative	15	21
0 - 15%	24	18	0	4	19
16 - 30%	22	26	1 - 5	18	27
31 - 60%	28	29	6 - 20	33	23
> 60%	24	9	21 - 100	22	5
			more than 100	8	5
Chi Sq.=10.1, α=0.04, DF=4			Chi Sq.=12.2, α=0.03, DF=5		

Source: Survey on gender entrepreneurship in Slovenia, 2004.

There are also meaningful differences by gender at the *level of indebtedness* for women entrepreneurs tend to have lower financial leverage: one-third of men-managed companies had an 80 per cent level of indebtedness, while only one-sixth of women entrepreneurs were leveraged to that extent. As far as *export results* are concerned, a weak third of companies (31 per cent) decreased their export orientation, one-third of companies increased it twofold (35 per cent), and one-third increased it more than twofold. As hypothesized, women and men entrepreneurs do not differ in terms of profitability ratios. The distribution of companies by *sales profitability* was the following: 20 per cent of companies had zero profitability, 46 per cent had between 1 to 3 per cent profitability; 21 per cent had 4 to 6 per cent profitability; and 13 per cent had sales profitability higher than 6 per cent. Another profitability ratio shows that some 36 per cent of respondents had between 1 Euro to 5,000 Euro profit per employee; 10 per cent had a loss; 16 per cent had more than EUR 10,000 per employee; and up to 24 per cent had EUR 1,000 per employee. There were no significant gender differences in the level of *added value per employee*: 39 per cent of companies had negative added value per worker, 8 per cent had it up to EUR 10,000, 21 per cent had between EUR 11 to 20,000, 23 per cent had between EUR 21 and 40,000 and the rest were higher.

The present study provides empirical support for anecdotal data which has traditionally shown substantial differences between women and men managed businesses in Slovenia. The most contrasting differences between women and man managed firms are with respect to support they receive from their families in start up and current operations financing and also through family social capital. Women managed businesses are more dependent in that respect. Second, male and female entrepreneurs differ in terms of the importance they assign to attainment of performance related goals, such as: sales volume; employment; and quality. Women tend to assign higher importance to such goals and on average also experience a higher level of dissatisfaction if goals are not implemented. Moreover, other performance related differences include: the level of internationalization; an index of sales growth; return on equity; employment growth; sales per worker; and the DaBeg index. The general observation is that women-managed businesses on average scored lower: a higher number of women businesses (as compared to men) tended to be in lower performance classes.

Conclusions

Contrary to some expectations found in Slovenian SME development documents, women have not become as strong a source of new businesses as their potential has previously been assessed. The general level of entrepreneurial activity in Slovenia has been declining after the first entrepreneurial wave has reached its potential. Moreover, with the recent looming of recession, women are even less inclined to start businesses, although globalization has seriously hurt industries where women hold the majority of jobs.

The survey we conducted, together with the analysis of financial data on companies according to the gender of managers confirmed some previous results. Women establish businesses that are smaller in employment and sales due to specific start up objectives, such as flexibility and personal social security. Women–managed businesses are less export-oriented due to the structure of the products and services but also due to the lower mobility of women in doing business, since many still have the duties of housewives and mothers. However, in terms of financial indicators women–managed businesses do not do fare worse although women are less inclined to consider profit as the main business goal. Overall, in most business aspects women-managed businesses do not significantly differ from their male counterparts, but some barriers persist mostly in their access to financial sources and in the character of their networks. In what follows we provide some implications for alternative activities to promote female entrepreneurship in Slovenia.

Implications

Although equality of gender is well established in Slovenia, at least at the declarative level, a decreasing trend in the number of women-managed businesses has been recorded in the last few years, although some experts and key informants (i.e. in GEM 2003 research) share a positive perception that a broad societal framework for entrepreneurship is well established and the number of start-up businesses, regardless of gender, should be growing.

On the other hand, this research showed that women entrepreneurs lack networking competence and social capital assets, since they have to contract those resources through strong ties they have with family members. It follows that the suggested strategies and initiatives to promote women's entrepreneurship build on soft measures of support, such as: building a network of women's entrepreneurship promoters to support women's business ideas and to advise beginners, building up a specialist network to support groups of women entrepreneurs, such as rural entrepreneurs via 'e-friendship-classrooms', family business successors, and internationalizing businesses.

Conversely, gender bias in some aspects of running a business is obviously present (e.g. acquiring finance). Given this drawback, one suggestion for women is to look outside their personal sphere when it comes to business. Since at the formal level no strong negative attitude towards women entrepreneurs has been identified, strategies and initiatives to promote women entrepreneurs could build on soft measures of support. Already some programmes to support women's business ideas have been developed, through a network of women promoters, to advise beginners and family businesses, were proposed and taken by the network of enterprise sector, but a substantial impact has not evolved.

Indirect gender bias in some aspects of running a business has been suggested by women; for example, in acquiring finance women's businesses look less attractive due to their smaller size and less pronounced growth in marketing; some 'old–boys' networks work in favour of men. Finding women looking for the (first source of advice from family, husband, and informal sources, while their male counterparts tend to look more often professionals, we are inclined to suggest that women should more often use professional help.

Our research is in line with some older findings that the first source of advice for male entrepreneurs was professional (accountants) and the second was his spouse, whereas the first source of advice for female entrepreneurs is her family (spouse), and informal sources (friends). A network of supporters and mentors, made up of other women business owners and professionals can provide a valuable insights into running a business that are usually not available from business consultants and other formalized sources. Such structures embed knowledge and tips on how to present funding applications to bankers, confront a difficult supplier, or even choose resources available to women.

Lastly, the message that the women entrepreneurs in our interviews and in the survey had for their companions 'out there in the jungle' is simply: 'go for it!'. If you have an idea, energy, and the need to succeed with the support of your family and your partner, there is no limit on where you can go.

References

Amit, R., MacCrimmon, K. R., Zietsma, C. and Oesch, J. M. (2000), 'Does Money Matter? Wealth Attainment as the Motive for Initiating Growth-Oriented Technology Ventures', *Journal of Business Venturing*, vol. 16, pp. 119-143.

Brush, C. (1990), *Local Initiatives for Job Creation: Enterprising Women*, OECD, Paris.

Cohen, R. J., Swerdlik, M. E. and Philips, S. M. (1996), *Psychological Testing and Assessment: An Introduction to Tests and Measurement*, Mountain view, Maryland.

Domeisen, N. (2003), 'Canada Releases Report on Women Entrepreneurs', *International Trade Forum*, vol. 4, pp. 11-13.

Douglas, E. J. and Shepherd, D. A. (1999), 'Entrepreneurship as a Utility Maximizing Response', *Journal of Business Venturing*, vol. 15, pp. 231-251.

Drnovsek, M. (2003), *Evaluation of Voucher System of Counselling 2002 – 2003*, Small Business Development Centre, Lubljana.

Frese, M. and Rauch, A. (2001), 'Giessen-Amsterdam Model of Small Business Owner's Success', *Encyclopaedia of the Social & Behavioural Sciences*, pp. 4552-4556, Elsevier Science.

Glas, M. (1986), *Delitev po delu v socialisticni druzbi*, Delavska enotnost, Ljubljana.

Glas, M. and Cerar, M. (1997), *The Self-Employment Programme in Slovenia: Evaluation of Results and an Agenda for Improvement*, paper presented at the 1997 Babson Kauffman Entrepreneurship Research Conference.

Glas, M. and Drnovsek, M. (1998), 'Zensko Podjetnistvo v Sloveniji', *Informator PCMG*, vol. 6, pp. 24-27.

Glas, M. and Drnovsek, M. (2000), *Slovenian Women as Emerging Entrepreneurs*, paper presented at the RENT XIII Conference.

Glas, M. and Drnovsek, M. (2000a), *Small Business in Slovenia: Expectations and Accomplishments*, paper presented at the RENT XIII Conference.

Glas, M. and Petrin, T. (1998), *Entrepreneurship: New Challenges for Slovene Women*, paper presented at the 1998 Babson Kauffman Entrepreneurship Research Conference.

Goffee, R. and Scase, R. (1985), *Women in Charge*, George Allan and Unwin, London.

Hisrich, R.D. and Brush, C.G. (1986), *The Women Entrepreneur, Starting, Financing and Managing a Successful New Business*, Lexington Books, Toronto.

Hribar, V. (1997), *Zensko Podjetnistvo v Sloveniji*, Faculty of Economics, Ljubljana.

Kanjou, M. A. (1996), *Zenske v Managementu*, Enotnost, Ljubljana.

Markman, G. D., Balkin, D. B. and Baron, R. A. (2003), 'The Role of Regretful Thinking, Perseverance, and Self-efficacy in Venture Formation', in J. Katz and D. Shepherd (eds), *Cognitive approaches to entrepreneurship research*, JAI Press.

National Foundation for Women Business Owners: http://www.nfwbo.org

Novak, I. (1994), 'Podjetne Zenske', *Podjetnik*, vol. 10, pp. 17-18.

Petrin, T. and Humphries, J. (1980), 'Women in Self-Managed Economy of Yugoslavia', *Economic Analysis*, vol. 14, pp. 70-91.

Ram, D. (1996), *Women entrepreneurs*, Publishing Corporation, New Delhi.

Rebernik, M. et al. (2004a), *GEM 2002 – The Winding Road to Entrepreneurial Society*, IESBM – Faculty of Economics and Business, Maribor.

Rebernik, M. et al. (2004b), *GEM 2003 – Spodbujati in Ohranjati Razvojne Ambicije*, IPMMP – Faculty of Economics and Business, Maribor.

Rebernik, M. et al. (2004c), *Slovenski Podjetniski Observatorij 2003*, IESBM – Faculty of Economics and Business.

Sexton, D. L. and Bowman-Upton, N. (1990), 'Women Business Owners and Terms of Credit: Some Empirical Findings of the Canadian Experience', *Journal of Business Venturing*, vol. 5, pp. 327-340.

Tigges, L. M. and Green, G.P . (1994), 'Small Business Success among Men – and Women Owned Firms in Rural Areas', *Rural Sociology*, vol. 59, pp. 289-309.

Turk, M. (2002), 'Entrepreneurship as a Challenge and Opportunity in Slovenia', in United Nations (eds), *Womn''s Entrepreneurship in Eastern Europe and CIS Countries*, United Nations, New York and Geneva, pp. 51-57.

UNDP (1998), *Human Development Report: Slovenia 1998*, Bureau for Macroeconomic Analysis and Research, Lubljana.

Wilkens, J. (1987), *Her Own Business: Success Secrets of Entrepreneurial Women*, McGraw-Hill, New York.

Chapter 8

West and East German Women Entrepreneurs: (Why) Are they still Different?

Friederike Welter

Introduction

Germany allows for a unique comparison between women's entrepreneurship in a mature market economy (West Germany) versus entrepreneurship in a former socialist economy (East Germany). After more than a decade of re-unification one would expect little differences between West and East German entrepreneurs, because the transformation in the former German Democratic Republic (GDR) was facilitated by a considerable transfer of capital, knowledge and institutions from West Germany. On the other hand, East German female entrepreneurship also might show distinctive characteristics because of the rapid transformation process, which was accompanied by a massive loss of employment and a renaissance of conservative values. This question so far has not been explored systematically.

Several studies analyzing East German entrepreneurship concentrate on paths into entrepreneurship, personal factors of influence and individual experiences (e.g., Hinz, 1998; Lang, 1999; Thomas, 1996, 2001). Other authors study regional and sectoral aspects of venture creation and small enterprises (e.g., Brixy, 1999; Brussig (ed), 1997; Fritsch et al., 2001; Harhoff (ed), 1997; May-Strobl and Paulini, 1994; Schmude (ed), 1998). Some authors compare single aspects of enterprise development in West and East Germany, such as determinants of employment growth (e.g., Almus, Engel and Nerlinger, 1999; Almus, 2001; Fritsch and Mallok, 1998). However, there is a lack of studies on women entrepreneurs in the specific post-transition context of Germany. Existing studies have mainly analysed different facets of the social and professional life of East German mothers or wage employees (e.g., Rocksloh-Papendieck, 1995a, 1995b; Gensior (ed), 1995).

This chapter sets out to explore whether West and East German women entrepreneurs and their enterprises still differ after 10 years of re-unification, if so, in what aspects as well as to explore the ways entrepreneurship in both parts of Germany changed over the past years. It adopts an institutional perspective in order to investigate patterns and development paths of women's entrepreneurship, because features of entrepreneurship also reflect the distinctive nature of the external environment.

The chapter is structured in six main sections. The first section explains the institutional concept and its application to entrepreneurship and women's entrepreneurship. The next section presents some data on the development of SMEs and entrepreneurship in Germany. Sections three and four deal with policies for women entrepreneurs and the economic and societal environment in West and East Germany, while section five reports evidence on similarities and differences of women entrepreneurs and their businesses, taken from official statistics and research studies. The chapter concludes, summarizing the main results in an attempt to answer the title question: (Why) are women entrepreneurs in West and East Germany still different?

Institutional Theory and Entrepreneurship

The Concept of Formal and Informal Institutions

Institutional theory, especially the concept of formal and informal institutions developed by Douglass C. North, appears to be a suitable theoretical framework for analyzing the influence of the environment on patterns of entrepreneurship and entrepreneurial behaviour. North's framework draws attention to external political, economic and societal influences on individual behaviour, discussing them in terms of formal and informal institutions. North (1990, 1995) understands institutions as the incentive structure of a society, because they assist in reducing uncertainty and risk for individual behaviour as well as the transaction costs connected with entrepreneurship. They 'define what actors can do, what is expected from them, or they must do, and what is advantageous for them. In this way, they give stability and predictability to economic interaction.' (Dallago, 2000, p. 305).

Applying North's concept to entrepreneurship, institutions are the 'formal' and 'informal' constraints and enabling forces on entrepreneurship. Examples of formal institutions influencing entrepreneurship include the political and economic constitution, the legal framework and the financial system. Informal institutions refer to codes of conduct, values and norms, i.e., those non-codified attitudes which are embedded in a society, regulating individual behaviour. Codes of conduct and values reflect the collective, tacit interpretation of individual mental perceptions (Denzau and North, 1994). North (1990) understands the informal institutions as part of a cultural heritage. Whilst informal institutions are the culturally accepted basis legitimating entrepreneurship, the formal institutions contribute the regulatory frame (Wade-Benzoni et al., 2002). In other words, formal institutions create opportunity fields for entrepreneurship and informal institutions determine opportunity perceptions of both a society and individuals.

However, a clear-cut distinction between formal and informal institutions is difficult to achieve. Both informal and formal institutions are mutually dependent, whilst mental perceptions of individuals and informal institutions co-evolve. Partly, informal institutions result from formal institutions, which they in turn (could) modify. In this regard, they evolve as a culture-specific interpretation of formal rules. For example, whilst each legal framework normally contains explicit regulations for implementing laws, over time these regulations are complemented by an implicit understanding of their content. This refers to unwritten rules, i.e., informal institutions fill in legal gaps which become apparent only through applying laws and regulations to daily life. In addition, informal institutions also contribute to the enforcement of the formal framework. Although legal sanctions such as penalties for unlawful behaviour play an important role in implementing new rules of the game, these means are far from being sufficient. In this context, North (1990) himself acknowledges that we need to know more about how norms of behaviour develop and how they interact with formal institutions.

Institutional Embeddedness of Entrepreneurship

Fundamental rules such as private property rights are a major influence on the existence of entrepreneurship whilst the legal frame determines its nature and extent. This refers to laws relating to bankruptcy, contracts, commercial activities, taxes, but it also involves organizations with the capacity to implement them. Laws might create new opportunity fields for entrepreneurship. For example, in Germany the introduction of rules for environmental protection fostered venture creation in recycling industries. Other key institutions include the financial system or sectors in the sense of sector specific technological standards. Here, technological progress allows for customized mass production, thus creating new market opportunities in sectors which were previously dominated by economies of scales and scope and consequently larger enterprise sizes.

With respect to informal institutions, i.e., values and norms, Busenitz et al. (2000) refer to a 'normative dimension' which measures the degree to which a society admires entrepreneurial activities. Empirical studies such as the Global Entrepreneurship Monitor demonstrate that this image of entrepreneurship differs across countries, thus explaining differences in the extent of entrepreneurship: 'Among the many factors that contribute to entrepreneurship, perhaps the most critical is a set of social and cultural values along with the appropriate social, economic and political institutions that legitimize and encourage the pursuit of entrepreneurial opportunity' (Reynolds, Hay and Camp, 1999, p. 43). Cultural norms decide whether a society tolerates profit making behaviour as one prerequisite for entrepreneurship. They also influence whether a society has a practice of saving for the future or a focus on 'living and spending to enjoy the moment' (Morrison, 1998, p. 9) which in turn determines the amount of personal savings available for a business start-up.

Institutional Change, Path Dependency and Entrepreneurship

Institutional change has a positive influence on entrepreneurship in those cases, where it removes or lowers barriers to market entry and market exit, thus creating opportunity fields for entrepreneurs, and vice versa. Examples for positive changes refer to the introduction of private property rights at the beginning of the transformation process in former socialist countries, or the efforts to deregulate industries in mature market economies. However, institutional change itself is affected by the complex relations between formal and informal institutions. In this context, North (1995) points out the path-dependent behaviour of informal institutions, which are deeply rooted in society. Whilst formal institutions may be easily modified and transformed, informal institutions such as norms of behaviour and values appear to be more persistent and change slowly. Mummert (1999) explains this as a result of societal sanctions for deviating individual behaviour.

That implies that the persistency of informal institutions influences entrepreneurship in those situations where a new regulatory frame and previous codes of conduct do not fit any longer (Mummert, 1995, 1999). In this context, research on transition economies (e.g., Gustafson, 1999; Smallbone and Welter, 2001) indicates that inadequate legal and financial systems during transition often re-enforced socialist norms of behaviour such as the Soviet 'legacy of non-compliance' (Feige, 1997, p. 28), thereby explaining rent-seeking forms of entrepreneurship or informal entrepreneurship. The social context inherited from the former socialist period appears to affect both the attitudes and behaviour of entrepreneurs and the attitudes of society at large towards entrepreneurship.

Institutions and Women's Entrepreneurship[1]

With regard to female entrepreneurship, the question arises if and if so, how the institutional environment determines and possibly restricts their access to entrepreneurship. Gender-specific formal institutions refer first of all to the overall constitution ensuring equal opportunities for women and men. Whilst gender equality is stipulated constitutionally in most countries, its application in a particular economy or society might still involve discrimination against women in practice. Open discrimination is one aspect, especially where wage gaps are concerned, but also, where traditional attitudes of society forbid women to carry out certain activities. In addition, hidden constraints, expressing themselves through the institutional environment, and reflected in policies and legal regulations might play an even more important role in restricting women's entrepreneurship.

More specific formal institutions apply to labour market rules giving equal access to employment positions, family policies such as specific tax regulations or the overall infrastructure for child care. Moreover, social and tax policies could influence women's entrepreneurship, for example, with respect to the level of social security, which is an important factor for potential women entrepreneurs, who might consider business ownership in some cases, as a means of improving household income.

Examples of gender-specific informal institutions include religion and traditions, which can lead to specific influences on the behaviour of women thus shaping their standing in society and their economic function. The image of an entrepreneur which could differ across countries implicitly reflects the traditional values of a society. In this regard, empirical studies have shown that most Western cultures still appear to portray the entrepreneurial role as being more masculine than feminine (Fagenson and Marcus, 1991). In a transition context, this takes an additional dimension, because gender roles have undergone minor or major revisions.

Moreover, women's entrepreneurship depends not only on the availability of market opportunities. It is also influenced to a large extent by the value that society attributes to women in employment. This can contribute to labour market discrimination, which in turn may contribute to women being pushed into self employment/business ownership (Holst, 2001; Munz, 1997), and the value attributed to the family. The latter includes attitudes towards gender-specific role distributions, which might leave potential women entrepreneurs little time to pursue economic opportunities. It also refers to the role of the extended family as, for example, in African countries where (women) entrepreneurs who are successful are expected to assist their extended family and clan, although this argument can also be applied to African entrepreneurs regardless of gender (Rocksloh-Papendieck, 1988). The informal institutions reflected here influence the responsibilities, tasks and the workload that women entrepreneurs would have to cope with as well as any assistance from their milieu they might expect when setting up their own enterprise.

Thus, with regard to women entrepreneurs, formal institutions mainly influence the nature and extent of female entrepreneurship. Cultural norms and values help to shape the way into entrepreneurship and more specifically women's intention to set up a business. Informal institutions gain importance in those cases where formal constraints fail or are absent. For example, in an unstable and weakly structured environment, networks and contacts often play a key role in helping entrepreneurs to mobilise resources, and to cope with the constraints imposed by highly bureaucratic structures and often unfriendly officials (Ledeneva, 1998). This indicates the importance of social capital in the form of personal trust for influencing initial entry into entrepreneurship, as well as for consequent business development and growth. In addition, the social context inherited from the former socialist period appears to affect both the attitudes and behaviour of entrepreneurs and the attitudes of society at large towards entrepreneurship, drawing attention to the constraining effect of path dependency in the sense of legacies from the past. Regarding female entrepreneurship, this refers to ongoing traditional gender values that persisted even during socialist times, despite an ideological commitment to promote emancipation through labour participation of women (Kerblay, 1977).

In addition, inadequate formal institutions in the transition process can block the adaptation of informal constraints inherited from centrally planned economies (Mummert 1995, 1999). Here, a transition context has often been characterised by a 'syndrome of mistrust' (Leipold, 1999), which refers to the role of trust in determining ways into entrepreneurship, and the forms that it takes, as well as entrepreneurial behaviour. In this context, gender could represent an additional dimension, in that the evolving institutional framework might constrain women's formal integration into the emerging market economy due to redefined and changed gender roles, restricting their access to external resources and organizations which are needed in order to realize a venture. Moreover, their often lower professional status during socialist times might prevent them from drawing on influential social networks in order to enter entrepreneurship.

Entrepreneurship and SMEs in a Re-united Germany

Entrepreneurship Development since Re-unification[2]

Whilst legal private entrepreneurship in the former GDR was restricted to small craft enterprises and some private shops, entrepreneurship boomed with the introduction of legal regulations allowing private enterprises in 1990. The number of East German entrepreneurs more than doubled from 154,000 in 1988 (Schrumpf, 1990) to 348,000 in 1991. Since then, entrepreneurship (i.e., self-employed business persons[3]) grew by 67 per cent and amounted to 583,000 in the year 2003. During the same period, West German entrepreneurship also increased, albeit at a considerably lower rate. The number of entrepreneurs grew by 17 per cent to a total of 3.1 million. Especially in the East the negative labour market development during the past decade appears to indicate a push towards entrepreneurship. From 1991 to 2003 the total labour force was decreasing by 1,449 thousand. In this context, a study on craft entrepreneurs shows that '(risk of) unemployment' played a more important role compared to West Germany. However, the study also shows similar motives in both East and West Germany: 'Interest in entrepreneurship' and 'market opportunities' had been the foremost motives mentioned by East German entrepreneurs (Welter, 1996).

Although in East Germany the number of entrepreneurs keeps growing, the rapid growth rate which could be observed during the first years of re-unification has slowed down. This indicates, that entrepreneurship development in East Germany follows the general pattern several studies outlined for post Socialist countries (e.g., Piasecki and Rogut, 1993; Tschepurenko, 1998), i.e., after an initial upsurge entrepreneurship development slows down. This 'explosion of entrepreneurship' (Piasecki and Rogut, 1993) happened in East Germany from 1991-1995 whilst growth rates have been decelerating since the mid-1990s. Despite the enormous initial growth, the overall level of entrepreneurship is still lower in East Germany, compared to West Germany. In 2003, the share of entrepreneurs in the labour force amounts to 9.2 in East Germany and to 10.6 in West Germany, whilst at the end of the 1990s the average density (entrepreneurs per 1,000 inhabitants) is 39 in the East and 47 in the West (also Table 8.1). In comparison to 1991 this indicates considerable progress made since the beginning of the transformation process and re-unification. However, the decelerating growth rates since 1996 suggest an ongoing gap in the extent of entrepreneurship between East and West Germany.

A closer look at the business environments reveals several external factors which might have influenced the development of entrepreneurship in the 1990s. In *West*

Germany the slightly increasing level of entrepreneurship could result from growing unemployment which might have pushed individuals into entrepreneurship (Bögenhold and Staber, 1990) as well as from an overall growing interest in entrepreneurship. Since the mid-1990s, federal and state governments set up several initiatives to support venture creation. This includes efforts of the federal government to reduce regulations for business starts or specific support programmes for venture creation of university graduates such as the EXIST programme of the Federal Ministry of Research and Education. Especially the latter efforts might have contributed both directly and indirectly, to today's higher share of entrepreneurs with academic education, although this question would need to be examined in more detail.

The initial boom of entrepreneurship in *East Germany* is attributable to the removal of legal and administrative barriers in 1990 which allowed private firms to operate in all sectors of the economy. However, whilst the former East German government enabled this entrepreneurship explosion to occur, other factors contributed as well. That includes the limited competition that existed in many markets, the market opportunities that resulted from the shortages of certain goods and services in the East German economy, the latent consumer demand that existed, the rapidly increasing unemployment, and the existing supply of (potential) entrepreneurs. In this context, the transformation process created opportunities which entrepreneurs were either quick or forced to take up, implying that in the first years of re-unification socialist rules and norms did not constrain the occurrence and extent of East German entrepreneurship at large. Data from a study on craft entrepreneurs underline that fact, showing that in 1994 more than 70 per cent of East German entrepreneurs attributed a positive image to entrepreneurship, compared to less than 50 per cent in the West (Welter, 1996).

Although in the light of rising unemployment one would expect the growth rate for East German entrepreneurship to go up again, informal institutions such as a changing overall attitude towards entrepreneurship might explain decelerating rates. Research analyzing the prevalence of nascent entrepreneurs across German regions confirms lower rates for East German regions in the year 2000 (Bergmann, 2002). The initial positive attitude towards entrepreneurial activities appears to have changed over the past decade. This might reflect fewer entrepreneurial opportunities, higher competition and the growing awareness of the difficulties connected with the regulatory environment for entrepreneurship in a mature market economy.

Sectoral and Regional Patterns

Sectoral patterns illustrate similarities and interesting differences in West and East Germany. In 1991, entrepreneurship in services dominated in both West and East Germany with 39 and 37 per cent respectively, followed by trade enterprises (28.7 per cent and 29.3 per cent respectively). 23 per cent of all West German entrepreneurs had firms in the manufacturing sector, compared to nearly 30 per cent in East Germany. The development of the sector structure in West Germany shows the overall shift towards service industries, even if we take into account that sector classification were changed in 1995 which exaggerates the changes in services. Compared to 1991, a decade later the share of services had increased to nearly 42 per cent, while the share of small firms in manufacturing had declined to 20 per cent. In East Germany, low entry barriers, in terms of low capital and skill requirements, and a formerly underdeveloped tertiary sector resulted in initially high numbers of start-ups in trade and services, and this share increased for both sectors to 30.5 per cent for trade and retail and 39.5 per cent for services. Small-scale privatization played an additional role in fostering entrepreneurship in these fields. Moreover, the higher share of industrial entrepreneurs in East Germany, especially in 1991, resulted from privatization. This also explains the larger share of enterprises with employees in East Germany, whilst in West Germany the share of micro enterprises without employees has been continuously growing over the past decade.

Doubtless, sector influences explain today's higher share of entrepreneurs in services. New computer technologies allowed for smaller enterprise size, whilst reorganization processes in industry such as downsizing or outsourcing created opportunities for new ventures in business-oriented services, sometimes also in manufacturing. However, this also resulted in a growing number of so-called 'dependent' entrepreneurs (*Scheinselbständige*) in those cases where enterprises outsourced employees in order to avoid social security obligations. All this is reflected in the decreasing enterprise size in West Germany, where today the majority of entrepreneurs has no employees. In the year 2000 the government introduced legal regulations distinguishing between entrepreneurs and employees in terms of the number of customers a new business serves in order to prevent 'dependent' entrepreneurship. This also constrained 'genuine' entrepreneurship because new entrepreneurs often set up their venture with the help of one major customer, thus contributing to the decline in start-up rates in both parts of Germany which can be observed since 2000.

Table 8.1 Entrepreneurship density in East Germany, 1991 and 1999

	Entrepreneurs		Entry		Exit		Net entry	
	number per 1,000 inhabitants							
States (Länder)	1991	1999	1991	1999	1991	1999	1991	1999
Brandenburg	23	38	19	8	7	8	12	1
Mecklenburg-Western Pomerania	18	31	16	9	5	8	11	1
Saxony	22	39	19	10	7	8	13	2
Saxony-Anhalt	22	29	16	8	5	8	10	0
Thuringia	21	35	20	9	7	9	13	0
East Germany (excl. Berlin)	24	39	18	9	6	8	12	1
West Germany	43	47	6	7	5	6	2	1

Source: Own calculations based on micro census and business registry data provided by the Federal Statistical Office.

Regional patterns of entrepreneurship across the East German 'Länder' are more distorted today than a decade ago (see again Table 8.1). They broadly follow the North-South divide which is also to be observed in the West German 'Länder'. Saxony has the highest entrepreneurship density, followed by Brandenburg and Thuringia, whilst the rates in Mecklenburg-Western Pomerania and Saxony-Anhalt are considerably below the East German average. Regional disparities in entrepreneurship density often follow historical spatial patterns, thus confirming the path dependency of entrepreneurship (Arthur, 1994, pp. 49-67).

In this context, Saxony and Thuringia are historically the earliest developed areas in terms of industrialization which could explain their comparatively high densities in 2000. In Brandenburg, regional factors such as its spatial neighbourhood to the German capital play an additional role in explaining the favourable development of entrepreneurship. In those states with low entrepreneurship densities path dependent economic developments appear to limit the opportunity field for entrepreneurs. The rural structure of Mecklenburg-Western Pomerania mainly explains its lower entrepreneurship density whilst the economic structure of Saxony-Anhalt has been dominated by large chemical firms. Here, the privatization of state industries resulted in a massive de-industrialization process which in turn restricted entrepreneurship opportunities, for example as suppliers to larger enterprises.

Fostering Women's Entrepreneurship in Germany

Support Policies on State and Federal Level

Whilst support policies for small and medium-sized enterprises (SMEs) have a long tradition in Germany going back to the 1950s, the late 1990s displayed a particular concentration on start-ups in an attempt to push new businesses and create new employment possibilities. Both federal and the state governments initiated a number of new approaches to support new and existing enterprises and entrepreneurship from the mid-1990s onwards, without this initiative losing its momentum after the elections in September 1998, which ended the 16-year-government of the Christian Democratic Union (CDU) and Chancellor Kohl. This was accompanied by a shift towards fostering women's entrepreneurship. The Federal Action Programme on 'Innovation and employment in the knowledge society of the 21st century' pursues the aim to increase the share of female entrepreneurs in entrepreneurship to 40 per cent.

Most policies for start-ups concentrate on extending and stabilizing the financial base of the new venture whilst consultancy played a less important role, although there has been a shift towards integrated packages in recent years. PFAU, a programme designed to support start-ups of universities in North-Rhine Westphalia is one such example where elements of financial support, consultancy and mentoring are combined. North-Rhine Westphalia finances a part time job as university assistant for one or two years during which time the potential entrepreneurs are requested to get their business started. Additionally, they can apply for so-called 'marketing' and 'general consultancy' cheques to partly finance external professional consultancy. Senior experts (managers or former entrepreneurs) act as mentors during the start-up period. Moreover, there are various networks participants of PFAU and the GO-Initiative (*Gründungsoffensive*) in NRW might join, such as round tables of new entrepreneurs.

Whilst PFAU and most similar programmes do not include separate instruments for fostering female entrepreneurship, support measures exclusively directed at female entrepreneurs refer, for example, to a programme that encourages mentoring for young female ventures (TWIN, i.e. 'Two Women Win'), which has been extended to Germany as a whole after a successful trial period in North-Rhine-Westphalia. Selected support measures, which are exclusively directed at female entrepreneurs, are mainly to be found on *state level*. Besides mentoring programmes as a new and recent trend, these often refer to small credit lines. However, all these programmes only support a small number of female entrepreneurs. State governments also frequently introduce specific regulations into mass loan programmes, especially where these programmes are jointly financed by federal and state governments. One such example refers to a loan program in North-Rhine Westphalia where the state government allows loan applications of female nascent entrepreneurs without previous industry knowledge. Another such regulation is to be found in the East German state of Mecklenburg-Pomerania, where the state investment bank hands out loans directly to female entrepreneurs, provided they previously were rejected by banks (Kehlbeck and Schneider, 1999, p. 29). These regulations aim at levelling out the possibly negative effects of the German 'housebank system', where commercial banks take on a gatekeeper function, i.e., all applications for financial support programmes are channelled through them.

Only in 1999, one of the two large public banks (i.e., the Deutsche Ausgleichsbank, now merged with the KfW Bank to the 'KfW Mittelstandsbank' – Bank for SMEs), introduced its first micro finance programme, allowing for initial part-time entrepreneurship and small loans. Nowadays, there are several programmes both on federal and state or local level, acknowledging the fact that specific groups of entrepreneurs need smaller amounts of loans, and, as in the case of many women entrepreneurs, frequently start as part-time ventures (Piorkowsky, 2001).

Support for female entrepreneurship on *federal level* shows a thematic focus, taking into account the specific tasks of federal ministries. The Federal Ministry for Women, Senior citizens, Family and Youth (BMFSFJ) sees its role in fostering societal change, which also implies support for networking initiatives between gender-specific support agencies and 'mainstream' business organizations as well as lobbying for gender-specific statistics and financing relevant research studies (e.g., IfM, 2001; Piorkowsky, 2001, 2002). The Federal Ministry for Education and Research (BMBF) supports measures that aim to orient women towards 'new' employment fields, as well as gender-specific research (e.g., Lauxen-Ulbrich and Leicht, 2002; Fehrenbach and Leicht, 2002; Leicht and Welter, 2004; Welter and

Table 8.2 Awards for female business founders and entrepreneurs

Award and year	Initiated by	Requirements	Prize
Anna-Westphalen-Award, 1999, 2000, 2001	Working party 'Female entrepreneurs' in Flensburg	Region Flensburg Female entrepreneur, female business founder	750-1,000 EUR, golden pin, certificate
Beate-Uhse-Award for Female entrepreneurs, 2002	Company Beate Uhse	Schleswig-Holstein Female business founders and young female-led businesses	10,000 EUR
Bizzy, 2000, 2002	Fair for female entrepreneurs in Hamburg	Implicitly restricted to Hamburg and Northern Germany Female business founder, support for female workers in enterprises, products/services relevant for women	2,002 EUR
Existenz-Award for female business founders, 1997-	Company for office services in Berlin, Checkpoint Charlie'	Berlin Female entrepreneurs, female business founders	Fully paid office for 6 months
Future Award, 1998-	Magazine 'Super-Illu'	East Germany	5,000 EUR
Award for female business founders in Saxonia, 2001-	State Ministry for Equality of Women and Men	Saxonia Female entrepreneurs Innovative idea for business start	No data
Award for female entrepreneurs in Emscher-Lippe 2001	Go-Emscher-Lippe Region, City Bottrop, City Gelsenkirchen	Region Emscher-Lippe Female entrepreneur	5,000 EUR
VISION-Female entrepreneur Award, 2000, 2002	Network for female business founders, Aachen	Region Aachen Female entrepreneur, female successor, female professional	3,000 EUR
IDEE-Award, 1997-	Company Albert Darboven	Female business founders or young female-led businesses < 3 years	75,000 EUR
Veuve-Cliquot-Award, 1983-	Company Veuve Cliquot	Female entrepreneurs, handed out in 11 countries	No data

Source: Updated from Welter and Lageman (2003).

Lageman, 2003; Welter, 2004). The Federal Ministry of Economics and Labour (BMWA) generally is responsible for SME support. Overall, there is an ongoing subtle shift in federal support policies. The underlying support paradigm currently focuses on an organization-based and institutionally oriented support approach.

This is aimed at integrating gender-specific support topics more and more into mainstream agencies and mainstream organizations such as chambers and business associations, although support policies are slow(er) to adapt.

Increasing the Visibility of Female Entrepreneurs

The last years saw a trend towards increasing the visibility of female entrepreneurs throughout Germany. Public-private or private initiatives offering awards for female entrepreneurs and female business founders gained importance. Whilst Sperling and May (2001) could identify only four regional awards, an Internet search in 2002 found eight regional or local and two federal/international initiatives (Welter and Lageman, 2003; Table 8.2).

Awards are handed out for innovative business ideas, new products or services, or innovative ways of combining work and family. Some of the awards, such as the IDEE-Award, also take into account employment creation through new enterprises. The latter often is considerable, as the example of the Vision-Female Entrepreneur Award demonstrates. The six best female entrepreneurs prized since its creation had created a total of 85 new employment possibilities (52 of them for women), which amounts to an average 14 new jobs per firm, compared to the overall German average of 4.5 new jobs per new venture within the first five years.

In principle, most awards, especially those on regional and local level, offer only nominal acknowledgements, whilst mainly federal and international awards are accompanied by considerable prize money. However, especially where large, well-known companies or mass media donate these awards it is the public recognition of the prized entrepreneurs that appears important. Thus, the German environment for female entrepreneurship is characterized by a trend towards increasing the visibility of women entrepreneurs.

The Environment for Women Entrepreneurs in West and East Germany

Gender Equality, Family, Tax and Social Policies

The institutional and legal contexts play an important role for female entrepreneurship, influencing its nature and extent as well as its potential economic contribution. Here, the question arises if (and if yes, in which ways) access to entrepreneurship is restricted in Germany, and it is here where West and East Germany differ, following a conservative path (West Germany) and a socialist path (East Germany). Whilst gender equality formally was codified in the German Constitution after the Second World War, its implementation throughout economy and society led to open and subtle discrimination (Holst, 2002). In West Germany, open discrimination could be observed until the early 1970s concerning legal regulations where women needed their husband's signature on a labour contract to become valid, regulations with respect to bank accounts where husbands were required to countersign a woman's application. Only in 1977, women gained gender equality by law, with the civil code stating that both partners are allowed to work (Holst, 2002, p. 102). Nowadays, hidden constraints, expressing themselves through the institutional environment, might play an even more important role in restricting women's entrepreneurship.

Childcare facilities play a role in supporting or constraining female entrepreneurship in practice, although in an indirect way (Delmar and Holmquist, 2004). The extent and nature of family policies depend on the prevailing understanding of motherhood, which differed widely between West and East Germany. While the East German state propagated and fostered gender equality in the labour market through installing an elaborate system of public child care, West German governments were (and are) oriented towards a more conservative role of mothers, who should stay at home to bring up children (Gottfried and O'Reilly, 2002). This is reflected in East German women only temporarily leaving the labour market, while West German women often retreat to their family for long periods, and when returning to the labour market they do so on a part-time basis (Letablier and Jönsson, 2003; Knijn, Jönsson and Klammer, 2003).

Although the socialist child care system was downsized enormously after re-unification and the privatization of state-owned firms, the infrastructure still remains a better one compared to West Germany. All this contributed to a high participation of East German women in the labour market. For example, in 1989 nearly 90 per cent of all East German women either studied or worked, compared to a 'mere' 55 per cent in West Germany (Gerhard, 2003, p. 80).

In addition, social policies could influence women entrepreneurs with respect to the level of social security connected to entrepreneurship. This is an important factor for potential women entrepreneurs who might also consider entrepreneurship for family reasons or in order to improve household income. Moreover, Holst (2002) refers to the gender-restrictive role of the German tax system that mainly favours male participation in the formal labour market and informal, unpaid work of women through discriminating against married women by burdening their income with high taxes. In general, a tax system with a high tax burden would decrease an individual's opportunity to save money, which consequently could be invested in her own venture (Delmar and Holmquist, 2004). Here, Gustafsson (1995) demonstrated that if West Germany introduced the Swedish tax system, women employment would increase by 10 percentage points, whilst vice versa women employment in Sweden would decrease by 20 percentage points.

Societal Values

Female entrepreneurship is also influenced to a large extent by the value society attaches to women employment, as the discussion around child care and working mothers above indicates. For example, empirical evidence for East Germany demonstrates that the decreasing labour market participation of East German women following re-unification can only partly be attributed to higher unemployment rates for women, but it also reflects an overall conservative trend in Germany, ascribing a home-bound role for women (e.g., Meyer and Schulze, 1995; Rocksloh-Papendieck, 1995a, 1995b) as well as the decrease in child-care facilities. An increased labour market participation of women occurred in Western economies only since the 1970s, as Birley (1989) describes: 'Until very recently, the major role of women was seen in most Western economies by both men and women to be that of wife and mother. Indeed, even should they take employment, this was almost always in addition to their role as homemaker.'

Despite a growing share of working women, the West German society still defines women mainly through roles connected to family and household responsibilities, thus conveying female entrepreneurship as less desirable (Welter 2004, also IfM 2003). The role distribution is one where men contribute incomes and women are mainly responsible for child care, which forces West German women even in the 21st century to choose between either having a family and children or entering the labour market (Gerhard, 2003). In East Germany, although conservative values have gained ground, this still differs. Gerhard (2003, p. 81) quotes East German mothers as stating that those women who stayed at home had been an exception rather than the rule.

As a result, we might expect a possibly reluctant attitude of West German women towards entrepreneurship. This is reinforced through the ambivalent image of entrepreneurs (Unternehmer[4]), which is still attributed with male characteristics. Since the turn of the 19th century entrepreneurs had been identified as 'heroic lone fighters' (*heroische Einzelkämpfer*), which led to entrepreneurship being understood as a male task (Schmidt, 2002). In most Western cultures entrepreneurship still is attributed with male characteristics. Research, studying entrepreneurial metaphors for Scandinavian countries where the environment favours female entrepreneurs, demonstrated for the late 1990s, that women assign controversial and negative metaphors to entrepreneurship, whilst men frequently emphasized idealizing aspects: 'It appeared that many females perceived entrepreneurship as perhaps requiring too full a commitment to business, thereby reducing the time and effort required to pursued other important avenues. (…) The traditional view holding that every man has to fend for himself and make due sacrifices in order to succeed surfaced again and again.' (Hyrsky, 1999, p. 29).

This is even more apparent in the German society, which still puts a higher value to male role stereotypes than to female ones (Holst, 2002, p. 92). All this is reflected in the way German media discuss women entrepreneurs, shaping their identity. Achtenhagen and Welter (2003, 2005) have been researching the discourse on women's entrepreneurship in selected German newspapers, concluding that they often paint a 'restricted' picture of women entrepreneurs. This applies both to implicit role models and traditional values. For example, several articles discuss the double burden of work and family for women, sometimes stating explicitly that this particular female entrepreneur chose not to have a family and children because of her entrepreneurial role. Moreover, women entrepreneurs are mainly understood as being hard-working power-women, showing enthusiasm, energy, firmness, and cleverness, in short: they are superwomen standing their 'woman' in a male-dominated business world.

All this clearly illustrates the traditional role model for (West-)German women, which also started to dominate the East German context after re-unification. Thus, societal values implicitly assess female entrepreneurship as less desirable, which in turn affects the self-perceptions and individual attitudes of potential female entrepreneurs. Interviews with women entrepreneurs in Germany demonstrate that most women entrepreneurs, especially those having set up a venture in the professions (e.g., as doctors or lawyers), do not see themselves as a female entrepreneur which term they attribute to those women who lead larger industry firms (Welter and Lageman, 2003). Here, research also confirmed that professional choices of women take into account what society deems desirable and 'correct' for their sex (Holst, 2002). If a society values for women a housebound role higher than a professional one, it is not surprising that women often deny their entrepreneurial identity. All this in turn could restrict both the inclination of women to set up a business as well as their attitudes towards business growth.

Business Associations, Networks and Networking

The 1990s saw a considerable increase in gender-specific public-private and wholly private networks for women entrepreneurs (for details cf. Welter and Lageman, 2003; Welter, Ammon and Trettin, 2004). Women entrepreneurs appear to be more reluctant to address chambers of commerce and industry and crafts, which traditionally play a major role in the German (support) system. The overall dominance of male entrepreneurs in business associations and chambers is reflected in the low shares of women entrepreneurs in boards and committees, although recently more women entrepreneurs showed interest in participating in these business organizations. For example, only one out of 82 chambers of commerce and industry is presided by a woman, another four have female CEOs, whilst there are one female president, one female vice-president and six female CEOs across the 55 chambers of craft (Welter and Lageman, 2003).

Women-related organizations fall into different categories: those organizations or networks aiming at working women in general (e.g., the Business and Professional Women Organization, which originally was founded in the 1920s in the USA, and in the 1930s in Germany) and specific associations/networks for female entrepreneurs or female business founders. The latter category includes the oldest and with 1,700 members also largest female entrepreneur association in Germany, the Assocation of German Women Entrepreneurs (*Verband Deutscher Unternehmerinnen* – VdU), which was set up in 1954. It still remains the only association of that kind on federal and regional level, whilst most of the other organizations either have a mainly sectoral focus such as 'Schöne Aussichten' with 700 members, which is concentrated on female entrepreneurs in professions, or 'webgrrls' which focuses on women entrepreneurs in new media, or an explicit regional and local orientation, respectively. This overall increase and the focus on regions or sectors reflect a general shift in the organizations' philosophies from general lobbying towards providing direct membership benefits (Frerichs and Wiemert, 2002).

With regard to East Germany, a recent study compared network emergence in an East German state (Mecklenburg-Western Pomerania) and a West German city region (Munich; cf. Welter and Trettin, 2005). In the East German State of Mecklenburg-Western Pomerania, network development, which occurred within a relatively short time period, was facilitated by the strong commitment of various private and public actors. Common experiences from the socialist period also played a role, as network initiators and promoters were able to draw on trusted relations and 'old' linkages. While this kind of behavior ('blat', cf. Ledeneva 1998) was a necessary response to the constant shortage of materials and consumer goods in the socialist period, its functioning was extended to the transition period. In Mecklenburg-Western Pomerania, this obviously helped to build a formal network structure in a relatively short period of time, as it facilitated identity creation in networks and amongst women (entrepreneurs) during the transition process.

On the other hand, network initiators comment on a general lower usage of networks and business associations by women entrepreneurs in East Germany, which is partly reflected in a lower membership rates of established women (business) organizations in East Germany (cf. also Welter, Ammon and Trettin, 2004). The reasons might include a mistrust of formal organizations, as socialist private and professional life was characterized by obligatory membership in all kinds of different organizations. Partly, this also refers to the 'persistence of friendship networks' (Howard, 2003, p. 129), which might render membership in 'formal' organizations superfluous. This also is reflected in our study on the regional embeddedness of networks, where during interviews, respondents regularly emphasized their 'socialist background', which helped them in knowing whom they had to contact in order to solve problems, where to get access resources and support for their network etc (Welter and Trettin, 2005).

Development and Characteristics of Women's Entrepreneurship in West and East Germany

Development of Women's Entrepreneurship: Gaining Ground

Women's entrepreneurship in Germany is growing, alongside with an increasing share in the overall labour force. In 2004, women accounted for 45 per cent of the total labour force, and there were more than 3.8 million entrepreneurs in both West and East Germany, 28 per cent of whom were women.

In *West Germany*,[5] female entrepreneurship has been rising slowly from 757,000 self-employed persons in 1960 to 890,000 in mid 2003, with a slump in the late 1980s and early 1990s, when the number of women entrepreneurs only reached 687,000 in 1991, thus being considerably lower than 1960. Overall, women's entrepreneurship has been growing by 17.5 per cent, compared to a 'mere' 4.7 per cent for men during the same period. Most of this growth occurred during the 1990s. From 1991-2003, the total West German female labour force (including self-employed persons) grew by 10.8 per cent (male labour force: decrease of 6.3 per cent), whilst female entrepreneurship increased by 29.5 per cent, which was considerably higher compared to the 13.1 per cent-increase in male entrepreneurship (Figure 8.1). Nowadays women entrepreneurs account for 6.7 per cent of all West German female labour force and 28.2 per cent of all entrepreneurs. However, women also still constitute the majority of unpaid family workers in small enterprises, with more than three quarters of them being female.

In *East Germany*, since 1991 total female entrepreneurship has increased considerably by 85.7 per cent, amounting to 184,000 in mid 2003. However, this growth started from a very low level with 99,000 women entrepreneurs and 249,000 male entrepreneurs existing in 1991. Moreover, the positive development of women's entrepreneurship went hand in hand with an overall loss in female

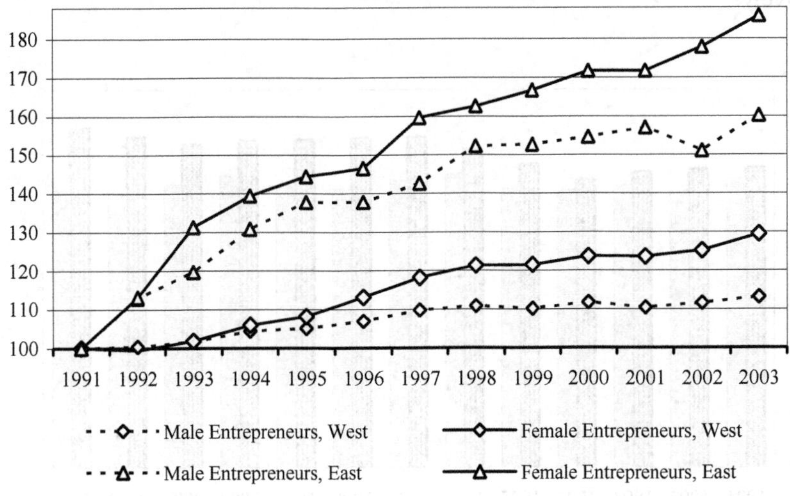

1991 = 100

Source: Own calculations, based on data from the Statistical Office.

Figure 8.1 Development of entrepreneurship in West and East Germany, 1991-2003

wage employment, which decreased by 18.2 per cent to 2.9 million. This appears to indicate a push towards entrepreneurship, especially as women were the first to be fired and the last to find new employment after transition started. On the other hand, the share of female entrepreneurs to all entrepreneurs has been high since the re-unification, on average 26 per cent in 1991 and nearly 32 per cent in 2003. This also can be attributed to the tradition of a high labour participation of women in the former GDR and not only to their rising unemployment after 1991.

Characteristics of Women-owned Businesses

Are there differences with regard to the characteristics of women-owned businesses in West and East Germany? With regard to *size*, statistical data confirms for Germany a fact well known from research on women entrepreneurs, namely, that women entrepreneurs more frequently work without employees, compared to men. Generally, the 1990s observed a trend towards micro firms, i.e., enterprises without any employees (Welter 2002), which is more pronounced for women entrepreneurs, as mentioned above. Whilst in 1991 55 per cent of all women entrepreneurs worked without any employees, compared to 42 per cent of all men entrepreneurs, in 2003 this share had increased to nearly 62 per cent for women and 49 per cent for men respectively.

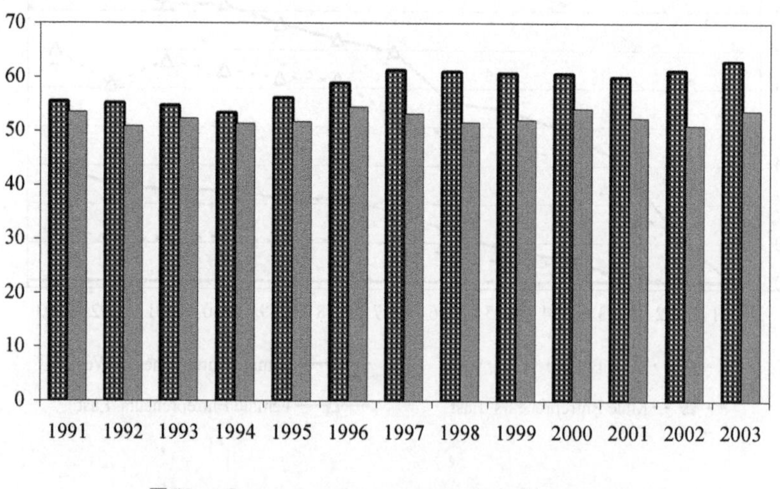

Source: Own calculations, based on data from the Federal Statistical Office.

Figure 8.2 Share of women-owned enterprises without employees in West and East Germany, 1991-2003

Interestingly, this differs considerably between West and East German entrepreneurs (Figure 8.2): In 2003 the share of women entrepreneurs without employees amounted to 63 per cent in West Germany and 54 per cent in the East. Figure 8.2 also demonstrates that the development towards micro enterprises has been more pronounced for West German women entrepreneurs than for the East German ones.

Sector differences might partly explain these size differences between West and East German women entrepreneurs. Across Germany as a whole, women entrepreneurs (similar to female wage employees) cluster in trade and services. They are still more likely to enter entrepreneurship in consumer-oriented and personal services such as laundry, cosmetics, hairdressing and personal care (Fehrenbach and Lauxen-Ulbrich, 2002). In 2002, the top four sectors for women entrepreneurs were trade (19.9 per cent of female entrepreneurs), personal services (18.2 per cent), social and health services (15.5 per cent) and business-oriented services (14.9 per cent) (Lauxen-Ulbrich and Leicht, 2004). Some female dominated business fields such as social and health services offer women less possibilities for entering entrepreneurship, obviously due to these fields being dominated by public employers and large organizations (Lauxen-Ulbrich and Leicht, 2004).

Comparing the sector distribution across West and East Germany, there are no fundamental differences with one exception (Table 8.3): the share of women firms in trade and catering had been considerably higher in East Germany both in 1991 and 2001. In 1991, this was probably a main result from the small privatization process, which took place in the early 1990s. Moreover, this might indicate an ongoing lack of resources on behalf of East German women entrepreneurs, which hindered them to set up businesses in sectors with higher entry barriers. On the whole, the sector developments in the first decade of re-unification illustrate similar shifts: a decrease in manufacturing and an increase in trade and catering as well as in other services.

Table 8.3 Sectoral distribution of women-owned enterprises in West and East Germany, 1991 and 2001

	West German female entrepreneurs		East German female entrepreneurs	
	1991	2001	1991	2001
Manufacturing	10.6	7.9	11.1	7.1
Trade, catering	27.8	31.8	34.3	36.5
Other services	54.0	55.4	51.5	54.1

Source: Own calculations, based on Statistisches Bundesamt (2003).

Another explanation for regional size differences of women-owned enterprises refers to the form of women's entrepreneurship in both parts of Germany. Table 8.4 presents data on full-time and part-time entrepreneurship, illustrating considerable differences between West and East German women-led firms: In West Germany, there is a pronounced trend towards part-time entrepreneurship, while the majority of East German women entrepreneurs owns full-time businesses. Not surprisingly, it is more frequently women in enterprises without employees who work part-time than those with larger firms.

Table 8.4 Share of full-time and part-time female entrepreneurship in West and East Germany, 1991 and 2001

	West German female entrepreneurs		East German female entrepreneurs	
	1991	**2001**	**1991**	**2001**
Full-time entrepreneurship	71.1	68.8	89.8	85.3
Part-time entrepreneurship	27.9	31.2	10.2	14.7

Source: Own calculations, based on Statistisches Bundesamt (2003).

Entering Entrepreneurship

An important question concerns possible differences in motivations for entering entrepreneurship. In general, research studies appear to confirm a 'push'-hypothesis for women towards entrepreneurship, although this apparently changes over time. Unemployment and fear of job loss are considered main push motives for entering entrepreneurship. These motives play a more important role for unemployed business founders, while pull motives such as personal independence or attractive business opportunities are more decisive for employed ones (Hinz and Jungbauer-Gans, 1999). This appears to change throughout entrepreneurship, indicating learning experiences and growing confidence: A 1997 study observed that nearly two thirds of the female entrepreneurs interviewed would never consider giving up entrepreneurship compared to 57 per cent of male entrepreneurs (Welter, 2001a). Although this may partly indicate entrepreneurship as an attractive employment possibility for women allowing them to balance work and household or family responsibilities, entering entrepreneurship was often a necessity for those women in order to be able to participate in the labour market, especially after child-rearing periods.

An overall push towards entrepreneurship is confirmed by statistical data. A large share of German women who changed or obtained employment in the year 2000 (47 per cent, were previously unemployed, another 32 per cent held a non-wage position, i.e., they were studying or at home as a 'housewife' before setting up their venture (Lauxen-Ulbrich and Leicht, 2002, p. 30). In East Germany, socialist values might initially have contributed to the higher share of female entrepreneurs and to them voluntarily entering entrepreneurship, because the former GDR, like all socialist states, supported and valued female qualified employment. This might have increased women's willingness to enter entrepreneurship, although growing unemployment also contributed to it, especially as women were the first to be fired and the last to find new employment after transition started. Here, data on craft entrepreneurs appear to confirm East German female entrepreneurship as a survival strategy (Welter, 1996): Nearly 30 per cent of female entrepreneurs in East Germany, but only 12 per cent in West Germany named unemployment as a motive for entrepreneurship.

All this is supported by recent GEM results for Germany, which indicate a higher share of necessity-based female entrepreneurship, compared to men: Nearly 36 per cent of the German women (8 percentage points higher than 2003) stated that they entered entrepreneurship out of 'necessity', compared to 21 per cent of the men (Sternberg, Bergmann and Lückgen, 2004, p. 35). Necessity entrepreneurship includes those that either did not find wage employment or who were dissatisfied with their previous job situation. Although the GEM does not report separate results for West and East German women, one might assume that this is even more pronounced in the East German context, as the overall share of necessity entrepreneurs has increased considerably from 2001 to 2003 (Sternberg, Bergmann and Lückgen, 2004, p. 14).

Case studies add to this showing that women often set up their own business when re-entering the labour market after a period of child rising (Welter, 2000b), although there remains doubt whether this reflects genuine 'necessity-based' entrepreneurship, the more so, as concepts such as necessity and opportunity-based entrepreneurship neglect that most entrepreneurs set up their business for a variety of reasons (Smallbone and Welter, 2003). Here, a pilot study researching nascent entrepreneurship in Germany illustrates that, compared to West Germany, a higher share of East German women appears interested in entrepreneurship, which would contradict the GEM results indicating the dominance of necessity-based entrepreneurship in East Germany (Figure 8.3).[6] East German women show a higher interest in entrepreneurship. Therefore, a larger share than in West Germany has a concrete business intention and has started realizing their idea (i.e., they are classified as nascent entrepreneur). On the other hand, more East German women than West German ones either discontinue working on their idea or never start this process, which might indicate both problems in accessing resources or less knowledge and skills needed for entrepreneurship.

An analysis for the transition from business wish to nascent entrepreneurship illustrates that overall German women have a four percent lower probability to express a business wish (cf. Engel and Welter, 2004). Interestingly, this only applies to West German women, confirming women employment and, consequently, entrepreneurship as being more accepted in the East German society (Welter, 2004). On the other hand, all interviewed female nascent entrepreneurs in East Germany claim that they started realizing their idea with assistance from employers. This way of starting a new business applies to only 19 per cent of the West German female nascent entrepreneurs, indicating possible resource problems in the Eastern context of venture creation.

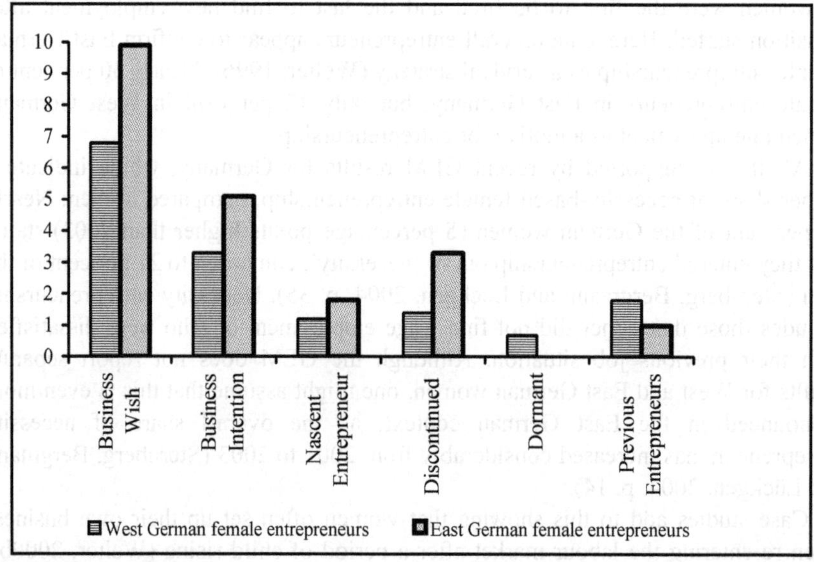

Source: Welter (2000a).

Figure 8.3 From business wish to nascent entrepreneurship, in per cent of German population, 1999

Developing the Business: Growth Intentions

Do women entrepreneurs want to grow their business? At a first glance results from the above mentioned pilot study of German nascent entrepreneurs confirm a well-known story, i.e., female nascents are less interested in growing their business, whilst male nascents are more inclined to plan for growth (Welter, 2001a, 2001b). When asked for their business aims, 18 per cent of male and 28 per cent of the female nascents had plans to work on their own without employees, and, regardless of gender, most aimed at moderate employment growth, planning an enterprise with some employees. Less than 7 per cent of female nascents, but nearly 25 per cent of male nascents intend to have a large enterprise. This differs across level of education and current job status. Interestingly, higher educated female nascents are interested more frequently in growing their enterprise to a large size than women with apprenticeship and highly educated male nascents. This might indicate growing confidence going hand in hand with higher qualifications. Growth intentions in terms of limited employment growth are also more pronounced for female nascents starting from wage employment.

Recent GEM results show a similar picture. When asked how many employees their enterprise will have five years after having been set up, 55 per cent of the female nascents planned for a firm with one or two employees, compared to 22 per cent of the male nascents, whilst 51 per cent of the male nascents aimed to have an enterprise with more than five employees (Sternberg, Bergmann and Lückgen 2004, p. 37). Around 85 per cent of the female nascents expect that in a period of five years time their enterprises will not offer more than five jobs. On the other hand, as shown above (see Figure 8.2), the majority of female entrepreneurs in Germany have micro enterprises without employees.

All in all, the results presented here cannot confirm a popular hypothesis, namely, that women entrepreneurs are less inclined to grow their enterprises, although the picture is a static one, as research on changes in growth intentions is lacking. Instead, the discrepancies between growth aims and growth realization[7] may indicate gender-specific access to external resources (especially capital). Additionally, more women entrepreneurs start a part-time business compared to men, and those businesses in general have lower growth potentials. Finally, the differences between business aims and realized growth might also indicate self-perceived and objective barriers (availability of growth finance) arising during venture creation and business development. This might prevent women entrepreneurs from realizing their growth plans.

While so far we have discussed results for women entrepreneurs in Germany as a whole, the question remains whether there are differences across West and East German women entrepreneurs? Table 8.5 presents data on growth intentions of female nascent in both parts of Germany, illustrating a considerably lower growth orientation of female nascents in East Germany. Overall, female nascents in both parts of Germany strive for a limited enterprise size.

Table 8.5 Growth intentions of nascent women entrepreneurs in West and East Germany, 1999 (in per cent)

	West German female nascents	East German female nascents
No employment growth planned	23.6	41.1
Limited employment growth	58.8	58.9
Large enterprise size	8.8	0

Source: Welter and Lageman (2003, p. 40).

However, the low overall growth orientation of East German female nascents was surprising, given the results presented above (see again Figure 8.2) that a larger share of East German women entrepreneurs owns micro firms. Moreover, none of the female nascents in East Germany named a large enterprise size as their aim, compared to significant 8.8 per cent of West German female nascents. These differences in growth orientations across West and East Germany could be a result of regional endogenous growth potentials as well as of the overall worse macroeconomic situation in East Germany, most probably reinforced by lower available income and access to resources needed for business development in East Germany (Welter and Lageman, 2003).

Conclusions

To sum up, the 1990s have seen an above average increase for women start-ups, although a gender gap remains. With regard to the development of female entrepreneurship, we can observe two main differences between West and East Germany: the growth rate has been higher, albeit from a low level, and the share of women entrepreneurs remains higher in East Germany, compared to West Germany. Differences are also apparent with regard to characteristics of the businesses such as larger enterprise sizes in East Germany, a larger share of full-time women entrepreneurs and generally a higher interest in entering entrepreneurship. From the sectoral perspective, the analysis confirms comparable structures of women's entrepreneurship in both West and East Germany after more than a decade of re-unification: Female entrepreneurs mainly operate in trade and services which reflects the overall shift towards service industries in West Germany as well as the transformation of the previously centrally planned East German economy.

The data and research results presented in this chapter thus draw attention to differing institutional influences on opportunity fields for entrepreneurship and opportunity perceptions of entrepreneurs. In comparison to West Germany, the share of East German female entrepreneurs has been higher since re-unification, reflecting the influence of differing attitudes towards female employment and the importance of path dependency in explaining these differences. The overall level of female entrepreneurship in East Germany is still lower compared to West Germany, although the above-average growth during 1991 to 1995 draws attention to the fact, that socialism apparently did not create a distinctive 'homo sovieticus' who would show no entrepreneurial initiative. Nevertheless, this is partly also explained by the worsening labour market conditions for East German women. Thus, the overall favourable development of women's entrepreneurship does not necessarily indicate better external conditions for entrepreneurship compared to West Germany.

In general, the German institutional environment constrains female entrepreneurship, both because of conservative values and the impact of the tax system which discriminates against paid work of married women (Holst, 2001). While there has been progress with respect to the legal and institutional environment for female entrepreneurship, especially in West Germany, several policy-related factors and societal attitudes still might unfavourable impact on women's willingness to enter entrepreneurship. Societal values implicitly understand female entrepreneurship as less desirable, which in turn affects the self-perceptions and individual attitudes of women. Moreover, while the East German society still values the labour market participation of women highly, empirical evidence illustrates that the rapid re-unification process, which transferred West German institutions, rules, laws and organizations to East Germany, also favoured a 'renaissance of conservatism', thus resulting in hidden conflicts between the predominant orientation of East German women and societal attitudes. In this context, research confirmed that professional choices of women take into account what society deems to be desirable and 'correct' for their sex (Holst, 2001). Consequently, this might (partly) explain lower rates of female entrepreneurs as well as the nature of female entrepreneurship and the still existing differences between West and East Germany.

The chapter set out to compare women's entrepreneurship in historically similar cultural settings, which experienced a different path of economic and societal development for 40 years. Overall, the findings draw attention to the institutional embeddedness of women's entrepreneurship, which is influenced by the regulatory framework, societal values and norms of behaviour. This allows to explore and to partly explain differences observed across women's enterprises, their ways into entrepreneurship and motivations, all of which are influenced by institutional legacies. Here, the chapter takes an important step towards a better understanding of women's entrepreneurship and its development in both mature market economies and former socialist economies.

Notes

1 This section is based on Welter et al. (2002) and Aidis et al. (2005, forthcoming).

2 Data reported in this and other sections come from the micro census and other official statistical sources of the Federal Statistical Office in Germany, unless reported otherwise.

3 This is a category in the micro census, a yearly 1 per cent-representative survey of the German population, conducted by the Federal Statistical Office. The classification of an entrepreneur refers to the question regarding employment positions. In case the respondent answered 'selbständig', (s)he is classified as entrepreneur. 'Selbständige' include both self-employed persons (i.e., genuine self-employed persons) as well as small business owners with employees. Data cited in this section are taken from the micro census, per cent and growth rates are calculated by the author, if not mentioned otherwise.

4 The German language distinguishes between 'Unternehmer' (male entrepreneur) and 'Unternehmerin' (female entrepreneur). In daily life, most people as well as the media, unless specifically reporting about women entrepreneurs, use the male term, meaning this to include women as well.

5 Longitudinal data are only available for West Germany, for East Germany we can observe the developments since 1991.

6 For more details on the study, modelled on the US Panel Study of Entrepreneurial Dynamics, cf. Welter (2000a, 2001a) and Welter and Bergmann (2002).

7 Of course, the differences between nascents with growth intentions and entrepreneurs who did grow in terms of employment could be a result of the fact, that mainly nascents with growth intentions might not realize their business formation, although this is not very realistic. Data on nascents for other countries confirm that between 30 per cent in the Netherlands, 33 per cent in Sweden and 14 per cent in Norway manage to set up a

business (van Gelderen and Bosma, 2000; Alsos, Ljunggren and Rotefoss, 2000). With respect to the realization of growth intentions, our pilot study thus only allow for very basic reasoning because we do not know how many nascents will finally realize their business idea.

References

Achtenhagen, L. and Welter, F. (2003), 'Female Entrepreneurship as Reflected in German Media in the Years 1995-2001', in J. Butler (ed), *New Perspectives on Women Entrepreneurs*, Information Age Publishing, Greenwich, pp. 71-100.

Achtenhagen, L. and Welter, F. (2005), *"The attractive blond lady in a pink business suit" – Analyzing the discourse on female entrepreneurship in German newspapers between 1997 and 2003*, paper presented at the IECER Conference, 2-4 February, University of Amsterdam, Amsterdam.

Aidis, R., Welter, F., Smallbone, D. and Isakova, N. (2005), 'Female Entrepreneurship in Transition Economies: The Case of Lithuania and Ukraine', *Feminist Economies, Special Issue 'Women Entrepreneurship'* (forthcoming).

Almus, M. (2001), *Das Wachstum junger Unternehmen – Eine Bestandsaufnahme 10 Jahre nach der Wiedervereinigung*, Discussion Paper No. 01-40, ZEW, Mannheim.

Almus, M., Engel, D. and Nerlinger, E.A. (1999), 'Determinanten des Beschäftigungswachstums junger Unternehmen in den alten und neuen Bundesländern: Bestehen Unterschiede hinsichtlich der Technologieorientierung?' *Zeitschrift für Wirtschafts- und Sozialwissenschaften*, vol. 119, pp. 561-592.

Alsos, G.A., Ljunggren, E. and Rotefoss, B. (2000), *Who makes it through the business formation process? - A Longitudinal Study of Entrepreneurs*, paper presented at the Babson College-Kauffman Foundation Entrepreneurship Research Conference, Babson, June 8-10.

Arthur, W.B. (1994), *Increasing Returns and Path Dependence in the Economy*, University of Michigan Press, Ann Arbor.

Bergmann, H. (2002), *Entrepreneurial attitudes and start-up attempts in ten German regions. An empirical analysis on the basis of the theory of planned behaviour*, Working Paper No. 2002-01, University of Cologne, Cologne.

Birley, S. (1989), 'Female Entrepreneurs: Are they really any different?' *Journal of Small Business Management*, January, pp. 32-37.

Bögenhold, D. and Staber, U. (1990), ‚Selbständigkeit als ein Reflex auf Arbeitslosigkeit? Makrosoziologische Befunde einer international-komparativen Studie', *Kölner Zeitschrift für Soziologie und Sozialpsychologie*, vol. 42, pp. 265–279.

Brixy, U. (1999), *Die Rolle von Betriebsgründungen für die Arbeitsplatzdynamik. Eine räumliche Analyse für Ostdeutschland 1991 bis 1996*, IAB, Nürnberg.

Brussig, M. (eds) (1997), *Kleinbetriebe in den neuen Bundesländern*, Leske + Budrich, Opladen.

Busenitz, L.W., Gómez, C. and Spencer, J.W. (2000), 'Country Institutional Profiles: Unlocking Entrepreneurial Phenomena', *Academy of Management Journal*, vol. 43, pp. 994-1003.

Dallago, B. (2000), 'The Organisational and Productive Impact of the Economic System. The Case of SMEs', *Small Business Economics*, vol. 15, pp. 303-319.

Delmar, F. and Holmquist, C. (2004), *Women Entrepreneurship: Issues and Policies*, Manuscript for the OECD, Stockholm School of Economics, Stockholm.

Denzau, A.T. and North, D.C. (1994), 'Shared Mental Models: Ideologies and Institutions', *Kyklos*, vol. 47, no. 1, pp. 3-31.

Engel, D. and Welter, F. (2004), *Dreamers and Doers – Who succeeds in the Process of Venture Creation?*, paper presented at the Interdisciplinary European Conference on Entrepreneurship Research (IECER), University of Regensburg, Regensburg.

Fagenson, E.A. and Marcus, E.C. (1991), 'Perceptions of the sex-role stereotypic characteristics of entrepreneurs', *Entrepreneurship Theory and Practice,* vol. 15, pp. 33-47.

Fehrenbach, S. and Leicht, R. (2002), *Strukturmerkmale und Potentiale der von Frauen geführten Betriebe in Deutschland,* Veröffentlichungen des Instituts für Mittelstandsforschung der Universität Mannheim, Grüne Reihe Nr. 47, Universität Mannheim, Mannheim.

Feige, E. (1997), 'Underground Activity and Institutional Change: Productive, Protective, and Predatory Behavior in Transition Economies', in J.M. Nelson, C. Tilly and L. Walker (eds), *Transforming Post-Communist Political Economies*, National Academies of Sciences, Washington, D.C., pp. 21-34.

Frerichs, P. and Wiemert, H. (2002), *„Ich gebe, damit Du gibst". Frauennetzwerke – strategisch, reziprok, exklusiv*, Leske + Budrich, Opladen.

Fritsch, M. and Mallok, J. (1998), 'Wie es vorangeht – Die Entwicklung mittelständischer Industriebetriebe in Ost- und Westdeutschland 1992-1995', in J. Schmude (ed), pp. 154-179.

Fritsch, M. et al. (2001), *Gründungen in Deutschland: Datenquellen, Niveau und räumlich-sektorale Struktur*, Technische Universität Bergakademie, Freiberg.

Gensior, S. (ed), *Vergesellschaftung und Frauenerwerbsarbeit: Ost-West-Vergleich*, Edition Sigma, Berlin.

Gerhard, U. (2003), 'Mütter zwischen Individualisierung und Institution: Kulturelle Leitbilder in der Wohlfahrtspolitik', in U. Gerhard, T. Knijn and A. Weckwert (eds), *Erwerbstätige Mütter: Ein europäischer Vergleich*, Beck, München, pp. 53-84.

Gottfried, H. and O'Reilly, J. (2002), ‚Der Geschlechtervertrag in Deutschland und Japan: Die Schwäche eines starken Ernährermodells', in K. Gottschall and B. Pfau-Effinger (eds), *Zukunft der Arbeit und Geschlecht*, Leske + Budrich, Opladen, pp. 29-57.

Gustafson, T. (1999), *Capitalism Russian-style*, Cambridge University Press, Cambridge.

Gustafsson, S. (1995), 'Public Policies and Women's Labor Force Participation: A Comparison of Sweden, West Germany, and the Netherlands', in P.P. Schulz (ed), *Investments in Women's Human Capital,* University of Chicago Press, Chicago, London, pp. 91-112.

Harhoff, D. (ed) (1997), *Unternehmensgründungen: Empirische Analysen für die alten und neuen Bundesländer*, Nomos, Baden-Baden.

Hinz, T. (1998), *Betriebsgründungen in Ostdeutschland*, Edition Sigma, Berlin.

Hinz, Th. and Jungbauer-Gans, M. (1999), 'Starting a Business after Unemployment,' *Entrepreneurship & Regional Development*, vol. 11, pp. 317–333.

Holst, E. (2002), 'Institutionelle Determinanten der Erwerbsarbeit', in F. Maier and A. Fiedler (eds), *Gender Matters: feministische Analysen zur Wirtschafts- und Sozialpolitik*, Fhw-Forschung, 42/43, Edition Sigma, Berlin, pp. 89-109.

Holst, E. (2001), *Institutionelle Determinanten der Erwerbsarbeit: Zur Notwendigkeit einer Gender-Perspektive in den Wirtschaftswissenschaften*, DIW Diskussionspapier, 237, DIW, Berlin.

Howard, M.M. (2003), *The Weakness of Civil Society in Post-Communist Europe*, Cambridge University Press, Cambridge.

Hyrsky, K. (1999), 'Entrepreneurial Metaphors and Concepts: An Exploratory Study', *International Small Business Journal*, vol. 18, no. 1, pp. 13-34.

IfM (2003), *Unternehmerinnen in Deutschland*, Dokumentation 522, BMWA, Bonn/Berlin.

IfM Bonn (2001), *Gender-spezifische Aufbereitung der amtlichen Statistik: Möglichkeiten respektive Anforderungen*, Materialien zur Gleichstellungspolitik, 82/2001, BMFSFJ, Bonn.

Kehlbeck, H. and Schneider, U. (1999), *Frauen als Zielgruppe von Existenzgründungen unter besonderer Berücksichtigung der Finanzierungsaspekte*, Eine Untersuchung im Auftrag des Senatsamtes für die Gleichstellung, Hamburg.

Kerblay, B. (1977), *La Société Soviétique Contemporaine*, Armand Colin, Paris.

Knijn, T., Jönsson, I. and Klammer, U. (2003), ‚Betreuungspakete schnüren: Zur Alltagsorganisation berufstätiger Mütter', in U. Gerhard, T. Knijn and A. Weckwert (eds), *Erwerbstätige Mütter: Ein europäischer Vergleich*, Beck, München, pp. 162-192.

Lang, C. (1999), *Was unternehmen?! Erfahrungen und Selbstinterpretationen ostdeutscher Unternehmer/innen auf dem Weg in die Marktwirtschaft*, IWH, Halle/Saale.

Lauxen-Ulbrich, M. and Leicht, R. (2002), *Entwicklung und Tätigkeitsprofil selbständiger Frauen in Deutschland: Eine empirische Untersuchung anhand der Daten des Mikrozensus*, Veröffentlichungen des Instituts für Mittelstandsforschung, 46, Universität Mannheim, Mannheim.

Lauxen-Ulbrich, M. and Leicht, R. (2003), *First Statistical Overview – National Report on Women (Start-up), Entrepreneurs and Female Self-Employment in Germany*, Small Business Research Institute, University of Mannheim.

Lauxen-Ulbrich, M. and Leicht, R. (2004), 'Wirtschaftliche und berufliche Orientierung von selbständigen Frauen', in R. Leicht and F. Welter (eds), *Gründerinnen und selbständige Frauen - Potenziale, Strukturen und Entwicklungen in Deutschland*, Loeper, Karlsruhe, pp. 72-96.

Ledeneva, A.V. (1998), *Russia's Economy of Favours: Blat, Networking and Informal Exchange*, Cambridge University Press, Cambridge.

Leicht, R. and Welter, F. (eds) (2004), *Gründerinnen und selbständige Frauen - Potenziale, Strukturen und Entwicklungen in Deutschland*, Loeper, Karlsruhe.

Leipold, H. (1999), 'Institutionenbildung in der Transformation', in H.-H. Höhmann (ed), *Spontaner oder gestalteter Prozeß? Die Rolle des Staates in der Wirtschaftstransformation*, Schriftenreihe des BiOst, 38, Nomos, Baden-Baden, pp. 133-151.

Letablier, M.-T. and Jönsson, I. (2003), 'Kinderbetreuung und politische Handlungslogik', U. Gerhard, T. Knijn and A. Weckwert (eds), *Erwerbstätige Mütter: Ein europäischer Vergleich* Beck, München, pp. 85-109.

May-Strobl, E. and Paulini, M. (1994), *Die Entwicklung junger Unternehmen in den neuen Bundesländern*, Schriften zur Mittelstandsforschung, 62 NF, Schäffer-Poeschel, Stuttgart.

Meyer, S. and Schulze, E. (1995), 'Die Auswirkungen der Wende auf Frauen und Familien in den neuen Bundesländern', in S. Gensior (ed), *Vergesellschaftung und Frauenerwerbsarbeit: Ost-West-Vergleiche*, Edition Sigma, Berlin, pp. 249-269.

Morrison, A. (1998), *Entrepreneurship and Culture Specificity*, paper presented at IntEnt98, Oestrich-Winkel, 26–28 July.

Mummert, U. (1995), *Informelle Institutionen in ökonomischen Transformationsprozessen*, Nomos, Baden-Baden.

Mummert, U. (1999), 'Informal Institutions and Institutional Policy – Shedding Light on the Myth of Institutional Conflict', Diskussionsbeitrag, 02-99, Max-Planck Institute for Research into Economic Systems, Jena.

Munz, S. (1997), 'Frauenerwerbstätigkeit im Spannungsfeld veränderter Lebensentwürfe und wohlfahrtsstaatlicher Regelungen', *Ifo-Schnelldienst,* vol. 23. pp. 21-35.

North D.C. (1990), *Institutions, Institutional Change and Economic Performance*, Cambridge University Press, Cambridge.

North, D.C. (1995), 'Structural Changes of Institutions and the Process of Transformation', *Prague Economic Papers*, vol. 4, pp. 229-234.

Piasecki, B. and Rogut, A. (1993), *Self Regulation of SME Sector Development at a More Advanced Stage of Transformation*, paper presented to the 20th Annual Conference of E.A.R.I.E., Tel Aviv, September.

Piorkowsky, M.-B. (2001), *Existenzgründungsprozesse im Zu- und Nebenerwerb von Frauen und Männern: Eine empirische Analyse der Bedingungen und Verläufe bei Gründungs- und Entwicklungsprozessen von Unternehmen unter besonderer Berücksichtigung genderspezifischer Aspekte*, BMFSFJ, Bonn.

Piorkowsky, M.-B. with assistance of S. Scholl (2002), *Genderaspekte in der finanziellen Förderung von Unternehmensgründungen. Eine qualitative und quantitative Analyse der Programme auf Bundesebene – unter besonderer Berücksichtigung der Gründung durch Frauen*, Bericht im Auftrag des BMFSFJ, Universität Bonn.

Reynolds, P.D., Hay, M. and Camp, S.M. (1999), *Global Entrepreneurship Monitor: 1999 Executive Report,* Kauffman Center, Kansas City.

Rocksloh-Papendieck, B. (1988), *Frauenarbeit am Straßenrand: Kenkeyküchen in Ghana*, Arbeiten aus dem Institut für Afrikakunde, 55, Deutsches Überseeinstitut, Hamburg.

Rocksloh-Papendieck, B. (1995a), *Verlust der kollektiven Bindung: Frauenalltag in der Wende*, Centaurus, Herbolzheim.

Rocksloh-Papendieck, B. (1995b), 'Lebensstrategien im Umbruch', in S. Gensior (ed), *Vergesellschaftung und Frauenerwerbsarbeit: Ost-West-Vergleich*, Edition Sigman, Berlin, pp. 219-248.

Schmidt, D. (2002), 'Im Schatten der „großen Männer": Zur unterbelichteten Rolle der Unternehmerinnen in der deutschen Wirtschaftsgeschichte des 19. und 20. Jahrhunderts', in F. Maier and A. Fiedler (eds), *Gender Matters: feministische Analysen zur Wirtschafts- und Sozialpolitik*, Fhw-Forschung, 42/43, Edition Sigma, Berlin, pp. 211-229.

Schmude, J. (ed) (1998), *Neue Unternehmen in Ostdeutschland*, Wirtschaftswissenschaftliche Beiträge, 164, Physica, Heidelberg.

Schrumpf, H. (1990), 'Selbständige in der DDR', *RWI-Mitteilungen*, vol. 41, pp. 105-116.

Smallbone, D. and Welter, F. (2001), 'The distinctiveness of entrepreneurship in transition economies', *Small Business Economics*, vol. 16, pp. 249-262.

Smallbone, D. and Welter, F. (2003), *Entrepreneurship in transition economies: necessity or opportunity driven?* Paper to the 2003 Babson College-Kauffman Foundation Entrepreneurship Research Conference, Babson, USA, 5-7 June.

Sperling, C. and May, M. (2001), *Aktivitäten von und für Unternehmerinnen und Existenzgründerinnen im Bereich der Klein- und Mittelbetriebe (KMU) – Bundesweiter Überblick, Band 1, Bundesweites Adressenverzeichnis, Band 2*, Recherche im Auftrag des Bundesministeriums für Familie, Senioren, Frauen und Jugend, Essen/Bonn.

Statistisches Bundesamt (2003), *Existenzgründungen im Kontext der Arbeits- und Lebensverhältnisse in Deutschland: Eine Strukturanalyse von Mikrozensusergebnissen. Materialband 1*, Bonn.

Statistisches Bundesamt (2004), *Leben und Arbeiten in Deutschland – Mikrozensus 2003. Tabellenanhang zur Pressebroschüre*, Bonn.

Sternberg, R., Bergmann, H. and Lückgen, I. (2003), *Global Entrepreneurship Monitor: Länderbericht Deutschland*, Universität zu Köln, Köln.

Sternberg, R., Bergmann, H. and Lückgen, I. (2004), *Global Entrepreneurship Monitor: Länderbericht Deutschland 2003*, Universität zu Köln, Köln.

Thomas, M. (1996), '…dass man noch da ist! Schwierigkeiten bei der Suche nach einem ostdeutschen Mittelstand', *Aus Politik und Zeitgeschichte*, vol. B 15, pp. 21-31.

Thomas, M. (2001), *Ein Blick zurück und voraus: Ostdeutsche Neue Selbständige – aufgeschobenes Scheitern oder Potenziale zur Erneuerung?*, BISS, Berlin.

Tschepurenko, A. (1998), *Die russischen Kleinunternehmen in der zweiten Hälfte der 90er Jahre. Teil I: Entwicklung, Leistung, Probleme*, BiOst, Köln.

Wade-Benzoni, K.A. et al. (2002), 'Barriers to Resolution in Ideologically based Negotations: The role of Values and Institutions', *Academy of Management Review*, vol. 27, pp. 41-57.

Welter, F. (1996), *Gründungsprofile im west- und ostdeutschen Handwerk: Eine vergleichende Untersuchung in den Kammerbezirken Düsseldorf und Leipzig*, RUFIS-Studie, Nr. 1/1996, Brockmeyer, Bochum.

Welter, F. (2000a), *Gründungspotenzial und Gründungsprozess in Deutschland - Eine konzeptionelle und empirische Betrachtung*, Schriften und Materialien zu Handwerk und Mittelstand, 4, RWI, Essen.

Welter, F. (2000b), *„Einmal im Leben darf jeder etwas Risikoreiches tun" - Fallstudien von Gründern und Gründerinnen*, Schriften und Materialien zu Handwerk und Mittelstand, 9, RWI, Essen.

Welter, F. (2001a), *Nascent Entrepreneurship in Germany*, Schriften und Materialien zu Handwerk und Mittelstand, 11, RWI, Essen.

Welter, F. (2001b), 'Who wants to grow? – Growth Intentions and Growth Profiles of (Nascent), Entrepreneurs in Germany', *Frontiers of Entrepreneurship Research*, vol. 2001, pp. 91-100.

Welter, F. (2002), *Entrepreneurship in West and East Germany*, paper presented at the Babson College-Kauffman Foundation Entrepreneurship Research Conference, Boulder/USA, 6-8 June.

Welter, F. (2004), 'The Environment for female Entrepreneurship in Germany', *Journal of Small Business and Enterprise Development*, vol. 11, pp. 212-221.

Welter, F. and Lageman, B. with assistance of Stoytcheva, M. (2003), *Gründerinnen in Deutschland: Potenziale und das institutionelle Umfeld*, Untersuchungen des Rheinisch-Westfälisches Institut für Wirtschaftsforschung, 41, RWI, Essen.

Welter, F. and Bergmann, H. (2002), '„Nascent Entrepreneurs" in Deutschland', in J. Schmude and R. Leiner (eds), *Unternehmensgründungen – Interdisziplinäre Beiträge zum Entrepreneurship Research*, Physica, Heidelberg, pp. 33-62.

Welter, F. and Trettin, L. (2005), 'The Spatial Embeddedness of Networks for Women Entrepreneurs', In M. Fritsch and J. Schmude (eds), *Entrepreneurship in the Region*. Kluwer, Dordrecht (forthcoming).

Welter, F., Smallbone, D., Isakova, N., Aculai, E. and Schakirova, N. (2002), *Female Entrepreneurship: A conceptual and empirical view*, Schriften und Materialien zu Handwerk und Mittelstand, 15, RWI, Essen.

Welter, F., Ammon, U. and Trettin, L. (2004), *Netzwerke und Unternehmensgründungen von Frauen*, RWI: Schriften, 76, Duncker & Humblot, Berlin.

Part 4
Policy Issues and Policy Perspectives

Chapter 9

Conclusions and Policy Perspectives

Friederike Welter, David Smallbone and Nina B. Isakova

The Current State of Women's Entrepreneurship in Different Transition Contexts

The Diversity of Women's Entrepreneurship across Transition Contexts

Enterprising women, as described in the book, live in a vast variety of transition environments. Some women are doing business in countries making rapid progress, with market reforms (East Germany, Slovenia and Lithuania), others are operating in countries within an intermediate stage of transition, (Kyrgyzstan and Uzbekistan); and the least fortunate are working in countries making slow progress (Ukraine and Moldova) (United Nations, 2003). Historical, cultural and religious diversity is also a feature of the group of countries included in the book.

Regardless of success in transition, female entrepreneurship in all the countries observed has not yet become a major economic force. Following a rapid growth in female entrepreneurship in the early 1990s, the rate of growth has slowed down in recent years in the more progressive transition countries (e.g. East Germany, Lithuania and Slovenia). As in developed countries, the development of women's entrepreneurship was associated with the growth of service activity, which opened up more opportunities for women in areas where specialized labour skills were not required. In addition, as the process of market reform proceeded, removing many of the administrative barriers to the entry of new firms also opened up opportunities for women. Although no reliable official statistics on female entrepreneurship are available across all the countries concerned, to allow for robust cross-country comparisons, the data presented in the book chapters lead to the conclusion that the potential of female entrepreneurs in transition countries is not fully developed and realized.

Women businesses account for approximately 1/3 of small business sectors in all surveyed countries, apart from Lithuania, where the figure amounts to 43 per cent (although against the background of a declining number of registered SMEs). Female entrepreneurs in transition countries, not unlike women in the rest of the world, tend to do business in a limited number of sectors. The vast majority of female entrepreneurs is doing business in the retail and service sectors. Those engaged in manufacturing activities, are mainly involved in sectors dominated by women, e.g., food processing or some branch of the clothing and textiles sector. In Uzbekistan particularly, traditional crafts (e.g., gold embroidery, carpet weaving, and silk weaving) play an important role in women's business activities. The choice of sector is accounted for by a combination of resource constraints, environmental uncertainty and specific female aversion to risk-taking, which lead them to engage in activities with low entry thresholds and low financial risk. The Lithuanian and the East German cases show that even at more advanced stages of the transformation process, retailing and simple trading activities account for a significant proportion of female entrepreneurship, particularly in very small enterprises.

Female businesses are typically smaller in employment and sales than their male counterparts, which is partly due to the start up objectives (flexibility, personal social security, the wish to be independent, family income), partly because of financial constraints. The majority of women-owned enterprises in all the countries are micro-enterprises, employing less than 10 people, hence their limited input into total employment in the featured countries. Female businesses in countries where market reforms have been slow are on average younger, compared to more progressive countries, which might indicate a greater maturity in the business stock in rapid progress transition countries.

Judging from the book chapters, unregistered economic activity is still a feature of transition countries amounting to approximately 70 per cent of total activity in Kyrgyzstan. In transition economies, unofficial business activity manifests itself in unregistered businesses and also in shadow operations of registered companies, which conceal turnover from state authorities. In Ukraine, for example, small companies tend to apply this approach to reduce the tax burden and survive. The vast practice of entrepreneurs working in the shadow economy implies there are certain difficulties in getting accurate numbers of female entrepreneurs (sole proprietors and enterprises), as well the sector, size and age of women-owned businesses in individual countries. In this context, qualitative research methods, based on case studies and in-depth interviews with entrepreneurs, along with observations of researchers, compensate for the drawbacks in more quantitative approaches with respect to offering process-oriented insights. One implication for policy is that provided the economic and regulatory environment is improved, transition countries may witness a sharp increase in the participation of women in business, as well as diversification of types of female business activity. Since female businesses are typically micro and small enterprises, they suffer the effects of the unfavourable business climate, along with other small enterprises.

Women Entrepreneurs and Routes into Entrepreneurship

Women entrepreneurs in all studied countries were mainly between 30 and 49 years old, married and had children, although East Germany experienced a sharp decrease in the latter respect after re-unification. The number of children depends on the country and varies from one child on average in Ukraine, two in Moldova and Slovenia, to four in Uzbekistan, reflecting cultural peculiarities of European and Asian family traditions. A high education level of entrepreneurs, which is a commonly reported characteristic of entrepreneurship in transition economies, is characteristic of women as well as men. In a number of countries, the majority of surveyed women had university level education, suggesting that there are few other employment opportunities for educated women under transition conditions.

The involvement of women in entrepreneurship and small businesses includes co-entrepreneurship, as well as women as sole, or majority, owners. Interestingly, however, there is evidence that in some transition conditions female co-entrepreneurs typically are leading their businesses (Kyrgyzstan, Ukraine), with their husbands/partners playing minor roles in management. This may be explained by the motivations of women, who very often come into business because of the necessity to provide an income for their families.

Until recently, the portrayal of female entrepreneurs in transition, in the mass media, depicted them as women forced by circumstances to trade in the market place in order to provide support for her family. The results of research reported in this volume provide evidence to support this type, particularly in the early stages of transition, although it is not the only type. A distinctive feature of female entrepreneurship in transition countries is a diversity of types, including the forced (often unregistered) female entrepreneurs mentioned above; former managers of state-owned companies privatised, professionals (teachers, medical doctors, accountants), who changed the legal status of their activities, as well as entrepreneurial female owners of fast growing companies. This implies different policies are required to cover the needs of all types of entrepreneur.

As material presented in the book demonstrates, both 'push' and 'pull' motives can be identified in transition environments, with regard to women starting entrepreneurial activity. Some female entrepreneurs are pushed by negative circumstances (i.e. unemployment), while others are pulled by positive opportunities. The push motives appeared relatively stronger in Slovenia, Moldova, and Kyrgyzstan. A desire to be independent (to work independently) was a strong motive in Ukraine. The extent to which entrepreneurs (of both sexes) in transition environments are pushed into business, by a need to find some way of supporting themselves and their families, has led some authors to suggest that a majority are better described as 'proprietors' rather than 'entrepreneurs'. Entrepreneurs are characterised by the reinvestment of business profits for the purpose of business growth and ultimately further capital accumulation, while proprietors tend to consume the surpluses generated (Scase, 2003). This implies that a large share of female SME owners in the surveyed countries would fall into the 'proprietorship' category, at least when their businesses are started.

However, our institutionally based analysis of female entrepreneurs cautions against the implications of such simplification. A more dynamic view is needed, which would recognize the learning capacity of individuals over time particularly where considerable human capital is involved, as well as possible changes in external circumstances. These can lead to changes in the aspirations of individuals and their ability to spot and exploit new business opportunities. As the chapter on women business owners in Moldova describes, even if specific entrepreneurial actions or events, such as creating a venture, are primarily driven by necessity or opportunity, it is inappropriate to place entrepreneurs, regardless of gender, into such categories, because of the need to incorporate a dynamic element. This is an important point from a policy perspective, since it has implications for the entrepreneurial capacity of an economy and what needs to be done to enhance it.

Gender Differences in Enterprise Development

With regard to gender differences in various aspects of enterprise development the evidence in this book is not conclusive. The results presented in the chapters are in the line with studies on the influence of gender on business performance and growth, which conclude that women-owned businesses perform less well. This may be caused by resources deficiencies at start-up (Carter et al., 2001), but also because financial gain is not such an important start-up goal as, for instance, independence or flexibility to interface family and work commitments (Brush, 1992, Rosa et al., 1996). In Slovenia, for example, female-managed businesses were smaller in the number of their employees than male owned firms. They also had lower revenues, significantly lower assets, less exports and less profit; but they experienced fewer losses. The Slovenian authors argue this weaker financial performance, compared with their male-owned counterparts was partly due to stronger competition in activities encompassing the majority of female-managed businesses and generally worse financial results. In addition, women were less profit-focused; they cared more for employment and a positive organizational culture.

An overall conclusion is that gender differences are not very explicit. Nevertheless, as demonstrated in the book, women do differ from men in a number of aspects:

- Women tend to have fewer resources to start-up business, which was manifested in personal savings being less available; women are investing less in their businesses; women appear less successful in the achievement of their business goals, in business performance and growth. According to the self-evaluations of entrepreneurs women are less oriented to risk taking, planning and problem solving in comparison with men. A certain gender bias was identified in evaluations of management skills. Men as a rule give lower ratings to women's abilities in production management, in exporting, innovation, networking, market development and growth of sales, while female entrepreneurs perceive that gender is irrelevant for successful management.

Almost no difference is registered with regard to external conditions for female and male businesses. In transition environments, entrepreneurs of both sexes have to start and run businesses in mostly unfavourable external environments, which are testified by the list of major start-up and current constraints. Both female and male entrepreneurs cited lack of finance (related to scarce external sources of finance), high taxes, regulations and laws. It is argued in the book that the slow growth of SMEs, in some countries, during the recent years of transition is caused by a combination of increasing regulations coupled with decreasing business opportunity.

Factors influencing the Nature and Extent of Female Entrepreneurship

Institutional factors are an important influence on the nature and extent of female entrepreneurship, which is particularly evident in those countries, which are still experiencing serious institutional deficiencies. The barriers to business described are related to the inheritance from the former command economy, such as a lack of personal initiative, political involvement and interest representation. In Kyrgyzstan, for instance, ownership and enterprise rights are not well protected; and a combination of corruption and political influence over the judicial system leads to an overwhelming mistrust on the part of business people towards public officers, particularly police and customs officials. Financial capital for enterprise creation is controlled by a few major banks which are politically manipulated by the Presidential Office.

Most countries described in this book (except for East Germany and Slovenia) have underdeveloped banking systems, which are not focused on small enterprises as clients. As a result female entrepreneurs very seldom apply for bank loans and prefer to use unofficial sources of finance, which has a negative impact on their growth capacities.

Among the key findings described in the book is the conclusion concerning the significance of networking and social capital for the development of female entrepreneurship. Networks and networking gain importance in transition environments, where the framework for entrepreneurship does not function properly or is not installed yet (Welter et al., 2004). Personal networks and contacts often assist entrepreneurs in getting access to resources; they can also facilitate market entry, and influence the business field chosen. Networking and personal contacts also assist in daily business operations in such environments. However, Slovenian research showed that women entrepreneurs are weaker in networking competence and social capital assets, since they have to contract those resources through strong ties they have with family members. In transition countries, family members and friends are an important source of providing tangible and intangible help needed by a newly founded firm, including financing at start-up and for current operations; offering emotional support; mentoring and counselling; and help with premises and business contacts, through social capital and personal networks.

A special place in the discussion of networking and social capital of female entrepreneurs is occupied by Central Asian bazaars, which provide the single most important commercial activity in these countries. Bazaars are increasingly evolving into entrepreneurial hubs with newly emerging business/entrepreneurial networks, providing the externalities of a market economy. Bazaars play a crucial role in income and job generation for women as well as for entrepreneurial development. Women from different ethnic backgrounds take advantage of these hubs and shape their businesses along with changing market opportunities. The effects of bazaar activity are described as horizontal and vertical expansions and capital accumulation used to move to new sectors. Bazaars are considered to be an intermediary operational level between the firm and the market in the Kyrgyz study.

Open air markets in other transition countries (Lithuania, Moldova, Ukraine) serve largely the same purpose of broadening the scope of micro environment used by women as a source of informal external support, information, management training and cooperation. Besides, for many women, trading is still an activity of the last resort to make an income when few other options are available. Open air markets could be a starting point for some women to expand activities and to lead to viable businesses.

The Role of Women Entrepreneurs in Relation to the Wider Processes of Social, Economic and Institutional Change

Women entrepreneurs in the transition countries featured in the book are contributing to the transformation process, both economically and socially. With regard to their economic role, empirical data demonstrate that some women are contributing through setting up activities new to the economy. Moreover, they provide employment and income possibilities both for themselves and for others, thereby contributing to greater social inclusion. They also manufacture goods to substitute for imports, thus contributing to the regeneration of national economy. Women entrepreneurs also contribute to social change and to alleviating some of the negative effects of transformation, through offering positive role models and adding to a more positive image of (women) private entrepreneurship. The participation of women in economic activities has not only resulted in the productive use of labour, but also contributed to improving the quality of life for women entrepreneurs and their households.

With regard to the social roles of female entrepreneurs, their main contribution is in terms of creating job opportunities. Typically, women entrepreneurs are more likely to employ women, thus providing jobs not only for themselves but for other women, which helps to reduce the effect of discrimination against women in the labour market. In addition, reducing female unemployment assists in fighting women trafficking, which is known as one of the most urgent issues in the Ukraine as well as in Moldova. Finally, female entrepreneurs serve as role models for the younger generations, demonstrating new employment (self-employment) opportunities.

Whilst female entrepreneurs contribute both to facilitating transition at the microeconomic and macroeconomic levels, their social role is even more important in a society, where cultural norms and values strongly influence the nature of female entrepreneurship. In Moldova, Kyrgyzstan and Uzbekistan, particularly, the nature and extent of female entrepreneurship appears to be restricted by their current societal role. For example, since the beginning of the 1990s, a revival of patriarchal values and religious norms could be observed in Central Asia. In rural areas particularly, traditional values did not change much during the Soviet period. However, after transition began, traditional values have gained importance across all layers of society in core and periphery regions alike. Nevertheless, research shows that transition contributed to the emergence of female entrepreneurs, despite contradictory attitudes of post Soviet societies towards working women (for a discussion of this issue cf. Welter et al. 2002, 2003a). In this context, female entrepreneurship has played, and continues to play, an important role in modernising (post Soviet) societies and changing public attitudes towards women, which in turn will enable governments to make better use of the economic potential of female entrepreneurs. Here, women entrepreneurs could offer positive role models, thus adding to a more positive image of (women) private entrepreneurship.

In Moldova, it is the traditional attitude of society, which influences women's entrepreneurship. Moldovan women appear to be less career-oriented than men, placing more emphasis on family relationships. This is partly due to the Soviet heritage, where men had higher incomes, and partly due to patriarchal traditions. The transition process added to this, increasing the workload of women at home and their family responsibilities. Nowadays, most women entrepreneurs in Moldova would not set up a business without the approval of their family. Interestingly, East German women also have experienced a renaissance of traditional values, as the re-unification process went hand in hand with a massive and quick transfer of formal and informal institutions and values.

Another important social role of female entrepreneurship in transition countries is in contributing to solving or preventing ethnic conflicts. The issue is relevant to all countries, but is of particular significance in Kyrgyzstan, Uzbekistan, and Lithuania. The transformation process in these countries is accompanied by a danger of ethnic and religious conflicts. Evidence from Kyrgyzstan bazaars show that entrepreneurial activities can help ethnic communities to survive, and provide opportunities for mutually beneficiary contacts with their fellow entrepreneurs of a different ethnic origin. In Lithuania, open air markets play a role in terms of employment for disadvantaged ethnic groups such as, for instance, Russian speaking Lithuanian residents.

In all countries depicted in this book, transition contributed to the emergence of female entrepreneurs, despite contradictory attitudes of post Soviet societies towards working women. This becomes apparent in Germany, where despite an implicit traditional attitude of the German society towards working women we can observe a higher level of female entrepreneurship in East Germany compared to the West. In this context, female entrepreneurship already has played and continues to play an important role in modernising (post Soviet) societies and changing public attitudes towards women, which in turn will enable governments to make better use of the economic potential of female entrepreneurs. As a consequence, assisting more women to start up businesses, and supporting existing firms to grow, can contribute to the development of a more competitive economy, as well as reducing social exclusion.

At the same time, there is a need to avoid stereotyping women entrepreneurs across transition countries, e.g. characterising all women entrepreneurs as 'necessity driven'. Whilst most may be driven by a need to raise family income at start-up, this does not necessarily determine their subsequent development path, which may involve more 'opportunity recognition', as external circumstances change and individuals grow in confidence, ambitions and competences.

In summary, in a situation where the overall level of entrepreneurship is at a very low level, the engagement of women in entrepreneurial activity is making an important contribution to the overall level of entrepreneurial activity in the economy. Although under-represented in the business owning population, the contribution of women to the emerging service sector is an important one in a post Soviet context. It can also be argued that the accumulated capital, knowledge and experience of women entrepreneurs are adding to what is a scarce human capital base of resources relevant to private sector development.

Policy Priorities for Fostering Women Entrepreneurship in Countries at Different Stages of Market Reform

The empirical results presented in this book suggest that female entrepreneurship is influenced by the interplay of various economic, institutional and transitional influences. Though formal institutions, such as rules and regulations allow for female business development, informal institutions, including gendered norms and values and discriminatory practices, can act as constraints. This also applies to formal institutional deficiencies, reflected in the lack of a market oriented regulatory system in most transition countries and adequate business support. The Soviet legacy of gender relations, combined with the emergence of newly formed national identities, as well as newly established international alliances (such as, EU membership in the case of Lithuania and Slovenia), play an instrumental role in shaping the expectations of female entrepreneurs in the differing transitional landscapes. In addition, environmental influences provide both pull factors into business ownership, such as new market opportunities, as well as push factors such as job loss and constraints to formal female labour market participation.

Whilst women entrepreneurs in the countries surveyed share many common features and problems, there are important differences, which indicates a need to recognize the diversity that exists between transition countries, reflecting different inheritances from the Soviet period, as well as differences in the pace of change during the transition period. More progress with respect to female entrepreneurship in East Germany, Lithuania and Slovenia can be considered a positive development, but it may also indicate that increasing numbers of women are turning to entrepreneurship (initially) out of necessity, including many without the skills and resources needed to successfully develop their businesses.

Women-owned businesses share many barriers with those owned by men e.g. tax laws, access to finance. As a consequence, improving the overall environment for business will help women as well as men. Examples in countries at an early stage of transition include measures to reduce corruption and the violation of rules at local level, which are among the most urgent issues of the business environment influencing women entrepreneurs. It also includes capacity-building and sensitisation of administrations at national and local levels, which is an issue in both in early and in advanced transition countries. State representatives need a better understanding of the issue of women's entrepreneurship, whilst women's business organisations need to work in partnership with other business associations to seek an improvement in the general business environment. Although the overall conclusion from the various transition studies suggests that the differences between male and female may be less striking than those identified in some studies in western countries, the concentration of women in trade and other low entry threshold activities is a distinctive characteristic. It means that policies aimed at, or influencing, these sectors can have a disproportionate impact on women.

Additionally, our studies demonstrate a need for a 'joined-up' policy approach. A good example is the relationship between access to childcare provision and the ability of young women to engage in entrepreneurship. The case studies show that female entrepreneurs can only combine business and family responsibilities, provided that their relatives (mothers) help to raise children. In this case, measures, such as raising funds for child care institutions, or benefits for private child care institutions to reduce prices for their services, are likely to have a positive effect on female business development, particularly in East Germany, Ukraine and Moldova. This aspect is particularly important in view of the contribution made by women entrepreneurs to household incomes in situations where there are often few alternative opportunities.

Judging from the results, in earlier stage transition countries female entrepreneurs do not typically use bank loans for start-up or investments, which significantly restrict the number of new female entrepreneurs as well as their subsequent business development. It can be argued that the insufficient supply of bank loans, on suitable terms for small businesses, is one of the greatest barriers to female entrepreneurs in transition countries. There is an urgent need for microfinance initiatives, particularly in transition economies, where market reforms have been slow, combined with reform and capacity building in the banking systems, which include businesses in sectors and activities in which women entrepreneurs are particularly active.

Governments, as well as international donors active in some of these countries, need to pay more attention to developing a sustainable business support infrastructure that seeks to meet the needs of female as well as male entrepreneurs and which is sensitive to women in the way that services are delivered. This means paying attention to the inclusion of women as role models in promotional literature and the recruitment of women business advisers. Most business support instruments operating in the surveyed countries in Eastern Europe and especially in Central Asia, including those focused on women, have been initiated by Western donors. The sustainability of the business support instruments created in this way should be addressed by governments and local authorities. This is especially important for female business support activities, which are typically less developed. The medium term aim must be to develop an effective business support infrastructure that can address the external support needs of women entrepreneurs at different stages of their business development. This would include business information, advice, training and help in accessing finance, which is sensitive to the needs of women as well as male entrepreneurs.

In Lithuania and (East) Germany (and other countries), mentoring programmes and increased positive visibility of successful women entrepreneurs would counterbalance the generally negative social attitudes towards female business owners. More specifically, there is an urgent need for policy makers to recognise the diversity of women's entrepreneurship in all these countries, which has consequences for their access to resources as well as their support needs. This needs to be taken into account when designing policies and programmes to support women entrepreneurs.

Special programmes targeted at women entrepreneurs may be justified in some instances, in view of the low level of women business ownership in 'early stage' transition countries. Evidence from policy analysis suggests that such programmes are limited in scale and funds currently. At the same time, local initiatives might give a new impulse for further development of different business services providers, including business centres, private associations of female entrepreneurs and business incubators. Initiatives to promote women's entrepreneurship should incorporate soft measures of support, such as building a network of women's entrepreneurship promoters to support women's business ideas and to advise beginners; building up a specialist network to support groups of women entrepreneurs, such as rural entrepreneurs, via 'e-friendship-classrooms', family business successors, and internationalizing businesses.

Women's business associations/membership organisations also have an important potential role to lobby on behalf of women, in order to protect their rights and interests, as well as assisting them. They could constitute self-help for women entrepreneurs and networking groups. In addition, they might also work as partners with mainstream agencies, drawing attention to the specific needs of women entrepreneurs and gender-sensitive issues.

The question remains whether we need specific policies to foster female entrepreneurship. In this context, Mirchandani (1999) draws attention to the fact that a barrier-focused approach towards female entrepreneurship 'makes it seem as though the barriers women face are removable through individual action. What is needed, it is argued, is for women to train or educate themselves better, develop more appropriate networks and mentoring relationships, and re-assign domestic work.' The author stresses that this shifts the attention of policy makers away from environmental constraints towards the needs of individual female entrepreneurs. There is an ongoing policy debate about how best to meet the support needs of female entrepreneurs, since it is clear that there are many underlying similarities between the support needs of female- and male-owned businesses, of similar sizes and sectors. At the same time, there is evidence that women entrepreneurs suffer some of the same problems more intensively than other small businesses, such as access to start-up finance. In some instances, they can also suffer from perceived discrimination (whether intentional or unintentional) on the part of providers of finance or support services (Johnson and Smallbone, 2000). Although this suggests that there may be a case for some programmes targeted at women, more importantly there is a need for mainstream agencies to monitor their penetration of 'minority' groups of entrepreneurs such as women. The aim should be to ensure that agencies are identifying and meeting the needs of different groups, within what is a very heterogeneous small business population, without institutional or individual bias, whether deliberate or inadvertent.

Are Women Entrepreneurs in Transition Countries Different?

Our book contributes to the ongoing theoretical discussion on the role of gender in entrepreneurship in bringing in a perspective from transition environments, where less research on women's entrepreneurship has been conducted. On the whole, the different chapters illustrate that in a transition environment there are more similarities than differences for female and male entrepreneurs and their businesses, thus echoing research results from established market economies, where studies researching personal characteristics of entrepreneurs find more similarities than differences to male counterparts (Carter et al., 2001). The main business obstacles mentioned in the book chapters are less gender-related, but they refer to an unfavourable environment, where business conditions are volatile and changing quickly. While male and female entrepreneurship in a transition context apparently show more similarities than differences, the question remains whether women's entrepreneurship in a transition context, as presented in the book chapters, differs from women's entrepreneurship in the West.

Profiles of Female Entrepreneurs and their Businesses

With regard to characteristics of female entrepreneurs and their businesses in mature market economies, Baygan (2000) summarizes the results from several empirical surveys, describing the average female entrepreneur as belonging to the age group of 35-44; being married and having children; having less formal or business related education or prior work experience. Women start a business because they are looking for job satisfaction, independence and achievement (Carter et al., 2001). Although the 'push group', which includes women who are forced into business, is comparatively larger, the 'pull group' of those who are looking for independence and self-realization in business, is argued to be growing (Baygan, 2000).

In terms of business characteristics, women entrepreneurs mainly start their business as sole proprietorships and set up their ventures with lower start-up capital than men. Evidence from different countries in the West indicates that female business owners prefer to start their business in sectors where female employment is concentrated (e.g., Luber and Leicht, 2000; McManus, 2001). Most women-owned businesses are in wholesale and retail trade, hotel and restaurants, and services because of low barriers of entry.

In transition countries, the socio-demographic profile of female entrepreneurs as emerging from the book is similar to the one known from studies on female entrepreneurs in a mature market context, with one notable exception being the generally high education level of female (and male) entrepreneurs in transition countries. The well educated profile of entrepreneurs in transition countries is a commonly described characteristic, with potential implications for business behaviour, because of the human capital involved.

With regard to routes into entrepreneurship, and again similar to Western economies, motivations are diverse. Although most women in the countries surveyed in the book emphasize motives such as 'independence' and 'self-realisation', the need to generate income is more apparent in countries with a poor economic situation such as Moldova.

Female businesses also show features similar to those in the West: they are on average smaller compared to male-owned enterprises; they were started with less capital and mainly set up in sectors with low barriers of entry. The sector distribution of women-owned businesses in transition countries reflects a picture well known in Western countries with most women-owned businesses set up either in trade or services.

Goals and Business Performance

Looking at business performance and success in the context of mature market economies, several studies appear to confirm gender differences in business outcomes for women and men entrepreneurs, both across representative samples of firms and within specific business niches (e.g., Du Rietz and Henrekson, 2000; Kalleberg and Leicht, 1991; McManus, 2001; Rosa et al., 1996; Srinivasan et al., 1994). However, gender-specific differences in survival and growth rates are marginal or disappear when data is controlled for industry and size (Jungbauer-Gans, 1993; Du Rietz and Henrekson, 2000; Rosa et al., 1996). Moreover, the sectors women generally prefer for starting a business also are characterised by high turbulence rates, thus providing but few opportunities for rapid business growth (Storey, 1994). Additionally, research often points out different success criteria for male and female entrepreneurs (e.g., Buttner and Moore, 1997; Stevenson, 1986). Overall, most studies of the influence of gender on business performance and growth from Western economies conclude that women-owned businesses perform less well, and this may be caused by under-resourcing at start-up (Carter et al., 2001). With regard to objectives, studies draw attention to the fact that women entrepreneurs aim at combining both business and family responsibilities whilst men concentrate on economic objectives. Here, while Rosa et al. (1996) indicate gender-related differences in quantitative economic and financial performance measures, they also emphasize non-conclusive results with respect to a more intrinsic goal-setting of women entrepreneurs, thus underlining the complexity of this topic.

In transition countries, the share of women wanting to grow is relatively high, contradicting previous studies from Western economies which often stated less growth-orientation (or less growth interest) of women entrepreneurs. Examples from cases indicate that in a hostile environment the aim of business growth often is linked to business survival and income reasons. Moreover, the woman's decision to enter entrepreneurship often is linked not only to her well-being (especially if she is divorced, single parent or a widow), but also to that of her household, whilst household and spouse attitudes might influence the amount and access to resources and assistance. This draws attention both to the unit of analysis in these cases (should it be the household instead of the entrepreneur?) and the interesting question for further research of how to re-define entrepreneurship to include this phenomenon of an 'enterprising household', which in our understanding differs from the concept of family business (Welter et al., 2004).

Networking and Networks

Gender differences in network structures and networking behaviour may influence both the decision to start and to grow a business as well as business survival and success (Carter et al., 2001). At a first glance, empirical studies for Western countries show several gender-related effects. For example, Allen (2000) reports women networks as including fewer entrepreneurs, which might restrict their outreach and usefulness for a female entrepreneur. Other studies report more homogeneous and less outreaching networks for women entrepreneurs as well as less frequent network activities of women entrepreneurs (e.g., Carter et al., 2001; Caputo and Dolinsky, 1998; Schutjens and Stam, 2003). However, the results on network contents and network frequency are not conclusive. For example, Aldrich et al. (1986) did not confirm gender differences in network size and the frequency of networking between female and male entrepreneurs. Moreover, Renzulli et al. (1999) indicate that women rely on homogeneous networks with a larger share of kinship relations. According to their results, it is less gender than the kinship, which creates disadvantages in starting a venture. All this leads McManus (2001, p. 82) to conclude that with respect to women 'it has yet to be empirically established that these entrepreneurial networks are effective at facilitating the transition to self-employment.'

For female networks in former Soviet countries, the material in the book shows similar results, with women entrepreneurs' networks being more homogenous on the one hand. On the other hand, the role of networks and networking gains importance for female entrepreneurship in a transition context, especially where the formal institutional framework for entrepreneurship does not function properly or is not installed yet. This results in a lack of trust on the part of entrepreneurs and government officials (Raiser et al., 2001). In this case, personal networks and contacts often assist entrepreneurs in getting access to resources (Ledeneva, 1998) in such circumstances. Here, the book shows that in an environment, where networks are much needed, women entrepreneurs often lack the established networks their male colleagues brought with them from Soviet times, which may raise further barriers to female entrepreneurship.

Implications for Future Research on Female Entrepreneurship

To sum up, the book shows a picture of female entrepreneurship in a transition context being similar in many features to female entrepreneurship in the context of mature market economies. However, the book also illustrates differences and the diversity of women entrepreneurs in and between transition countries, indicating the context-specificity of entrepreneurship. Here, Mirchandani (1999, p. 230) draws attention to the fact that there is 'little analysis of how gendered processes may in fact shape the size of firms, or the tendency to focus on certain industries'. She explicitly raises the point that most research on female entrepreneurship is not based on feminist theories, therefore explaining possible gender differences in terms of how women entrepreneurs deviate from a so-called 'male norm'. With regard to a transition context, this indicates a need to pay attention to the changing role of women (entrepreneurs) in the transition period as well as the role external conditions play in shaping patterns of women's entrepreneurship. In terms of implications for further research on female entrepreneurs, this emphasizes a need to look at entrepreneurship within its social and economic context, thus stressing the embeddedness of entrepreneurship, which also might explain differences often taken as gender-related ones.

References

Aldrich, H., Rosen, B. and Woodward, W. (1986), 'Social behaviour and entrepreneurial networks', *Frontiers of Entrepreneurship Research*.

Allen, W.D. (2000), 'Social Networks and Self-Employment', *Journal of Socio-Economics*, vol. 29, pp. 487-501.

Baygan, G. (2000), *Improving knowledge about women's entrepreneurship*, paper presented at the OECD Second Conference on Women Entrepreneurs in SMEs: Realising the Benefits of Globalisation and the Knowledge-Based Economy, 29-30 November, http://www.oecd.org/dsti/sti/industry/indcomp.

Brush, C. (1992), 'Research on women business owners: past trends, a new perspective and future directions', *Entrepreneurship: Theory & Practice*, vol. 16, pp. 5-26.

Buttner, E.H. and Moore, D.P. (1997), 'Women's Organizational Exodus to Entrepreneurship: Self Reported Motivations and Correlates with Success', *Journal of Small Business Management*, vol. 35, no. 1, pp. 34-46.

Caputo, R.K. and Dolinsky, A. (1998), 'Women's Choice to Pursue Self-Employment: The Role of Financial and Human Capital of Household Members', *Journal of Small Business Management*, vol. 36, no. 3, pp. 8-17.

Carter S., Anderson, S. and Shaw, E. (2001), *Women's business ownership: a review of the academic, popular and Internet literature*, Report to the Small Business Service, University of Strathclyde, Glasgow.

Du Rietz, A. and Henrekson, M. (2000), 'Testing the Female Underperformance Hypothesis', *Small Business Economics*, vol. 14, pp. 1-10.

Johnson, S. and Smallbone, D. (2000), *Support for Minority Entrepreneurs in Europe: Specialist Agencies or Mainstream Provision?*, paper presented to the 30th European Small Business Seminar, Ghent, Belgium, September.

Jungbauer-Gans, M. (1993), *Frauen als Unternehmerinnen*, Frankfurt.

Kalleberg, A.L. and Leicht, K.T. (1991), 'Gender and Organizational Performance: Determinants of Small Business Survival and Success', *Academy of Management Journal*, vol. 34, no. 1, pp. 136-161.

Ledeneva, A.V. (1998), *Russia's economy of favours: Blat, networking and informal exchange*, Cambridge University Press, Cambridge.

Luber, S. and Leicht, R. (2000), 'Growing self-employment in Western Europe: an effect of modernization?', *International Review of Sociology*, vol. 10, no. 1, pp. 101-123.

McManus, P.A. (2001), 'Women's Participation in Self-Employment in Western Industrialized Nations', *International Journal of Sociology*, vol. 31, no. 2, pp. 70-97.

Mirchandani, K. (1999), 'Feminist Insight on Gendered Work: New Directions in Research on Women and Entrepreneurship', *Gender, Work and Organization*, vol. 6, no. 4, pp. 224-235.

Raiser, M., Haerpfer, C., Nowotny, Th. and Wallace, C. (2001), *Social capital in transition: a first look at the evidence,* EBRD Working Paper, No. 61, EBRD, London.

Renzulli, L.A., Aldrich, H. and Moody, J. (1999), 'Family Matters: Gender, Networks, and Entrepreneurial Outcomes', Manuscript, prepared for submission to Social Forces.

Rosa, P., Carter, S. and Hamilton, D. (1996), 'Gender as a determinant of small business performance: Insights from a British study', *Small Business Economics*, vol. 8, pp. 463-478.

Scase, R. (2003), 'Entrepreneurship and proprietorship in transition: policy implications for the SME sector', in R. McIntyre and B. Dallago (eds), *Small and Medium Enterprises in Transitional Economies*, Palgrave, Hampshire, UK, pp. 64-77.

Schutjens, V. and Stam, E. (2003), 'The Evolution and Nature of Young Firm Networks: A Longitudinal Perspective', *Small Business Economics*, vol. 17, pp. 15-134.

Srinivasan, R., Woo, C.Y. and Cooper, A.C. (1994), 'Performance Determinants for Male and Female Entrepreneurs', *Frontiers of Entrepreneurship Research.*

Stevenson, L.A. (1986), 'Against All Odds: The Entrepreneurship of Women', *Journal of Small Business Management*, vol. 24, no. 4, pp. 30-36.

Storey, D. (1994), *Understanding the small business sector*, Routledge, London, New York.

United Nations (2003), *Small and medium-sized enterprises in countries in transition.* Series: Entrepreneurship and SMEs, UNECE, New York and Geneva.

Welter, F., Smallbone, D., Isakova, N., Aculai, E. and Schakirova, N. (2004), *Social Capital and Women Entrepreneurship in Fragile Environments: Does Networking Matter?*, paper presented at Babson College-Kauffman Foundation Entrepreneurship Research Conference, University of Strathclyde, June.

Index